Joscelyne

Beach

Best wishes

Elaine Hurry

(nee Joscelyne)

Arthur Joscelyne

DESERT ISLAND BOOKS

First published in 2004
(Second impression)
by
DESERT ISLAND BOOKS LIMITED
7 Clarence Road, Southend on Sea, Essex SS1 1AN
United Kingdom
www.desertislandbooks.com

British Library Cataloguing-in-Publication Data
A catalogue record for this book is available from the British Library

ISBN 1-874287-85-6

Printed in Great Britain
by
4edge Ltd, Hockley. www.4edge.co.uk

Joscelyne's Beach extends for 200 yards on the north shore of the
River Thames and adjoins what became Chalkwell station on the
Southend Central to London Fenchurch Street railway line.

Cover photograph shows Joscelyne's Beach around 1925.
The breakwater marks the barrier with the public beach beyond.
The author, Arthur Joscelyne, stands with hands on hips in a white
sweater by a row-boat next to the breakwater. He is in his early 20s.
'Mother' is in the left foreground, wearing a long brown dress,
her hair in a bun, looking down.

Publisher's Note

In January 2004 Clare Harvey rang me to ask if I wished to have a look at her late father's 'book'. I was going abroad the following day, but said I would ring her back on my return. I am glad I did. There was something in the brief description Clare gave me that suggested she might have something special.

No sooner was I back home than I telephoned Clare, and the following afternoon she turned up and presented me with a typed manuscript bound in green cloth. It bore on the front and spine in faded gold lettering the words SEAWEED, SAND & SALTWATER BY A. W. JOSCELYNE.

It takes a matter of moments to judge whether a manuscript is worth pursuing. Flipping through the pages, my eyes were arrested by almost every sentence – free from obvious spelling errors, and most important, their content utterly fascinating. It was, even on that small acquaintance, something out of the ordinary. I asked Clare to leave the manuscript with me. Over the following days I read it with a mounting sense that I was holding in my hands a minor treasure.

I never knew that 200 yards of beach by Chalkwell railway station had been in private hands for almost forty years, up to just after the Second World War. That in itself is justification for this remarkable tale. It should be accepted that Arthur Joscelyne was reminiscing as an old man, when recall of dates and events might not have been as exact at they once were, and his words are better treated as personal memoir than history. He writes in a gentle, diffident style, fearing to upset or offend those he names, and his book is all the more beguiling in consequence.

The background to the book is worth recording. In 1982, at the age of 79, Arthur Joscelyne penned and printed this memoir. It lay untouched in a trunk in the garden shed for twenty-two years, until Clare chanced upon it and 'wondered if anyone might be interested'. Arthur himself had died in 1993.

His tale is part local history, part autobiography, and offers a vivid insight into Leigh-on-Sea and its characters before, during and after the First World War. He has a sharp eye for detail: the first motor car struggling down from London, adenoids removed in the kitchen, a German Zeppelin shot down in a nearby field, attempts to launch a glider with a seven-year-old at the controls, beer crates that served as 'luxury' benches.

Above all, the sea, its smells, the inlets and creeks, razor-edged barnacles on the boats, seaweed clogging the sand, the flounders caught for folk-medicine, the moorhens on the marshes guarding their eggs – all viewed and recorded by a small boy grown to manhood on his parents' beach.

Other than break up a few long sentences, and add the occasional comma or hyphen, I am able to present the reader with the text unchanged from how Arthur Joscelyne left it. His intended title 'Seaweed, Sand & Saltwater' could as easily apply to Blackpool or Scarborough as Leigh-on-Sea, and gives little hint of the tale that unfolds. With his daughter's permission, I therefore changed the title to *Joscelyne's Beach*, for that – as the reader will shortly discover – is exactly what the book is about.

I should like to thank Clare Harvey for bringing her father's manuscript to me. Had she not done so, this classic tale of almost a century ago might – like those who come alive in its pages – have been lost for ever

CLIVE LEATHERDALE

T. 1 & 2; 8/13.

An Agreement made the ———— Ninth ————

day of ———— November ————1915 between the MIDLAND RAILWAY COMPANY (hereinafter called "The Company") by William Henry Christy Clay their Estate Agent of the one part and Arthur Joscelyne

of May Bank, Cranleigh Drive, Leigh-on-Sea, Essex.
hereinafter called "The Tenant" of the other part.

Whereby it is agreed as follows:—

1. The Company agree to let and the Tenant agrees to take All that plot of land or foreshore situated at Leigh-on-Sea with a frontage of 210 feet to the foot path as shewn by red colour on the plan attached hereto with permission to place a portable shed thereon and also to store boats

From the twenty ninth ———— day of ———— September ————1915 for the term of one ———— half ———— year and so on from ———— half ———— year to ———— half ———— year until the said tenancy shall be determined at the yearly rent of Five pounds
———————— (£5. 0. 0) ———————————— payable halfyearly ————————
and the first payment to be made on the ———— 25th ———— day of ———— March ———— next.

2. This agreement may be determined by either party on the expiration of ———One ———— month's notice such notice to be in writing and to expire at any time hereafter without reference to the commencement of the Tenancy. The Tenant shall have no claim upon the Company for any damage or loss that he may sustain by giving up the said Premises pursuant to such Notice (except the reasonable value of any growing crops which may be then unfit to get) and shall pay a proportionate part of the said rent for the fraction of the current ———half———year up to the day of the expiration of such notice.

3. The Tenant shall pay the Rent on the before-mentioned dates free from all deductions whatsoever except Landlord's Property Tax and Land Tax and shall also pay all Rates Taxes and other out-goings (except Landlord's Property Tax and Land Tax) assessed or imposed upon the Company or upon the Tenant in respect of the said premises and in the event of neither party being separately assessed by reason of the premises being included in the general assessment of the Company's Property or should there be any alterations or adjustments in such assessments the Tenant shall pay for rates and taxes such reasonable yearly sum as may be fixed by the Company's Rating Surveyor as being applicable to the said premises.

4. The Tenant shall not remove or in any way damage or destroy the existing Gates Doors Fences Ditches Quicks Drains or Buildings and will keep the same in good and tenantable repair and shall permit the Company's Officers and Servants at all times to enter upon the said Premises to repair or drain the Railway Works or to view the state and condition of the said Gates Doors Fences Ditches Quicks Drains or Buildings.

5. The Tenant shall not carry on or permit to be carried on upon the said Premises any noxious or offensive trade and shall not manufacture or bring or suffer to be brought upon the said Premises any Fireworks Fog Signals Petroline Paraffin Naphtha Turpentine or any

Part of the lease for Joscelyne's Beach. This one dates from 1915. They were granted from 1909 until after the Second World War

About the Author

My father, Arthur (better known as 'Sonny') William Joscelyne, was born in Castle Road, Hadleigh, in Essex on 20th March 1903. He was the first of his family to be born outside of Leigh Old Town since the arrival of his Great Great Grandfather, John Joscelyne (Blacksmith) from Black Notley in Essex in 1758.

In 1909, Arthur's father (Arthur senior), purchased the lease on a strip of beach behind what is now Chalkwell Station. From then on the family built this into a business, and Sonny – together with his five younger brothers and sisters grew up as 'beach children' – swimming, sailing, fishing and helping with the business as children did in those days. Sonny was born with a lively interest in life, as well as all things to do with the water. He was a keen bird-watcher and an avid collector of birds' eggs and butterflies. At twelve, his book of watercolours of birds and their eggs, with notes, was passed around at Leigh North Street School. He gained a scholarship to Southend Art College where he produced beautiful enamel work and jewellery.

He left school at fourteen to take up an apprenticeship at Leigh Engineering works in the Old Town. This, however, came to an abrupt end with the death of his father. At fourteen he had to become a man and assist his mother with running the beach and bringing up the younger children. Once the last sibling was out at work, Sonny decided to hand responsibility for the beach to younger brother Vincent and strike out for himself. Firstly he worked at Shuttlewood's yard in Paglesham (boatbuilding). Then he moved on to working for a charter company at Wallasea. By this time, another brother – Harold – had decided to try building for a trade and asked if Sonny would join him.

In 1935, Sonny married a local girl – Rose Harvey. When the Second World War struck, all three brothers went with the little ships to Dunkirk. Harold and Sonny later moved to Wiltshire to work on aircraft at Hullavington airfield. It was here that Sonny and Rose's only child – Clare, myself – was born.

By 1949 Sonny was fed up with the dour living conditions in Britain and decided to try his luck in South Africa, running a café and general store. This was a disaster and he lost everything. At forty-eight he returned to England and 'started again from scratch'. He resumed his work in the building trade. Later, Harold, who had also emigrated to South Africa, returned and their building partnership lasted until Sonny retired at sixty.

I doubt if one could call it retirement because the years from sixty until his death at ninety in 1993 were full. He often said he worked harder in the thirty years of retirement than when at work. He pursued his love of birds and was renowned for breeding parakeets – breeding some of the first albino cockatiels in Britain. Some were taken down to Lady Bailey at Leeds Castle. Sonny was also sent one of only eight pastel lovebirds in the world, by a breeder in Belgium who knew that if anyone could breed them it would be Sonny Joscelyne. His aviaries were expanding, so he purchased the house at the back of his own so that he could use that garden too.

Sonny then started what was to become the obsession of his life – genealogy. He would set off most weeks with his sandwiches and flask and catch buses to the Records Office in Chelmsford, or out into Essex Churchyards with his notebook and pen. He never did quite get the hang of cars, although in his youth liked motorcycles. He tracked down quite a family tree and made contact with others who were interested. Eventually the 'The Josselin Society' was formed, of which he was the first President.

In the 1980s he started writing things down for his grandchildren. First a family history called 'The Twig was on the Branch'. He had noted down as much as he knew, including the story of John Joscelyne who made two Voyages to America in the 1600s. He also researched Ralph Joscelyne, roundhead vicar to Cromwell's troupes [sic], and also vicar of Earl's Colne for forty-three years. He followed this with his own story 'Seaweed, Sand & Saltwater', which is now open in your hands as *Joscelyne's Beach*.

Then he donated a small book of his Dunkirk Memories to raise funds for Leigh Heritage Centre, and this has been reprinted numerous times. He also wrote a series of short stories about Leigh and its characters, 'See yer termorrer'. Apart from the Dunkirk book, he did not want the others published until after his death.

At eighty-seven he again took up water colour painting. He remained full of life and interest in the world until at ninety he could no longer see or hear. At that juncture he took me aside and said that, as it was a Bank Holiday, I should have a day off work to look after mum, because he had decided to die. He was going to go on 'hunger strike'.

There was nothing morbid in this. Quite the contrary. He was upbeat and positive to the end. He called in his loved ones to say a personal goodbye and, ever practical, told mother to remember to clean the leaves out of the gutters on his shed and creosote the fences each year – yet she was eighty herself! He died, calmly, shortly after stating his intention to do so, then complaining that it was taking so long, almost as if he was conducting an experiment.

It was the best of deaths, with no loose ends, and he had been preparing for it for months. His books were labelled 'First Editions', 'Keep This'. Clothes had secretly been sorted out and dumped so there was the minimum to dispose of. Probate papers were in a folder for me to execute.

My father was determined, self-educated, creative, eccentric, practical, a skilled fisherman, sailor, boat builder, builder, engineer, writer, and always in charge of his own life and those around him. He could not abide waste and raided many a skip. His grandchildren knew that he could make or mend anything. Rose outlived him and also reached ninety after a happy and busy life caring for this complex, not always easy, but interesting and lively man.

CLARE HARVEY (née Joscelyne)

Preface

To those who read this I make no pretence, either as a storyteller or author. There is nothing spectacular: no heroes or heroines involved in the whirlpool of sex or illicit love, no voyages to other worlds. Just a flotsam and jetsam of bits and pieces, some rubbish, odd bits picked up and looked at; here and there something that might 'come in useful', all washed up by the tide of remembrance, on the seashore of the past, around 'Old Leigh'.

ARTHUR W. JOSCELYNE

The cast of 'Joscelyne's Beach'
Left: The author's father – 'Dad' – shortly before his death in 1917
Right: A torn photo showing the author (left), brother Harold, and 'Mother'

Introduction

Curiosity is a natural human instinct and I have little doubt those reading the dedication of this book, 'To Charlotte and those that went before,' will think it strange there is little or no further mention of her. I would blame no one if the suspicion crossed their minds that here was a secret love, the culmination of perhaps previous affairs of the heart for 'those that went before', the romance ever remembered, the jewel hidden deep and secretly cherished in one's memories and sacred from the world outside.

A delightful and satisfactory explanation, plainly an obvious conclusion, and no one is more sorry than I that it is so far from fact. The truth is, *I never even met Charlotte* (how I wish I had), but I firmly believe that this chronicle would never have been written but for her (and in lesser degree those others who preceded her). I have over the years come to feel a closeness difficult to describe, but very real, to her.

My first knowledge of Charlotte was not a particularly happy one but it was for that very reason she remained in my memory. I was, I think, around eight or nine years old and taking the shorter way through the churchyard to the Broadway with Dad. When we neared the East gate he pointed to a stone tomb, a vault he called it, and said, 'A lot of the old Joscelynes are buried in there.' He pointed to the panel nearest the path with the inscription –

In Memory of Charlotte Sams
Who Departed This Life August 2nd 1871
Aged 70 Years

and added, 'She was one of your great aunts.' Then he said, quite unemotionally, 'She was supposed to have "done away" with her husband.'

My interest flared up immediately. 'How did she do it, Dad?' I said, full of enthusiasm.

'Well, it was said she poisoned him, but it was long before my time so I don't rightly know much about it,' and there, in spite of further questions on my part, it finished. But it left sufficient impression on me to always remember it.

It was many years later when Auntie Polly gave me a little note book kept by this same Charlotte and dated 1830. In it she draws aside the curtains of time for a brief moment to allow a peep at the past and gives a brief summary, all too brief unfortunately, of happenings among the family and relatives, previously or at that time. But it was sadly lacking in length or detail and, although it satisfied a little of my curiosity, it left far more questions than answers and little or no hope of ever solving them.

She talks of her father John Joscelyne the blacksmith but gives no information on why he left his home in White Notley, married Mary Woodwards at St. Mary's, North Shoebury, and the following year settled in Leigh. Nor does she tell how this same John, when he came to Leigh in 1780, made sufficient or had enough money to own 'Joscelyne's Square' of seventeen 'tenements', a black-smith's shop, coach house, Great and Little Shorefields – land which extended from the road to Leigh Hall Farm (but now The Broadway), right over the cliffs to the sea – and 'Turner's' corner field, wherever that was. All this I have found out for myself.

Yet she quaintly records that, 'Walking to Hole Haven in the heat of midsummer the sun melted his blood and, turning it to water, he died out of his mind.' What in modern medical terms could have caused his death? Was it sunstroke or possible diabetes? And why, with all that wealth was he *walking*, at seventy-four years of age? Should he not have been riding a horse or driving a vehicle that distance from home? It just doesn't make sense. And just what was his business at Hole Haven, so many miles from Leigh, and what part does the family legend of smuggling play in all this?

His elder son John owned the 'King's Head'. His other son William (my direct ancestor) was a victualler as well as a black-smith, and to add further mystery to it all, John, with all his pos-sessions and property, gives in the 'Court Rolls' his 'domicile' as 'a barge on the foreshore'.

I can only assume that from time to time extra storage facilities free from Customs inspections might have arisen both there and in the 'King's Head' and victuals were supplied to the many ships moored in the estuary. And what more convenient place could one find than 'a domicile on the foreshore' to unload a cargo, be what it may? The Leighmen, both fishermen and farmers, were an iso-lated but tight-knit community. Mostly they obeyed the laws of

God but had little respect for the laws of their King, if it interfered with their way of life. Many were the cargoes of illicit goods that found their way up the creeks and marshlands hereabouts while the Revenue Officers slept or followed false trails, or sometimes it is said 'turned a blind eye' for personal gain. And I don't expect John and his sons were any different from the rest. In fact his position of councillor and overseer of the poor probably helped rather than otherwise.

But what he didn't foresee was that all his wealth and efforts would be dissipated and wasted by the gambling and drinking habits of his eldest son and by the marriages of six of his ten daughters, thereby going out of the family. Truly 'the mills of God grind slowly' and in this case leave only a wealth of unanswered questions in their wake.

And Charlotte continues: 'My family are related to the Parsons family, farmers and barge builders of South Shoebury, many of whom lie dead by the porch in N. Shoebury churchyard.' Then she goes on to mystify and add more queries: 'My uncle, 1st Lieutenant James Woodwards of the King's Royal Navy, was captured by the French and in a French prison for two years living only on horse beans and black bread. But, making love to his jailer's daughter, escaped in woman's apparel, leaving his chest and all his belongings, his two companions and two hundred coins of gold well hid.'

Now here is a pretty story. It tells so much but leaves so much unsaid, and is worthy of so much more research than I have so far given. Did he return after the war and marry his French maid, as is customary in the best stories? After all, she probably risked her life for him. It was the honourable thing to have done. But did he? – she doesn't say. And what of the 'chest and all his belongings' and more particularly 'the gold coins well hid'? Had it been English money, surely she would have said 'sovereigns' or 'guineas'. And how did he come by this large sum of money, chest and belongings? It is obvious that he was not caught in the heat of battle and was no ordinary prisoner of war. She doesn't say.

The most likely explanation, backed by some recent evidence given me, is that he was the leader of a small reconnaissance party, put ashore to spy out enemy positions and the money was entrusted to him to bribe or buy his way to information. Is it still tucked safely away in some secret hiding place, or buried in the soil of

France? And even if his love waned for his French lady love, did the natural human desire to retrieve this money take him back to recover it? After all, it was quite a large amount at that time. But if it had been so, surely Charlotte would have said. But could it in some way be connected with her father's 'secret', which I refer to a little later? And how much did this same James Woodwards, First Lieutenant in the 'Temariere' and previously six other ships of the line, who fought with Nelson in The Battle of the Nile, figure in the affairs of Lord Nelson and Emma, Lady Hamilton?

John Joscelyne had married Mary Woodwards on the 11th May 1779. On the same day, in the same church, St. Mary's, North Shoebury, Mary's stepfather Christopher Parsons (the elder) entered the bonds of matrimony for the third time. He had previously been married to Elizabeth Woodwards, herself a widow and the mother of both James and Mary. She died, leaving Christopher a widower for the second time, a situation it would seem not to his liking, so he made it a double wedding, this time by marrying John's sister Elizabeth Joscelyne of White Notley, Essex, a very young bride no older than Mary herself. Mary had continued to live at 'The Lawns', his farm in Southchurch, after her mother's death. It is highly probable that the double marriage made things more convenient for both ladies now a new mistress presided. Mary was, by profession and training, a midwife.

Rumour, backed by considerable evidence, has it that Lady Hamilton gave birth to a child, born out of wedlock, at 'The Lawns' and that Nelson was present. It is said that Mary in her professional capacity, but under the supervision of a local surgeon, a Dr. Seacole of Prittlewell, was present. It was all very hush-hush, but confirmed when Charlotte in her little book wrote: 'My father had a secret of which he would tell no one until on his deathbed, but dying "out of his mind", no one learned his secret.' But I suppose it could have equally applied to James and his hidden gold.

James, Mary's brother, having served with Nelson, must of necessity have been close to him, if only as a senior officer, but just how close? Could it have been that it was James' suggestion that the very comfortable and homely farmhouse 'The Lawns', isolated in the countryside of Essex, would make an ideal retreat for such an event? On the face of it, it makes sense, particularly bearing in mind his sister's profession. Charlotte doesn't say, but all

12

these events took place in her parents' time, so maybe she only wrote of hearsay and she herself knew little more than family gossip.

Perhaps, Dear Charlotte, it would have been better if your little notebook had been lost before it came into my possession – before I read and re-read it so often that I nearly knew it off by heart, trying to find answers to so much you had written, without it creating the additional, heartbreaking mystery of disappearing completely, leaving no trace of its whereabouts. I have searched high and low for it, and will never forgive myself for losing it.

The interesting, yet confusing unfinished oddments of information in her faded but beautiful script with which Charlotte recorded these scraps of family happenings whetted my appetite but did little to satisfy the need to know more. But she had sowed the seed: to search for answers but more particularly to continue – not where she left off, that was too far back – but to follow her example, so that my grandchildren, Ben and Daniel, and if God willing others that follow them, will have some idea of the family of my day and age. But I determined also that my effort would contain more detail and information, even if most of it was, I fear, only trivial, and even that seems to have 'misfired', as although my intention was to write entirely of my family and my own life, I seem to have strayed down many side-roads in the process. It contains nothing of historical value – that is being done by more skilful hands – but possibly presents a clearer picture of my everyday life and those around me, hopefully leaving less unanswered queries.

Perhaps it should have read: 'To Charlotte and those that come after', but what about 'those that went before'? Here again I feel some explanation is necessary. My researches into my family history, extending over the last fifteen years, have thrown much interesting light on the family since its arrival in England from Brittany in 1070 A.D. and much else besides, and it would seem that at various periods in history one or another of the growing family of Joscelyne felt the need to put into print an account of their lives and those about them. The first I know of was 'The Chronicles of Jocelyne of Bracklond', a monk, almoner in the abbey of St. Edmund, and elected prior in 1200 A.D. It is now translated from its original Latin to English and I am fortunate in having a copy.

Then came the scripts of John Joscelyne, born in 1529, secretary to Archbishop Parker who, it is said, was the original 'nosey parker' (owing to the length of his nose and his habit of minding other people's business). John wrote many learned works and much of the known history of the Anglo Saxons, but claimed that the bishop took all the credit of it for himself.

Then came another John Joscelyne, who made the dangerous journey twice to the 'New World', once in 1637 and again in 1647, staying eight years. He wrote a complete pedigree of his forefathers and 'Rarities of the New World' and later, 'Two Voyages to the New World', and to add to the interest mentions 'the vessel anchored off Lee waiting for the tide to take us up to Deptford'. I also have a copy of this rare book (and how I got it is a story in itself).

Again in the 1600s came Ralph Joscelyn', Vicar of Earl's Colne in Essex. He kept and wrote an explicit diary of all the events around him, social conditions, and his personal and family life, and that of his numerous children and it is now a valuable source of information for researchers into that period.

In 1880 a John Henry Joscelyne of Ipswich wrote the genealogical history of the ancient family of Joscelyne and later, in 1903, a Henry Joscelyne of Braintree recorded in a book much of his immediate family's story and some generations back.

I am not claiming or suggesting they were all in my direct line as Charlotte was. I wish they had been, it would have made my own research so much easier, but they all came from the same root stock and whether this did in any way influence me to add my small contribution I cannot say. Certainly they helped me with a wealth of general knowledge I could have found in no other way, and were 'those that went before', so they also played their part and deserve the acknowledgement that is their due.

So to Charlotte and the others, I add my small effort, claiming the indulgence of those who read on and asking them to heed my opening remarks in their judgement of it.

ARTHUR W. JOSCELYNE
(aged 79)
1982

Dad Buys a Beach

Born in Hadleigh, Essex, in 1903 I was probably the first member of the 'Joscelyne' family to see the 'light of day' outside of the Old Town in Leigh for over 120 years. In 1780 my ancestor John Joscelyne arrived in Leigh, a newly married man and started both a family and a business in his trade of blacksmith at the Old Smithy that used to stand in Horse Hill, right opposite the bottom of Church Hill. The smithy, alas, has gone, but the old weather-boarded house that served for both coach house and family home still remains to this present day [1982].

But Hadleigh was still within walking distance of Leigh and my father retained all his associations with his relatives and the other inhabitants there and I can only think that working spasmodically for Mr. Upson, a Hadleigh builder, and perhaps the chance of buying a plot of cheap land, had persuaded him to move even that far from home. He still kept his old 'Green Boat' (named after the colour it was painted) at Leigh, and even at the tender age of three months I was a frequent passenger on it in the summer that followed my birth, although, of course, I remember nothing of it. Like more of my story, I rely on hearsay to some extent for the truth or otherwise of those early days.

I have, in fact, frequently tried to recall my first and earliest memories, a milestone on which I could place a date of some accuracy, and it would seem that my earliest impression was walking with my parents along the cinder path, a narrow ash-covered track between the railway and the seashore that led to Chalkwell fields and what is now the Westcliff end of Chalkwell promenade. Eventually at the end we came to a padlocked five-barred gate leading to the brickfields and I particularly remember the whole circumstance through the difficult and unsuccessful attempts by my parents to lift the large pram containing my twin sisters, Lily and Rosie, over this obstacle.

Of course, there was no Chalkwell bridge at that time, so having failed to negotiate this barrier they turned back a few yards to where a rail crossing existed over a low step. I seem to remember crossing it into the narrow tunnel of undergrowth existing on the other side, but overcome by tiredness went to sleep and was

15

probably dumped on the pram with the others and on home. But little did my parents or I realise that the small triangle of pebble and seaweed we had just passed would play such an important place in our lives or how my later life would be influenced by it, and by no stretch of the imagination could we know it would bear our name for some fifty or more years after. But what it did do was to establish in my mind that being only one year and five months older than my sisters – and they were still in a perambulator – I was at that time most likely between two and two and a half years of age. But it was four years and four more children later [in 1909] when I was six years old *it* happened. It came without warning.

Saturday, about one o'clock, and we children sat at table awaiting the arrival of Dad, and immediately I saw him it was evident something exciting had or was about to happen. He was an unpredictable man at all times. He was hurried and breathless, told Mother to put his meal back in the oven, went to the china jug on the mantelshelf where the family fortunes were so obviously hidden, tipped the contents out and into his pocket, informed us he was about to obtain a beach of our very own, and that he must get back immediately to the Old Town to secure it.

I pleaded hard to accompany him but it seemed it was all to be done in a public house and no child would be allowed in, so I never really knew exactly how it was acquired. I do know he had no knowledge until about twelve o'clock that same day when he called in at 'The Smack Inn' for his usual pint and heard that the London, Tilbury and Southend Railway was about to auction the lease of a small strip of foreshore at Chalkwell that very afternoon at, as they put it, 'precisely two o'clock'. I could see my mother was considerably disturbed, but it was more curiosity on my part at this sudden and unexplained turn of events.

I asked what we would do with a beach of our own and she seemed equally at a loss to find an answer. Perhaps we could have picnics on it, she suggested without enthusiasm. This hardly seemed an answer when there were many beaches and better sand much nearer home we could play on, and we didn't go on the beach much anyway, so when Dad arrived home later and proudly announced that we possessed a beach I am afraid it made little impact other than surprise.

But my father was full of optimism, which apparently was not shared by any other bidders at the auction, and I gathered his was the only bid and no other saw any future in this little triangular-shaped strip of sand and pebbles on the edge of beyond, too far from Leigh or Southend, just the end of the cinder path and the brickfields. So, for the princely sum of £9 for a four months' lease, June to September, renewable yearly, he was now the tenant of what was shortly to become known as 'Joscelyne's Beach'.

I doubt he had any clear idea himself what he intended to do with it. He outlined various wonderful schemes and suggestions of possibilities and intentions, more I think to convince himself than us. But it was eventually agreed we could have a shed or hut on it, being more permanent than a tent, and spend our school holidays on it and perhaps even sleep there if we wished. Gradually, as all sorts of weird and wonderful suggestions were proposed, we all caught my father's enthusiasm and were won over, excusing ourselves that while £9 was an awful lot of money, maybe it would not be entirely wasted. So with this somewhat doubtful family blessing, the foundation of Joscelyne's Beach was established in the early summer of 1909.

The excitement had hardly worn off, when a few days following I came home from school to find timber and shining bright sheets of corrugated iron dumped in the back garden. Within a week or so a portable iron shed with a wooden floor some 10ft. x 12ft. constructed by my father and uncle was ready to be transported by horse and cart to its site at Chalkwell and our summer home for the next forty years or more came into being.

With the new holiday home established, the family just couldn't wait to try out the possibilities of such a place, so when free from school over the weekend, amid very considerable flurry and disturbance, the whole family started from our home near 'The Elms Inn' and London Road on the long journey to Chalkwell. Father, with a two-gallon stone jar full of fresh water, led the way, followed by Mother, with the same large old perambulator but with two recently acquired babies, another pair of twins, a number of large packages, food, buckets and spades and other oddments that filled and overflowed any vacant corner and the handles. The remaining four of us children, carrying nets and other bits and pieces we felt necessary for the occasion and our well-being, trailed at various distances behind.

Fortunately we were saved the longer journey through the Old Town, as now a fine new iron bridge had been constructed over the railway about halfway between Old Leigh and Chalkwell (Queens Bridge). This we reached after a series of stops, starts and diversions, such as meeting 'Henery', a mild and timid little man but a brilliant musician and local character living in Leigh Hall Road, our route for today. (About this time the music halls and public places were all ringing with the popular song of the day – 'Henry the Eighth, I am, I am' – and poor Mr. Henry, unable to defend himself, was made the butt and ridicule of it. His life was made a misery by children chanting and following him from the nearby North Street School, until he was almost afraid to go out. I expect I was as bad as the rest and I only realise now how cruel and unkind children can be.)

But to return to my story: reaching the cinder path we then faced the worst part of the journey. The path was covered with a loose, sharp layer of cinders and ash, no doubt supplied by the Railway Company. Deep potholes and subsidence made some parts almost unnegotiable where the sea had undermined and washed away or eaten into the narrow path, and this made difficult travelling for all and more particularly the heavy perambulator. The babies, now awake and protesting loudly, added a new dimension to our troubles. The youngest of those of us walking, who used to have an extra seat on the pram, was tired and lagging far behind, in constant danger of slipping or failing down the sea wall. Dad was struggling with his two-gallon jar of water, lifting and helping Mother with our heavily laden vehicle, and trying to look after us at the same time, and all in all the journey was a nightmare. Nor was it helped by the knowledge that we had to face the same again that night or go the other long way round up the unmade road and cart tracks through Chalkwell Hall and on to the London Road, which was almost as bad.

However, we did eventually arrive, very tired and hungry, and there at last it stood, on the highest corner near the Westcliff boundary of the pebbly beach, resplendent in a coat of my father's favourite green paint (almost everything in Leigh was either tarred or painted green in those days), bearing on the side facing the path 'GRANTEE OF THIS FORESHORE A. JOSCELYNE' in large white letters and below in rather smaller script 'Anglers supplied with bait'.

So it was plain Dad had decided on one means of income at least and as he was at that time a member of the Southend Amateur Angling Society, a reasonable market for this commodity was more than likely. There was also nearby a large white board with black lettering newly erected, proclaiming to all and sundry that 'THIS FORESHORE IS THE PROPERTY OF THE LONDON, TILBURY AND SOUTHEND RAILWAY COMPANY' and this it continued to do until the beach was taken from us, in spite of the changes of ownership by the railway companies.

In a short while the horrors of the journey were forgotten and the promised picnic became reality. We searched for crabs and little fish in the.pools, gathered driftwood and made a fire and generally enjoyed ourselves as children do on a beach the world over. I suppose all in all it was a success, but with beaches so much nearer at Bell Wharf and 'The Gipsy Yacht Club', there seemed little or no point or advantage in undertaking this tiresome and difficult journey often. Besides, the other beaches usually had children we knew on them to play with, so we lost our enthusiasm and I doubt we visited it half a dozen times as a family that summer. But I [aged six] was my father's constant companion and many a time he kept me with him instead of going to school, excusing himself by telling me there was more knowledge outside school than in it, a view certainly not shared by Mr. Thatcher, our headmaster of North Street School.

Our visits become more and more frequent until it became almost routine. Dad gave up the odd decorating jobs he used to do and gradually it was part of our lives. We took our lunch and boiled a kettle of water for tea on an old 'Beatrice' paraffin stove. We went fishing often, or foraging on Canvey Point, and even across the water to Yantlet. He taught me about boats and tides, sea birds and their nests and the creepy crawlies that inhabited the creeks and pools, and how to find the best bait holes and dig them, which was by now a flourishing source of income. How to distinguish the hideout of the big 'ragworm', which unlike the smaller 'lugworm', left no casts on the surface of the mud.

But most exciting of all was going out in the 'Green Boat' and searching for the 'Old Wreck'. This was a sailing vessel bringing a cargo of china clay from Cornwall to Leigh for the 'Victoria Potteries' (which were situated near where the Grand Hotel now stands), and also a large number of boxes containing the old-fashioned clay pipes, destined for London and I think sold for the sum of one penny each. Some of these by strange chance I have just found tucked away in an old shed by my cousin's grandfather, who was chief of the Customs & Excise or Coastguards at that time.

The great storm of 1880 sank the vessel in the deep water of the Fairway, almost opposite our beach and, some thirty years afterwards, its rotting timbers were infested with boring worms and became a paradise both for fish and those that sought them. Codling, whiting, pouting and occasionally the odd lobster or eating crab and spider crabs all lived there in its shelter and it was this uncertainty of what one could catch that was so exciting.

There were just two snags: first you had to find the wreck in the murky depths of the river, and secondly you had to be on or within a few yards of it. How much of it existed by then I don't know; it was never uncovered by water. Any small distance away you rarely caught a fish; on top of it, it caught you, and I dread to think of the number of anchors and ropes we lost or fishing tackle we left behind. We dare not use a chain cable; we could cut the rope when firmly caught, but it would mean losing all our chain. Once found, you couldn't fail to get a large catch. It was my favourite spot and in spite of the heavy price we paid we returned again and again to it after carefully lining up the marks on the shore and pierhead until we found it. It was our secret and as far as I know no others knew it and this was an added bonus to my joy in going there and still leaves a warm feeling in my heart to this day. I question now, over one hundred years after the ship sank, if there is anything of it left but at that time and for many years later bits of clay pipe stems could be found in the little eddies in the creeks and among the sand and pebbles of the tide line on the beaches and seashore.

Perhaps this is an opportune time to tell something of the father so frequently mentioned and my mother, whom I speak of much less at this time, but who were both in their own way to guide and shape our lives.

My father was the youngest of a family of seven and born late in the life of his mother. The family had lived in Leigh since 1780. In that year his great grandfather John – a blacksmith combined with innkeeper, and a comparatively wealthy tradesman and owner of considerable property known as 'Joscelyne's Square' on the south side of Horse Hill (or Leigh Hill as it is now known) – started business opposite the bottom of Church Hill at his trade. He built a smithy, and combined it with innkeeping by buying the 'Kings Head', which at that time stood somewhere near or on the site of the Old Leigh Station, where rail lines now run over its foundations, if it had any.

The business of blacksmithing flourished and passed from father to son or sometimes two sons and eventually descended to my father's eldest brother, as was the custom at that time. The other brothers and sisters had to be content with a small legacy of £100 each, although I suppose this was quite a considerable sum in those days, when a clay pipe cost a penny. The two other brothers were apprenticed to large London firms and two sisters married, leaving my father still very young at home and weak with asthma. His school was no doubt the 'Old Schools', now rebuilt and converted to 'The Rectory' on Church Hill just below Leigh Church. It was built, so my father told me, of the stone from the ruins of Hadleigh Castle, which was most likely true as I have read that much of it was destroyed and sold for road-making etc.

When Dad left school, not strong enough to work, spoilt by both his mother, now a widow, and elder unmarried sister, and left to his own devices with all and every day free, much of his time was spent in the blacksmith's shop. Perhaps more so when the comfort of the forge glowed red during the winter. But his summers were occupied mostly by bait digging and fishing, collecting winkles and cockles, long lining, sailing his little boat through the creeks and marshes around Old Leigh and Canvey Island or just wandering over the mud and cooking the shrimps he had caught with his little trawl in Leigh Creek.

These things he could do at his leisure and with them his health improved in a remarkable manner. It did little to discipline his life but as he grew stronger he did undertake decorating work and other building jobs for his friend Charlie Phillips. Charlie had a workshop at the bottom of the garden of the 'Bell Inn' and a small sweet and general shop nearby on Leigh Hill. I suspect Dad only worked when he needed the money for his boat or other activities and he seldom allowed work to interfere with the life he had chosen.

But to lead this life, as he grew older, became more and more difficult; times were changing and circumstances forced him to adopt a more normal existence and go to work more often, but living still at home he never completely gave up his old life and was always a rebel.

However, the 'system' won in the end and when he was around thirty-five he was working full time for Mr. Upson, a builder in Hadleigh, and was now quite a tradesman. When the opportunity arose and Dad was offered some land in Castle Road, Hadleigh, he gave up his job and started to build a detached house with the small inheritance he had received under his father's will. In the meantime, his brother Henry had returned from Australia and bought land in the then unmade and outlandish Cranleigh Drive, Leigh. The other brothers and sisters were persuaded to buy adjoining plots, and on completion of the Hadleigh house my father was asked to supervise the building of a small row of villas, some seven on one side and later four on the other.

By now most of the family were doing fairly well and Leigh was developing and expanding fast. All this, of course, slowly but surely steadied my father and he became quite ambitious and more settled in his ways, but never completely gave up his independence and right of choosing to do what he wanted, and still slipped off fishing whenever circumstances allowed. Quick to take offence and equally outspoken, he upset many people. But, being always willing to help, providing he got his own way – much due, I suspect, to his upbringing – he also made many friends and joined in the social life, such as it was, in the village. I learned this from my old Auntie's accounts, to whom I owe so much of this information.

Dad had an extremely fine singing voice and his rendering of 'The Stowaway' was always one of the highlights of the Christmas gatherings of the old folks at 'The Sailors' Rest', a large wooden hall almost opposite where the 'Coliseum' cinema now [in 1982] stands in Elm Road, Leigh. At the end of this ballad many of the audience were, it is said, in tears, something I can vouch for. A typical song of those sentimental Victorian times, it told the story of a small curly-headed boy little more than a child found stowed away in the hold of a sailing ship. It starts something like this:

22

'From Liverpool across the Atlantic
The good ship was sailing o'er the deep,
The sky bright blue above her
And the water below her asleep'

The story continues how the first mate, a terror to the crew, dis-
believes the child's story that his parents could not afford to keep
him and had hidden him away, hoping that like a stray dog someone would love and keep him. The mate insisted that it was a
member of the crew who was responsible and wanted the
little one to name the man or be thrown overboard, allowing him
only the time to say the Lord's Prayer before carrying out his
threat.

All, of course, comes right in the end, as almost all of these
ballads did, but in that day and time it tore the heartstrings of all
those who heard it, not the least me. As a child I would pester my
father to sing it, each time trying to fight back the tears that invariably accompanied it, and it became a most important challenge to
me to listen to it without crying. I never did succeed and to this day
I still wonder if I heard it sung whether I could listen dry-eyed. It
would seem foolish that I even mention it now. I can only say no
other song has ever made quite the same impression on me.

My father also played a banjo quite well and whether this was
the reason for his frequent social visits to the newly opened imposing hotel 'The Grand', complete with its ballroom and all modern
amenities, I am not sure; suffice to say they became even more frequent when a certain Miss Setterfield, niece of the licensee, arrived
on holiday from Margate. They danced together and found enjoyment in each other's company. She was due to stay a month but
within a fortnight events took matters into their own hands. A
telegram from Margate told of the sudden death of her father,
leaving her mother alone. She packed immediately and caught the
paddle steamer home to Margate.

When my father arrived in the early evening he was told the
news; he promptly returned home and without stopping caught
the train to Margate to offer both help and his hand in marriage.
Shortly afterwards they were married at Holy Trinity Church,
Margate. As I have said, an unpredictable man. They had known
each other just over a fortnight, not perhaps the best way to enter

into a lifetime of wedlock. So maybe to compensate the risk, circumstances or the 'powers that be', they decided to make their path easier than it was for most in those days, at least domestically. My father still had the house he had built in Hadleigh; true it was let, but tenants had few rights other than the option of plenty of property to rent. Their furniture was basic and not cluttered up with all the aids to modern living of these times, so the tenants moved a few doors up the street, and 55 Castle Road, Hadleigh, became the family home.

The widow, Mrs. Setterfield, had been running a guest house in Trinity Square, Margate. As both her sons were in Africa, having fought in the Boer War and later decided to return there, and her daughter was now married, she decided to sell up and join the newly married couple in Hadleigh, making all the furniture, linen and domestic appliances freely available to complete the new home. So by the June of 1902 they were installed with every 'mod con', if one discounted main drainage, piped water and little, if any, transport and shopping facilities. But they had a good view of Hadleigh Castle, and work again available with Mr. Upson, builder and decorator, Hadleigh.

And now a few words about my mother, and they must of necessity be only a few as I had no kindly old aunt on her side of the family to put me in the picture. I only once met any relative, so I know little of her history or life before her marriage except odd memories during her conversations and rarely touched on. Born in 1874, she was one of four children – two sons, two daughters – her father a master carpenter and wheelwright, and her mother, who as I have said, ran with the help of her daughter a small guest or boarding house. One daughter, Jessie, died at eighteen, the brothers William and Thomas were both well educated at Margate College and went to Africa. My mother's uncle was manager for a large brewery company and this necessitated him moving to many hotels in Essex – 'The Grand' at Frinton, 'The Crown' at Rayleigh, the 'Anne Boleyn' at Rochford and the newly opened 'Grand Hotel', Leigh-on-Sea – among them.

It was customary at the end of the holiday season at Margate for my mother to spend a month or so with her uncle for a holiday wherever the firm had sent him, so she must have known Essex quite well. But it was her first visit to Leigh and within two weeks her whole life was changed and Miss Setterfield became Mrs. Joscelyne.

My grandmother, who never really settled in Hadleigh after her busy and full life at Margate, lost heart and died soon afterwards. Mother was saddened by the loss, lonely, cut off in a backwater from all interests and with a life totally alien to anything she had previously known. To add to this, an intensely jealous streak that had developed in my father prevented any social contacts from forming and I dread to think how unhappy and miserable her life had become. On the other hand it made little or no difference to my father's way of life. He worked a little but continued in his old ways, except that now he had to walk from Hadleigh to Leigh and back to meet his folk and companions or go on his fishing or other trips. I doubt he was different to the majority of the men of those days, particularly from the narrow confines of a village like Leigh, and his upbringing had not helped, either, to learn tolerance and understanding. Those first few months of marriage must have been a nightmare and it showed amazing courage and character for such a gentle and loving person that my mother was. I think perhaps if she had had somewhere to run to she would have done so, but now her uncle was in Canada and she had not a single relative left here.

To complicate matters still more, she was expecting a baby – me – and fortunately with my arrival a complete change took place. My father, so my mother told me later, became a changed man. He doted on me, he couldn't do enough for Mother or me, and most important of this sudden change was his decision to move to one of the houses he had built in Cranleigh Drive and leave Hadleigh. Here, for my mother, among my father's relations was the companionship and a move away from the loneliness and solitude of Hadleigh and strangers.

Leigh was blossoming; houses and shops were going up all around. Even London was only an hour's journey away and Dad's boat or the beach within a short walk. With all this, a greater understanding grew between my parents, coupled with the fact that Aunt Polly – my Dad's eldest sister, whom he respected and feared more than anybody – lived two doors away. Polly never failed to say what she thought and made him behave with more consideration and understanding. Although by some standards he never became a model husband, he loved us all passionately. As the family grew, he gave all he could for our happiness and cared for mother with a deep affection as the mother of his children; and she on her part respected him and mothered him with all of us. This was the situation when my father made his decision to own a beach.

That first summer of 'Joscelyne's Beach' was from my personal and my father's point of view quite a success. Not only were our fishing trips fun but the bait digging enterprise was a financial success. Often we would combine the two by spending all day in the Ray [a deep-water channel off the coast] digging bait when the tide left the banks uncovered and doing a little fishing until the tide allowed us to come home. Here again was the added bonus that the tide reached our beach almost an hour earlier than Leigh. Also, my Dad was letting his boat out to friends and fishing parties and was considering buying another. A surprising number of local retired people and others were finding their way to 'The Shed' to meet and talk about boats, and this led to their sale and commissions on them and, in turn, to the sinking of moorings for clients.

All in all a business was taking its own shape and in between times we could always fall back on rock shifting. All along the lower part of the beach, from the tide line to some twenty or thirty yards out, it was littered with heavy stones or rocks that had been used to build the apron wall protecting the cinder path. I can only assume that the barges that had brought them, probably from Kent – they looked like Kentish ragstone similar to those of Hadleigh Castle – had unloaded them on this patch of sand and left them there when the job was complete.

They were now half buried in sand or mud and weighed up to 2cwt. each, a danger to any boat or bather when just covered by the tide. It was a killing job removing and carrying them up the beach and stacking them safely and I think I hated struggling with the little ones as much as my father did with the big ones. The job seemed always there, particularly when there were so many nicer things to do. It was so tiring: we couldn't do many at a time and other than the pile of rocks at the top of the beach there was little proof that we had made any impression; there were such a lot and that year little to show for our efforts. Financially it was not really paying its way, in fact it was a loss as it was preventing my father from working at a proper job. Had it not been that my mother had inherited a small sum from her mother, things would have indeed looked black.

As it was, at the end of September when the four-month tenancy ended, we obtained the Railway Company's permission to keep 'The Shed' on it and the option again for the following year. Dad had now to go seriously to work to help the family's exchequer and get us back on our feet again. And now with six of us to feed and clothe, he finally accepted defeat and really settled down to working for his friend Charlie Phillips or others on a sub-contract system of painting and decorating.

To some extent we were like many of our neighbours, self-supporting. Nearly everybody around kept chickens, like ours running loose in the fields around us and coming home only to be fed and shut up in their enclosures – a weird selection of sheds made mostly from orange boxes, strong wooden crates in which at seasonable times the oranges arrived and which could be bought for a few pence. It was incredible what my father could make with them, from sheds to fences and even mend boats. With a coat of tar from the gas works at 4d [four old pence] a gallon, they lasted many years. We were thus assured of plenty of fresh eggs and with a large back garden planted mostly with potatoes, which when planted suffered the indignity of just being dropped into holes made by a dibber.

It was only later that my father adopted the idea of a trench lined with seaweed which we used to drag up from 'The Beach' in sacks because we found this method increased the yield threefold. We also had beans and cabbages in profusion and, coupled with a fair supply of fresh fish and Mother's home-made jam and bread, we never went short. With all of our ages within a year or two of each other, and growing quickly, clothes were passed down as a matter of course, so in spite of everything we were well fed, healthy and happy. We had very few luxuries; our wants were simple and basic, but I feel sure our childhood was equally as happy as the children of today or possibly more so, and those around us were much the same. If there was any 'keeping up with the Joneses' I don't remember it, and certainly there was more neighbourly friendship in the streets.

The fact that the shed still remained on 'The Beach' obscured any idea that we no longer had any rights over our beach. At weekends and on spare occasions we still used it as if it remained in our tenancy. Whether the Railway Company knew or just didn't bother, I don't know. I expect as with most of these larger companies, the property was in the hands of agents, who acted for them and we were just a name on a file and the necessity of renewal the only reminder. So Joscelyne's Beach remained a full year in spite of only a four-month agreement, and it seemed natural that it should be so.

At weekends it became a favourite meeting place for the locals, who were now coming in increasing numbers from the newly built 'Grand Parade' and 'Woodfield Road' areas. A frequent visitor and friend of Dad's was Mr. 'Bill' Hales, a far-seeing businessman who visualised the potential and scope of development of this area. He developed his own water works at the top end of Woodfield Road, Leigh, a factory-like structure, complete with a huge water storage tank on top, an 80ft. well and pumping engine, and started a piped water supply. I have little doubt it was this available supply that started and helped the incredibly rapid growth of property in and about this district. It was later taken over by the Southend Water Company but no longer functions as the supplier of water but as the Woodfield Garage, started just after the First World War by Mr. Grisley and his brother.

Mr. Hales then turned his attention to the catering business and built 'The Bungalow Tea Rooms' opposite the bottom of Woodfield Road at the top of the Undercliff. Owing to the road height, one entered it over a wooden drawbridge. It had a magnificent view over the beach and estuary and was a magnet to the many school treats and outings that were customary in those days. He spent very many hours with my father, and I believe influenced and encouraged him to expand and use the beach for its business potential, stressing the expansion of both Leigh and Westcliff. Unfortunately he was unable to benefit by his foresight as he died a few years later after building his tea rooms and I doubt he is now remembered by many.

Another far-sighted businessman, who also saw the ever-growing prospects of the area and was a frequent visitor to the beach, was Mr. Brewer. He opened his grocery store at the corner of

Woodfield and Leigh Road and it is still in the family to the present day. Then there was Mr. Bull, who opened an off-licence on the opposite side of Woodfield Road. He has passed on, but his wine store is still there. These and many others were part of the regular gatherings that developed, mostly on Sundays.

The Beach began to lose its isolation and, knowing that someone was around most of the time, some of the boat-owners suggested that for a small fee they would bring their boats to be stored for the winter if my father would keep an eye on them. This was, of course, contrary to our agreement but, as nobody seemed to care, worth trying and a half a dozen or so boats settled for the winter on this little corner, another small but welcome source of income. So the winter passed and the question still remained: 'Was the beach to become a business or a playground for our summer holidays?'

In point of fact it answered itself and became both. With the renewal of the lease for another four-month period the following year, it became a part-time business at weekends. As the summer progressed, more and more during the week the new residents – and those on holiday staying at the increasing board and lodging establishments – began to find the peace and quiet of the Westcliff beaches as their numbers grew. Dad had bought two tents for us to use as our own dens but he found a growing demand to let them daily to families with children, so he bought more and soon we had half a dozen. A similar demand for rowing boats for hire decided him to buy two more and to retain the old one for fishing parties.

On very hot days (and we seemed to have a lot more then), and particularly on August Bank Holiday, many visitors wanted to hire a bathing costume and a tent to change in. The nearest other bathing facilities were 'Davis's Bathing Machines', near the Crowstone; undressing on the beach was unlawful with heavy penalties, so once again a ready market became available. A stock of bathing costumes and towels was acquired from Mr. Partridge, who had a wholesale store in the old Customs House in Leigh High Street. The use of a tent for half an hour including costume and towel, if I remember rightly, was 6d. After some busy days, when we arrived home after the long walk from the beach, Mother and Dad would have maybe a hundred costumes and towels to wash in fresh water and dry for the following day.

We only had one cold tap, on which a hose was fitted and passed through the scullery window into two large zinc baths, which at other times served us, one to soak the costumes and towels, and one to rinse. They were both on the ground and it was a back-aching job. Afterwards, with two lines strung along the full length of our garden, it looked more like a laundry than a dwelling house. When eventually they had finished – and all this came after a long, hot, tiring day and walk – the fear their efforts would come to nothing if it rained, or the washing didn't dry, was a perpetual problem with them. Only now as I write this do I realise how far we have come from the slavery of those old days, and yet it was accepted and suffered without question as part of normal living; one got what one worked for and that was precious little, but clearly understood as a way of life. If you didn't work you didn't eat; it was as simple as that.

But to continue. The increasing scope of the business answered the playground problem automatically. My father couldn't cope with the work and difficulties of meals etc. He was there sometimes twelve and fourteen hours a day, according to the tides and his fishing parties. So immediately the school holidays started, the old pram was loaded with all our drinking water and food for the eight of us and other necessities. The long trek to 'Our Beach' was undertaken regularly each day for the whole of the holiday period. Whether we liked it or not, it became our second home, Mother doing most of the cooking on two 'Beatrice' paraffin stoves. So the camping out and picnic atmosphere became reality after all.

The beach had now become alive, there were people, and children to play with; we were in and out of the water, playing around in boats. Best of all was the little wood on the other side of the railway and Undercliff Gardens, a mass of almost impenetrable thicket, but a living paradise of small creatures, butterflies, moths, rare birds and flowers. The reason for this can only be explained, I think, by the rapid growth of the property encircling the whole area, driving all wild life into this one last stronghold, but cut off by the railway and sea from escaping further. Coupled to this, the conditions, environment and complete safety of the thick thorn bushes and scrubland made the ideal conditions that were necessary. It was also private land and the owners of the one or two properties that existed on it maintained this privacy very strongly and few strangers ever passed that way unchallenged if they set foot on it. I never ventured too near the first house, 'Seabrink', except with caution and an escape route open, so it was mostly the 'little wood' or the first 100 yards of the undercliff, and only in later years, as they began to build a few more houses and it became a little more public, was I able to venture further.

Perhaps it might be of interest to mention two rather unusual things that register in my mind about this further building that took place.

Owing to the fact that both ends of the undercliff were either too steep or sealed off, no vehicles could get down easily to bring building materials to the sites, so quite elaborate chutes were constructed, mostly of corrugated iron or scaffold boards on substantial frameworks, from the Grand Parade down the cliff to the site, and all materials and equipment passed down this way. The second matter of interest was that owing to the steepness of the bank adjoining the proposed roadway, it was necessary to cut into this bank at road level for such distance as the building to be erected required, plus a small back area. This in turn necessitated a high retaining wall to hold the cliff back. But more troublesome still was where to dispose of the enormous quantity of displaced earth, resulting from this excavation, plus the excessive amount of scrub and undergrowth that had to be removed before even starting to dig, there being no easy way of getting it out of the undercliff. So the contractors piled all this undergrowth on the flat area in front of the proposed building, set it on fire, and when it became a fiery mass of ash and charcoal, proceeded to dump all the clay and earth of the excavation onto this fire, and by some strange trick of nature this also slowly began to burn.

The mounds formed, if I remember rightly, were about 30 feet long, 20 feet wide and 8 feet high, and for the whole of at least one summer they smoked quietly like sleeping volcanoes, getting a little smaller all the time. One could feel the latent heat when close to them. I was sometimes tempted, as children are, to run up and over them, but I am grateful that common sense or fear prevailed, as the possibility of them caving in with the weight of someone and precipitating them into a fiery mass could, I suppose, have been very real. When they eventually cooled the result was known as 'burn bake', a crumbly material that looked like crushed brick and was used later on these same buildings mixed with lime and called 'slapdash' as a form of outside wall covering, and to my knowledge is still on them after all these years. But the amount used made only a small impression on these mounds and the remnants are there still, in spite of the developments that have taken place since.

I trust I will be forgiven for so frequently diverging in other directions from the main theme: my only excuse is that later residents of the area might find it of interest, so once again I will continue my interrupted story.

That summer came to a close and if there had been any doubts of what to do with 'Our Beach' they were now finally and completely decided for us. No decisions were needed. No doubts were left. It had to be a business, but the best of both worlds because it was a holiday home for us as well. My father secretly believed it was his foresight that saw all these possibilities. I rather feel that we just happened to be there at the right time. But chance or foresight, it only confirms in my mind more than ever my belief that to a greater or lesser degree our lives, in spite of ourselves, are ordained and in the main planned by a Higher Authority or influence outside ourselves. Many will disagree, and quite rightly so, but it will not change what I feel I have learned in my own 79 years of life. I am convinced that events shaped themselves and it had to be so and little or nothing could have altered the course of events. 'Joscelyne's Beach', an established, although very small, business came into being as much by circumstance, but not by chance.

That autumn a minor tragedy hit both Dad and me. His well-loved old 'Green Boat' was either lost or stolen. He had been out hoop netting, a method of fishing I think now completely gone and forgotten, and I doubt practised anywhere now in England. For many of our later generation, should they be interested, perhaps I will be forgiven if I once again branch off with a short description of this and other fishing methods in use in Old Leigh, whose inhabitants mostly depended in some form or other on collecting the 'fruits of the sea' for a living.

The bawleys, or shrimpers, were the most important. Some thirty feet or more in length, broad of beam and drawing around

5ft. 6in of water, they were crewed by two men, skipper and mate, and sometimes a boy. They were capable of weathering heavy seas between Leigh and Harwich, working all the year round trawling for shrimps. In the early days the catch was brought ashore and cooked in coppers on Bell Wharf, but later was cooked on board and sent to the London market in wicker baskets known locally as pads. Leigh railway goods yard was usually filled with returned empties and it was a favourite habit of my father to go over these pads searching and collecting the stray shrimps caught in the wicker work to start fishing with until the sandbanks uncovered to dig bait.

To a lesser degree came the stow-boats or whitebait and sprat catchers. These only worked during the winter months, and unlike the shrimpers, remained stationary to make their catch. Anchored in the strong tideway, they lowered a large (but small-meshed) net on a framework much like a huge mouth, into which the tide swept the shoals of little fish. It must have been a very haphazard way to fish, but with their skill and expert knowledge of tides these boats seemed to make both good catches and a fair living.

Unfortunately, while the smaller quantities of whitebait caught found a ready market, heavy catches of sprats were difficult to dispose of, and had to be sold to farmers to spread over their fields as fertilizer. Judging from the huge flocks of gulls accompanying the operation, how efficient this was is doubtful, and I always felt saddened at what seemed a waste of good food. But with herrings so plentiful and also very cheap, I suppose no one cared. And having now got on the subject of sprats, this brings to mind one of those little incidents that remain in a child's mind for no particular reason.

Catches of sprats that autumn had been particularly heavy and, for the price of a drink, Dad had brought home a large basket of prime, large sprats. Some few days previously he had been given a fairly large oak tree on some vacant ground in Elm Road that needed clearing, and with much effort had sawn off most of the branches and was tackling the trunk. This resulted in large quantities of sawdust and small oak logs. Whether in view of this he had got the sprats I don't know, but on his arrival with them he announced his intention of smoking them, a very popular tea-time delicacy in Leigh.

33

He proceeded to knock both top and bottom out of a forty-gallon oak water butt we had, and drilled a series of small holes at various distances and heights in the sides. Through these he passed strong, thick fencing wire threaded thickly with sprats, which he skewered through the gills. He then lit his oak chips and sawdust fire under and inside the barrel. With curly wisps of aroma-laden smoke coming from it, all of us around excitedly joined in, anticipating our tea.

The sprats were some time later considered cooked and ready, and not only did we have ample for ourselves, but aunts, uncles and neighbours all had a share. It was voted such a success that it encouraged Dad to thread up all the remaining sprats and start a second cooking. Having got it 'under way' again, he informed us that all this was thirsty work, he felt the need of his usual pint or two, and as it was opening time at 'The Elms' just across the way said he would slip across for ten minutes. Ten minutes became an hour and he had still not come back. It was the younger children's bedtime and, following Mother up to the bedroom, with them I looked out of the window. The darkness was now lit by a glorious bonfire, the barrel and sprats, helped by their natural oils, were a flaming mass, and it was fortunate that it was in the middle of the garden. It was a bonfire night to be enjoyed and was better fun than if the sprats had cooked as before, but it was the first and last time we had home-cooked sprats!

Having covered shrimpers and stow-boats, lower on the list came the hoop netters. I am still not sure where they stood in the hierarchy of fishermen. They were Leighmen, but not fishermen in the true sense of the word, as the dabbing season – and dabs were mostly what they caught – only lasted for about three months and ended around Christmas. As far as I remember, 'the dabbers' were usually engaged in other activities associated with yachting, beach combing, shellfish, bait digging and the hundred and one casual jobs that go unnoticed in a community like Leigh.

There was no expensive outlay on nets or equipment. If one owned or could borrow a 'skiff' – the local name for the heavy, strong dinghies built by local boatbuilders, mostly for the shrimpers to get back and forth from the 'bawleys' – and had a hoop net, one was in business.

The hoop was some 3ft. or 4ft. in diameter, in heavy round

iron, with three iron rods forming a lifting triangle and made usually by the local blacksmith. It had a bag-like net, weighted at the bottom and fastened round the hoop at the top. The hoop was bound with sail-cloth to prevent the rust damaging the net. Two or three lines of strong twine – which when in use were threaded with sprats, herrings, or disembowelled crabs – were strung across the centre of the hoop. The whole contraption was lowered to the sea-bed on a rope, where it was left for ten or fifteen minutes. It could only be used until the tide run became too strong for it to remain quietly on the sea-bed. The secret of success was tautening the rope accurately without moving the net and frightening the fish feeding on the bait; then, with a sudden mighty jerk, lifting the net and the fish without warning or chance of escape. Sometimes as many as twenty-five or thirty dabs were caught, other times only one or two at each haul, according to the skill of the operator. It was heavy, back-breaking work, with little or no protection from the elements on their small, open boats.

My Dad, who only did it for fun and not to sell his fish, always enjoyed it, but he could choose his weather. Whenever I could go with him I did, and in between the waiting we fished with a hand line and what he called a 'sprool' or 'sprawl', a lead weight with three strong wire prongs sticking out at equal angles each about one foot long, with on the end of these, a 12-inch length of twine with a fishing hook attached. Dad made them himself, and although crude they were very efficient and on good days often caught three fish, one on each hook, at the one time.

Hoop netters mostly worked two nets, so there was no time lost if one was being emptied or re-baited, usually with the crabs that were caught with the fish. On some days as many as three or four stone of dabs were caught and sold to one of the three fishmongers in Leigh. These were 'Lumpy' Cotgrove, whose tiny shop adjoined Bell Wharf; Juniper, next to 'The Smack' in Leigh High Street, whose shop and dwelling must have been one of the earliest built in Leigh – and most likely there when it is reputed the 'Mayflower' of Pilgrim Fathers fame called at Leigh for food and stores – or, lastly, 'Wap' Robinson, whose shop was one of the half dozen or so small cottages and shops at the foot of Leigh Hill between 'The Bell' and the rail crossing. Between them they bought the catches and disposed of them by size or weight to the ever-growing numbers of commuters using Leigh railway station, which was at that time in the very centre of the three shops. It must have been difficult to know how to buy on days of plentiful catches – they dare not acquire too many as they had no modern fridges or means of keeping the fish fresh – or on bad days when not enough were caught to satisfy their customers. But the loss usually fell on the hoop netters and made it a precarious living, with little alternative.

Last of all came the 'long liners'. They pegged lines, known as 'cod lines', about 100 yards long, with short lengths of twine every three feet or so and about 15 inches long with a baited fish hook attached, on the mud flats around Leigh Creek. After each tide they collected the catch, mostly flounders, and re-baited for the next tide. This method was used by very few and mostly for home consumption, but with a good catch sold if possible. But as flounders had little market value, it was not in general use. It was a cruel form of fishing, as the fish that were caught took so long to die. Even worse, when baited, particularly with sprats and the tide just flowing over them, the lines attracted both gulls and curlew. The birds, by swallowing both sprat and hook, died a slow agonising death by drowning. So the only time Dad used a long line was from our boat when the tide was in, weighted at one end and slowly released from a circular cheese box, weighted and buoyed at the other end, and left ready to pick up again on returning from fishing.

Eels there were in plenty in the sea-grass just off Bell Wharf and sometimes caught with eel spears, a four-pronged fork-like tool used when the tide was out. But I never remember Dad using one; his favourite method was 'sapping'. 'Lob worms' were threaded through their length by a big needle, usually made from an umbrella spoke, attached to about a fathom length of 'worsted', a coarse knitting yarn. When the length was completely filled it was folded like a bunch of sausages the length of a worm. A short piece of line was attached, which in turn was tied to the end of a short stick or broom handle. Anchoring the boat in the shallow water above the gently swaying sea-grass, the 'sap' or bunch of worms was lowered among it. The eels would rush at the worms and swallow one completely and my father used to claim that their teeth caught in the worsted. With a quick lift out of the water the eel would drop off and, if quick enough, into the boat. The trouble with this method of fishing was that it necessitated taking up all the floorboards in the boat when arriving on the moorings, and chasing and catching the catch a second time – sometimes in the dark, as Dad always maintained quiet, dull, thundery evenings were the best and easiest time to catch them.

Unlike today's sophisticated and expensive equipment, the only thing we bought were the hooks, and these were sold in boxes of one hundred of one size. The line and twine came usually from the sailmaker, and odd ends were in great demand. I remember one day when Dad was fixing a new hook he casually remarked how things had progressed since his young days, when fish hooks were made from rose-bush thorns. I wish now I had enquired further about the method and construction of this form of hook, as I have never heard or read of it since. I can only assume it was a short piece of rose twig about one inch long, with a thorn left on it, but do not know, and it must have been very inefficient.

Once again I make no apologies for this long diversion on fishing. Nothing makes me more angry than, when writing, the author assumes the reader knows all about the obscure devices and instruments used in a past age or is not interested in anything but the story. So from time to time I shall continue to do so, leaving the reader to skip it if he so wishes.

As I have said, the loss of 'The Green Boat' saddened us all. It had been a faithful friend of many years. We had had great fun with it. Innumerable fishing trips paid its way by hiring out, and it became part of our lives. It was a shock too; no one stole boats in Leigh, it was like robbing a blind man, or a carpenter or craftsman of his tools. A boat was a man's livelihood and it was stealing his bread and butter.

It was a mystery and became quite a subject of discussion among the inhabitants of the Old Town, when they lowered their pints and expounded their ideas and theories. It was generally agreed that it was a 'foreigner', most likely one of the many sailing barges that visited Leigh. They enlarged further; perhaps the barge men had walked ashore, and lingering too long in the local had need to help themselves to a boat to get back, and Dad's barge dinghy was just the thing. Maybe they cast her adrift. Maybe they had put her in the hold of the barge to sell somewhere. After all, they went all over the rivers of Essex and Kent and travelled great distances. But all agreed that it was unlikely now that it would be found, as with the wind on-shore, if cast adrift it would have come ashore somewhere between Leigh and Southend.

Then Dad heard a rumour that a green boat had been found at 'Hole Haven' on Canvey Island. I was with him, but it made no difference, he immediately caught the train to Benfleet. It was about mid-day when we found the ferry man in his little wooden hut beside the causeway and stepping stones that crossed the creek at low tide. But the tide was too high to cross by foot, so for 3d each we were ferried over in his ancient dinghy and started the long trek down the 'Long Road' until we reached Canvey village with its thatched roofed pump, Dutch Cottage, and cluster of little cottages and shop. My father seemed to have boundless energy but already I was so tired I could hardly drag one foot after the other. So he hired one of the few ancient traps, drawn by an equally ancient horse, that lined up by the pump to take us down a similar long road to Hole Haven (possibly the very same road that my great great aunt Charlotte had referred to in her diary of 1830) and we eventually arrived at the 'Lobster Smack'.

The first need was for my father and the driver to quench their thirst, a ceremony that took quite a time. Then enquiries were made about the boat. The landlord said he'd heard of a boat found down by 'Kynocks Hotel', a remarkable Victorian structure some three or four hundred yards along the sea wall to the east. It was hinted with a nod and knowing wink by the locals that its isolation was its greatest asset. There were 'goings on' there best not looked into, and certain 'High Society' members 'lived it up' at holidays and week-ends. Just how true this was is anybody's guess. All I can say is, that it was a remarkably strange location for an hotel.

So we walked along the sea wall, having asked our driver to wait, and on arrival at the hotel eventually found someone who knew about a dinghy washed ashore. He told us where to look, and a hundred yards or so on the inner side of the sea wall we found it. It was not our 'Green Boat'; a useless wreck with a large gaping hole in one side. Only the transom was painted green, the rest tarred or scraped bare, and only about 10ft. long.

Completely and utterly disappointed we returned in the 'trap' right back to the ferry at Benfleet and caught the train to Leigh. I suppose I walked or was carried home – I don't remember until I woke up next morning.

It seems Mother had been frantic at our unexpected absence, terrified something serious had happened, and had for once read the Riot Act in a most unexpected and very outspoken manner on our arrival. My father was a very quiet and docile man for several days after. In fact I have a feeling that this was a crisis point in their relationship. He was surprised and shaken and never quite regained his supreme power and control of all family matters. From then on, Mother asserted herself and had an increasing say in affairs which, strangely enough, Father seemed to accept with relief.

Also, with Mother now an active and almost irreplaceable partner in the affairs of the beach, there was little he could do about it. The change in her character was almost unbelievable. As time went on, women in all ranks of society were beginning to change their image and throw off the shackles that to a greater or lesser degree had bound them in the past, and Mother among them. No doubt the contact with the outside world and the cross-section of the public she encountered in the summer months also had its place. She had had, before marriage, in a lesser degree, some experience of the excitement and demands of the holiday season in her mother's boarding house at Margate, and of mixing with all types on her brief visits to her uncle's hotels. An added advantage was that we were getting older and less demanding of her time.

So, all in all, she began to feel a confidence that had been lost in those first unhappy years of marriage and those that followed. Slowly and imperceptibly she took over the reins and began to run the home and the business her way, and equally slowly but surely my father relinquished his power as head of the family and business, except for his fishing parties, but without rancour or bitterness. In fact I think he was pleased. The strain of acquiring so rapidly a family and all that it entailed, with the unfamiliarity, and I suspect frustration at the loss of freedom and complete right to please himself, was constantly at loggerheads with his desire to accept responsibility and do his best for Mother and his children, and yet reconcile this with his previous way of life.

But we, for our part, were happy and little thought of the stresses of matrimony and certainly not of the future, when Fate decreed that the sole upbringing of the family should be left in her hands. And but for the strength of character now emerging, that future would have been bleak indeed. But with no knowledge or fore-warning of that in mind, I come back to the loss of the 'Green Boat'.

After the wild goose chase to 'Hole Haven', Dad seemed to accept that it was gone for good, and this was so; it was never seen or heard of again. But the loss was not only that of an old and trusted friend, it also hit him financially. He had been accustomed to letting it to small parties of anglers, or taking the rather more privileged and wealthier anglers from London. These were prepared to pay for his knowledge of the more choice fishing grounds he alone knew, so it was important that he replaced it before their custom was lost.

The answer came quite unexpectedly. As was his usual practice, he called at 'The Smack' for his pint. This served the double purpose of quenching his thirst, but more than that, kept him informed of all the 'goings on' in what was far more his 'home' than where he now lived. And here, quite by chance, he got into conversation with two strangers, fishermen from Gravesend. They told how, with the shortage of shrimps and fish, they had hoped to do better here in Leigh and had sailed down river and fished with little or no success. They were now desperate and their boat, lying just outside in Leigh Creek, would have to be sold. It was a Gravesend shrimper, about 22ft. long, beamy, and open except for a 6ft. foredeck, under which was a fo'c'sle containing a chain locker, two bunks and a small cast iron coal stove. It had a loose-footed mainsail and foresail of heavy canvas, one long oar, and a beam trawl. With a little bargaining an agreed price of £20 was arrived at. Like the auction for the beach, history repeated itself. The rush home, the collection of the money and the hurry back to secure it happened all over again, and the sale was completed.

I have often wondered why, with this method of business, more trickery, thieving and sheer roguery did not happen, and why Dad, having just lost or had his own boat stolen, was so trustful with two complete strangers. But it was a normal way for transactions to take place; the money always in cash and likely as not no receipt, or if receipted the stamp steamed off an old envelope and heavily signed and dated to cover any postmark, and the system seemed to work quite satisfactorily.

Dad immediately took the craft down to Chalkwell and moored it off the beach and next day I went with him to see it and soon caught his enthusiasm for its possibilities – larger fishing parties and the luxury and comfort of the fo'c'sle, and even trawling with a net. It had a name I don't remember, but cut into the transom on the inside and filled with white paint in large letters was A. J. SOPER, GRAVESEND, and from that day onwards, as far as I was concerned that was its name.

The 'A. J. Soper' was a success from the start and was immediately hired on the following Sunday by members of the Southend Amateur Angling Society. The system of hiring was simple. A number of members agreed among themselves to pay £1 collectively for the day, the bait was extra. There were usually about eight; less than that number made it expensive, and more spoilt or overcrowded their fishing lines.

Whether it was too large to manage alone I still don't know, but we always took 'Hictor' Johnson, a fisherman and boyhood friend of Dad's, with us. He was in my opinion as great a character as Gotty, who was so well known, both from the book 'Gotty and the Guvnor' and his exploits on the greasy pole at Leigh Regatta. 'Hictor's' remuneration was a one-third share of the hiring fee, one share being for Dad and one share for the upkeep of the boat, which, of course, Dad retained. This was the customary practice among the fishermen of Leigh and I think still is. The party were ferried aboard, the sails hoisted, the coal fire started and the large iron kettle on top was soon singing merrily. Later, large mugs of hot strong tea were handed round and the food baskets opened. Just after the pierhead was passed, the fish trawl was dropped over and dragged along the seabed until we reached the fishing grounds. Sometimes it was a good haul, sometimes poor, but it ensured that the party always had some fish to take home, however poor their individual fishing efforts were.

For a whole day's work, plus the use of the boat, Dad received 13 shillings and maybe eight shillings for bait. This was typical of the times but the 'A. J. Soper' was paying her way and gave us confidence for her future. In fact she paid for herself that season and

I was sorry when it was over and finished for that year. A new love had taken the place of the 'Green Boat' in our hearts, and many a happy day in the following year the whole family spent on her, in the Ray. The comfort of the fo'c'sle was a great blessing and generally a vast improvement on the now almost forgotten 'Green Boat'.

But its loss was still being felt in another way. The new and more important 'A. J. Soper' did not – although a great improvement – entirely fill the gap left by the smaller boat, which was usually hired out without the services of either skipper or mate to smaller parties, mostly of four, or trippers with families needing a safe and nearly unsinkable old boat for fun.

The larger boat having already paid for itself, the following spring my father decided to replace the 'Green Boat' and strangely enough it was Gravesend that again supplied the answer.

I don't know how he heard of or found it, and can only speculate that his original source of knowledge, i.e. the 'Smack Inn' was responsible. The first I knew was being told to be up early, as Dad was going somewhere, and the following morning about seven o'clock we left home, making our way to Leigh Station, picking up 'Hictor' on the way. Arriving at Tilbury we crossed by ferry to Gravesend and walked some distance along the seafront, and among the happenings of that exciting day a curious memory still remains in my childhood mind. I had to relieve a call of nature and my father ushered me into a strange-shaped cast iron contraption standing in the open street which exposed both the legs from the knees downwards and head and shoulders if one was tall enough. I had never seen such a place before and although only a child was deeply embarrassed, such was the upbringing in those days. It made a surprising impression on me. I only mention it now to record that what I always thought to be a purely Continental custom was a feature of Gravesend's seafront.

Shortly afterwards we arrived at a large shed-like structure built on piles over the water and open at the further end. There was a big expanse of floor with a ramp sloping into the river and men hurrying around. I had the impression that they were sailors, all smartly dressed in nautical clothing and what I used to call 'captains' hats', which were quite unlike the peaked caps worn in Leigh.

After a few enquiries Dad found an even more impressive one with gold braid very much in evidence and a great contrast to Dad's and 'Hictor's' fishermen's jerseys and seaboots. A few words and we were taken to where the object of our journey rested.

I doubt if I shall ever see the like of it again, or that there are craftsmen in this age of fibre glass that could reproduce one comparable. A yacht's tender, some 14ft. long, beautifully moulded and yet with a good beam, and built of teak throughout, it shone with the sheen of highly polished furniture, and that was almost the impression it gave. It was not so much a boat as a creation. Even the floorboards both for'ard and aft were works of art, inlaid by gratings of American rock elm. A pure white cotton rope painter lay coiled on a raised platform in the bow. White cylindrical fenders hung round the sides, and to me the most remarkable thing of all, fastened on either side of the bow were two carved plaques framed in a curved rope pattern and in the triangle a blue and white flag intersected with a gold-entwined anchor and rope.

This alone made me offer up a silent prayer that Dad would buy it and my prayer was almost immediately answered. There was no haggling; I don't think he would have dared, with the gold braid he was dealing with, and the purchase price was passed over in sovereigns carefully counted, a receipt on impressive headed paper given, and it was ours. It was launched into the river and with almost reverence we stepped carefully aboard and were away.

They had timed it as far as possible for high water and to catch the ebb down river, and with its aid Dad and his companion rowed for five long hours until we reached 'Hole Haven', a distance of twenty miles at least. It was almost low water when we arrived. There was no chance of getting to Leigh except by way of the lowway, another six miles. Also, the 'Lobster Smack' was at hand and they both disappeared into its open doorway, leaving me outside, as I was too young to be allowed in. Later Dad came out with a thick sandwich and bottle of ginger beer and left me to my own devices on the wooden bench outside.

I remember exploring along the dyke, full of reeds and rushes, that went all along the base of the sea wall, a very old farmhouse, barns and carts about 100 yards from the inn, and the desolation and silence, broken only by the cries of gulls and seabirds, and ducks on the farmhouse pond, and the sudden rush of chickens as a woman came out of the farm door and threw them food. Eventually, bored, I climbed aboard our new boat and was soon fast asleep. The journey round Benfleet Creek on the incoming tide in the dark, the train from Benfleet where they moored it, and the walk home are a complete blank and I remember nothing more until waking up in my own bed next day.

The boat had been left in charge of the ferryman overnight and the following day Dad and I again took the train to Benfleet and caught the ebb tide through the marshes to Leigh Creek and the Old Town. Its arrival in Old Leigh was quite a sensation. Boats played a major part in the life of its inhabitants and all the knowledgeable Leighmen were unstinted in their praise. Compared, if it were possible at all, with their rough, heavy and very strong 'punts and skiffs' (I never learned the difference), it was as different as 'chalk from cheese'. I suspect only a handful, like Mr. Wilder or Mr. Kirby, who had skippered some of the famous racing yachts like 'Britannia', 'Valkyrie' and 'Meteor' (which incidentally were responsible for those roads of a similar name in Westcliff to commemorate their visits) had ever seen such a lovely craft. And when I again saw it, even fresh glories come to light. A gold-leafed band was inset all around the gunwale. There were four strong, light and brightly varnished oars and four solid shining gunmetal rowlocks. In fact every fitting was shining gunmetal and these were fresh assets to those previously seen, and all duly noted by those around.

That my father had got a treasure was agreed. Then the doubts and fears began to creep in. Would it be lost or stolen like the Green Boat? He moved it to Chalkwell and the fears followed. Also, it was too good for hiring out. Nobody could be relied on to take the care it deserved. Sand, mud, bait and dead crabs in it were unthinkable. It couldn't be hired for fishing or let to strangers, so there it sat on its moorings most of the summer, except once or twice when as a special treat he took us for a row in it. The five or six years it was in his possession were a dead loss and financially a complete failure, but its unique beauty held him like a mistress and he would not part with it. He kept it varnished and did everything possible to retain its prestige but it was never quite like its original perfection; it should never have been left in the open. Its rightful place was in a boat shed or tarpaulin-covered on the deck of a yacht and used only on the few occasions that such boats are called on, with no care or expense withheld.

The real answer was probably to take it home and build a shed to keep it in and cherish it like a valuable heirloom, just to look at and show to friends, but from a practical angle it was a complete mistake and remained so. Even its name, done in gold lettering by a signwriter and intended as a supreme compliment to my mother – 'Minnie' – his special and affectionate nickname for her, while suitable for an ordinary boat, was an insult to it. It was a white elephant to the last but nothing would persuade him to part with it.

Of course, while these incidents had some small bearing on our future they were merely highlights in our normal life. The beach had little influence on us children during the months following Christmas until the renewal of the lease, always a matter of some fear. These months of cold short days and long evenings seemed for at least the five weekdays to consist of just going back and forth to school. Mealtimes and evenings, with none of our modern methods of entertainment, were passed playing either an old battered gramophone or cards, 'Beggar Your Neighbour' being favourite. The great occasions were when it snowed and Grand Drive, Leigh Cliff and other steep roads were taken over both by adults and children on home-made sleighs of a weird and wonderful variety, the roads being free of cars. Spasmodically I made model boats or aeroplanes driven by elastic, but never remember being bored.

At weekends with our chosen school mates, we wandered over the fields that stretched from the London Road to Eastwood and beyond. Roads were cart tracks, in some cases almost impassable owing to the herds of cows driven over them. Prittle Brook was a favourite, but we ventured through mud above our ankles to the top of Elmsleigh Drive to Hill's Pond, a great place for sticklebacks and frog spawn and a bathing place for both gipsies and their horses in summer. I collected stamps, cigarette cards and odd bits of anything that caught my eye, and as the time and season came round, to my present regret, birds' eggs and butterflies. But with wildlife so plentiful it did not at that time seem wrong, and many adults, including the curate of St. Clement's Church, were keen collectors. And how delighted I was when Mr. Saunt, a well-known solicitor in Leigh with connections on Lundy Island, gave me some rare sea-birds' eggs from that isle. In fact it became my overriding hobby and I produced an illustrated book of British birds and their eggs, mostly, I confess, poached from other books and cigarette cards, which I showed to Mrs. Nicholson, my teacher. To my surprise it was passed round to Mr. Thatcher, the head-master and all the other teachers and was, I think, instrumental in my obtaining the evening scholarship at Southend School of Art the following year.

And my mention of Mrs. Nicholson, for whom I had the great-est respect and even affection, calls to mind a curious incident when I was very much older, in fact I think in about 1957. I was in the front garden of my present home in Fernleigh Drive when two very elderly ladies stopped and admired the roses. One had an amazing likeness to, and allowing for age, was the image of my for-mer teacher, so with great delight I put out my hand and said:

'Aren't you Mrs. Nicholson?' She looked at her companion in a curious way,' then turned to me and said:

'Why do you ask, young man?'

I replied, 'Well, if you are Mrs. Nicholson then you were my favourite teacher at North Street School.'

She looked at me for a moment, then again at the lady with her, and exclaimed:

'Extraordinary! Yes I am a Mrs. Nicholson, and I was a teacher.' Then she added, 'Of music. But I live and have always lived at Ilford and this is my first time in Leigh, to visit my friend.' After a brief chat they passed on their way and I didn't see her again but the coincidence was so remarkable that it left me wondering what the odds are of meeting a complete stranger in the street, asking if their name is Nicholson and being answered 'yes', irrespective of the fact she was a teacher also.

I was now nearly thirteen years old. My personal hobbies and a growing independence and the companionship of boys of my own age slowly but surely eroded my loyalty and friendship with Dad and I spent less and less time with him. But for the Easter holidays of that year we had a fortnight together.

Many a time when fishing in the Ray in, the far distance, at the mouth of 'Oyster Creek' near Canvey Point, I had seen this old black hulk complete with high deck house silhouetted against the evening sky, and in my mind built romantic stories of pirates and sea rovers. It had always been there, ever since I could remember and was part of the seascape, so it seemed completely unbelievable when Dad calmly announced he had bought it and was going to have it towed onto the marshes near the sea wall. A few days later he took me to see it. The great black hull looked enormous and written in large weather-worn lettering on its bows was 'Ye Olde Watch Boat'. The spelling alone showed its age, even if it had been repainted some time more recently. He explained that many years before, back in the 1800s, oysters were cultivated all around this area and, to prevent pilfering and stealing, this was the guard boat where two men lived, much like lighthouse keepers, to protect and conserve the beds and shellfish.

I was somehow pleased that, if not quite so romantic as a pirate ship, it was at least a guard ship, and spent the morning exploring it from cabin to keel. The deck house was filthy with dirt but even so the varnished pine and teak panelling was quite impressive, the cabins spacious, and it would, I think, have made a delightful home. It was quite possibly a hundred or more years old, but still sound even then. But my father had other ideas; he had bought it and it was very cheap only £5 – entirely for the timbers in it. The lovely pine matchboarding that comprised the deck house was just what he wanted to build a long box-like structure to store the ever-increasing number of tent poles and oars the business was acquiring. So he started its destruction by removing the linings of the deck house, and on a flat spot at the base of the sea wall built this storage box, about 12ft. long, 4ft. wide and 3 or 4ft. high with two sloping lids extending the whole length and hinged at the back.

I would have thought (looking back) that it would have been best to have built it in sections and bolted or screwed it together, but for some reason it was built complete, and when the tide was at its highest, floated into the creek and towed with the tide to Chalkwell, where it was moored overnight and next day floated to high-water mark, put on rollers and levered to its allotted place. There it stayed until the beach was taken from us, so it speaks well of his workmanship.

When this was accomplished he took little or no further interest in the vessel and left her there, where she stayed all through the

Great War. After his death, in 1919 or maybe even 1920, Mother was approached while on our beach by two young men. They enquired if she still owned it. Long forgotten, she said, 'Yes.' Would she take £5 for it? Once again she said, 'Yes.' The whole transaction took about ten minutes. The money was handed over and they were gone. I don't know what they eventually did with it but that was the end as far as we were concerned. In any case we had almost forgotten it belonged to us, but I did hear later that they had approached Mr. Parsons, a well-known local boatbuilder, with intentions of again making it seaworthy.

The beach was now our main source of income; the rapid growth of both residents and visitors left no lingering doubts as to its possibilities. We had the 'A. J. Soper', more tents were ordered from 'Francy' Tunnidge, our local sailmaker, more tent poles (the tents were square with a pole in each corner), and two second-hand rowing 'skiffs'. These boats built specially for hiring to visitors have now gone completely out of existence but I will try to describe them. They were very much a standard type, used all along the sea front from Leigh to the Kursaal by those who let out rowing boats and at a rough guess there were maybe 150-200 all told, as it was a flourishing summer trade, particularly in Southend and Westcliff. Fourteen or fifteen feet long, they were lightly built, rather low freeboard and rather narrow in beam, with a chair-back rear seat and rudder steering by lines. In fact they were really just a more substantial version of the river skiffs seen on the upper reaches of the Thames, but strangely seaworthy, although they didn't look it, and I never heard of a fatal accident involving one. The charge was 6d per person, children half price, per hour. They were licensed by the Foreshore Office to carry up to four persons but this was never, I think, enforced, as quite often the hirers picked up others further along the foreshore to avoid paying for the extra passengers.

My father never quite got over the loss of the Green Boat. He needed it or one like it but he wouldn't buy another, because then he would have no excuse to keep his Gravesend pride and joy, and he had no intention of parting with that, so when the chance came to buy these two skiffs, it satisfied his conscience and provided a solution to some degree. He would now only take fishing parties in the 'A. J. Soper' and the hiring of the skiffs to visitors would amply compensate. But it was no real answer. The skiffs were suitable for one purpose and one only – hiring to trippers. They were completely unsuitable for the many, many uses of an all-purpose boat. But here again chance, Fate, call it what you will, took a hand and in retrospect it would seem a common factor running through most of his dealings with the beach. The acquiring of it – the 'A. J. Soper' – the boat from Gravesend – the two skiffs – the rapid growth of the surroundings – all had required little of the usual struggle and effort to establish a business. Things just seemed to happen. Not that Dad didn't work very hard when they had happened and make full use of the opportunities so created.

And so it was that once again this factor came up with an answer. My uncle and aunt had an only son. They were in the position to buy him the most wonderful toys. They had marvellous Christmas parties and November 5th was looked forward to with joy and anticipation by us all, as we were always invited. In fact to us his life was all that could be desired, and for his school holidays they bought a dinghy, not as one would expect from a local boat builder, but from the biggest toy store in London, 'Gamages'.

It arrived by rail to Leigh. Unlike the elm-built local boats, it was spruce, light, strong and very beamy, almost round. We christened it almost immediately 'The Tub Boat' and the name stuck, irrespective of its proper name. The arrangement was that Dad would maintain and look after it and we in turn would have the use of it when needed, providing it was available for my cousin's use at any time he wished, which in actual fact was about three times during the many years we looked after it. And when I think of our happy-go-lucky carefree existence, and later his life, which seemed to consist of school, homework and study, all the toys in the world wouldn't compensate for the responsible and remunerative job that he later acquired. But my cousin's health suffered and he never lived to enjoy the retirement he richly deserved and which I had hoped in some degree to share, as I had the greatest respect and admiration for him and he was a fine, principled man.

The Tub Boat was a great blessing. It towed well, rowed well and was as safe as any dinghy could possibly be. I was able to row it with ease, take my brothers and sisters in it and even go fishing on my own if I kept in sight of the beach. It did all and more than what we asked of it and, to all intents and purposes, as it turned out, was as good as ours, and as time went on we never thought of it otherwise.

That year was also notable for an event that had far-reaching results on our lives. The powers that be, i.e. the Railway Company, built Chalkwell Bridge. Previously one had to cross over the rail track at Leigh or the more recent 'Queens Bridge' halfway along the cinder path, or alternatively through a 'kissing gate' and across the rail track where the new bridge at Chalkwell was proposed. Surprisingly I remember little of its construction, other than railway trucks depositing huge loads of sand and gravel on our beach. As it was, I think, early spring, and the lease not renewed, the Railway had every right to do so, but my father was furious. He seemed to think the beach was his now for the whole twelve months and in a way it had been.

This again showed Fate working in the background, as it forced him to face facts. The upshot was he entered into negotiations successfully to renew the lease yearly for a larger rent and secure our occupation on a more permanent basis, and this in turn gave the sense of security which persuaded him to expand the business even more. He now had five boats, more tents, costumes and towels on order and invested in a dozen deck-chairs. These proved a menace as the ordinary deck-chairs he bought could not withstand the ill-treatment they received, unlike those of the Corporation, who had them specially made.

All this had to be paid for, and it was necessary for him to take out a loan. Many times that summer I remember calling at one of the large houses on Cliff Parade and the passing over of sovereigns, the ritual of signing and the small glass of wine that accompanied these visits. I sometimes now try to identify the house but I only remember it was opposite the gas lamp that stands solitary on the grass patch above the Essex Yacht Club. This lamp always fascinated me. Two sides of the four glasses were red and two normal, clear glass. There was another, similar, gas lamp at the bottom of Queens Road but I think all the glasses were red. My father explained that these lamps were especially placed to act as a guide to the fishermen at night, plotting the channel of the 'low-way' to the Ray, a stretch of water that remained deep at all states of the tide and was the mooring place of as many as sixty bawleys and fishing boats at low tide. The lamps are still there but I doubt whether they are used, as the sands in the estuary are constantly moving and the low-way channel is no longer in its previous position.

I was at school during the building of the bridge and most weekends were fully occupied with my own devices, which probably accounts for my lack of interest in its construction, but I do recollect how surprised I was at the time taken. It seemed only a few weeks until I was able to cross the line with confidence and safety to my beloved undercliff. There I constructed a secret hideout in the dense undergrowth and spent the best part of my holidays, only revealing it to my closest friends of the moment. As these were generally children of customers on the beach, it remained secret from the locals and the danger of them knowing its location. From it, I watched the comings and goings of the wildlife that lived there.

That summer all Dad's hopes were realised; it was a glorious year. In fact, although he had ordered more tents and costumes, they were not nearly sufficient and more orders were placed for both and quickly obtained as it was 'Francy's' slack season. With the increased number of tents, Dad decided to leave them up all night, when previously he put them up each day – an hour or more of tiring work as four post-holes had to be made for each tent. He now decided that the increased number made this impossible, so they remained up. The danger of fire from the adjoining railway trains which sometimes belched out showers of sparks was ever present, so it was decided we needed a night watchman. And in that same curious way that things seemed to happen in those days, it was not long before we had an applicant.

I plainly recall this oldish man, limping on a crutch, struggling down the entrance to the shed. The sand made the going even more difficult and he accepted a seat on a beer crate with relief. He informed Dad his name was Mr. Tye, that he had been an employee of the Gas, Light & Coke Co. in London and retired on a very small pension, suffering severely with arthritis. He had heard we wanted a night watchman and was hoping we would consider him for the job.

It was obvious to anyone that he could never have coped with a fire or protected the tents from petty thieving. But for some unaccountable reason my father decided he was suitable and it was arranged that he should be on duty from eight in the evening until eight the next morning. The first night he turned up at six and stayed until ten o'clock the following day. He slept in a large bell tent near The Shed on a camp bed. We supplied an oil lamp, 'Beatrice' stove and kettle and he settled in.

There was an almost immediate change in him. That he liked the life was plain to see and he stayed longer and longer each day, until he was only going home for an hour or two, or not at all, and Mother began to include him in our meals. The sand made it almost impossible for him to use his crutch and after struggling with it for a while he abandoned it, except for going home. With the aid of a stick he managed somehow to keep mobile and even began to help in a small way. Every week showed a little improvement in his general health and we were worried and frightened when he started wading, trousers getting soaked above his knees, to push a boat off the beach, expecting him to fall or at least undo all the improvement we had seen. But it had entirely the opposite effect and he became so useful that Dad engaged him both day and night. Soon he was proving his worth in taking out families for a row in one of our skiffs and more than earning his wages.

He almost lived on the beach now. I never knew where he really lived, except it was somewhere off Leigh Road. My world was still the beach and where he lived didn't interest me. By the end of that summer the change was remarkable and while he still limped badly he was able to get about in a manner that had to be seen to be believed. He was now accepted as part of the beach among the customers and regulars, and until 1918, in spite of the War, helped us every summer. His health continued to improve, although he never lost his limp and he became known affectionately – but behind his back – as 'Old Hoppy'.

Reading this one could be excused for thinking Mother took little or no part worth mentioning in our lives and The Beach, but in actual fact none of us could have survived as a family, or the beach continued as a business, without her. Her role was less spectacular and interesting but equally, or perhaps even more important, to the general well-being of us all. With six young children to wash, mend, sew, cook, feed and care for, and without the modern aids of today, she had more than sufficient to do. Now, with the added work during the summer months that the beach required, I am still amazed at the courage, resolution and sheer hard work she uncomplainingly faced each day. Perhaps if she had been otherwise we would have realized it more and even tried to help; as it was we all just accepted it without thought or question.

Owing to the increasing demand of the business, she now started going to the beach from June onwards, usually with heavy bags of food and other necessities required each day and she normally walked both there and later back. There were no buses and the trams and trains were of no help from where we lived. The summer school holidays did not start until the last week in July, so she had to prepare our dinners and leave them ready for us when we came home just after twelve. The older of us had to look after the younger members and I was mostly in charge of opening and locking up the house at mid-day. In the afternoons we made the long journey straight from school and had tea in the shed or just outside, sitting on the ever useful beer crates. In the late evening we journeyed back, usually along the Broadway to get next day's shopping. The shops were open until quite late at night and the gas lamps in them glowed brightly on those warm summer nights. Quite often I would stop with Dad, who usually followed later along the cinder path. There, through the railway railings in the grass of the embankment, the tiny lights of the glow-worms that abounded there shone with a phosphorescent and greenish glow. They were usually just out of my reach, as I badly wanted to catch them, and even long after sunset a nightingale would break the evening quiet with its powerful song from the thicket across the way.

But once again, as always it seems, Dad has slipped into the picture and Mother again into the background, which was the last place she deserved. My closeness to Dad was, I suppose, natural, as my twin sisters were next in line to me, and girls had very little place in my father's way of life. Four years younger than me came my brother Vincent, too young to take much part in Dad's everyday doings, and lastly my youngest brother Harold and his twin sister Edna, so much younger still and quite unable to do the things my Dad and I could do. The fact that I was his oldest son made me his constant and favourite companion. He was probably living his youth over again in me, and while he loved us all, I was the favoured one and I in turn enjoyed every moment with him. Mother understood and welcomed it. The responsibility of the rest of the family and all it entailed fell on her but she seldom received the credit due. But it did build her character and made her strong to face the future.

As the modern child is now interested in [outer] space, my mind was turning to the new flying machines. Cigarette cards, stamps, birds' eggs and butterflies had all in their turn filled my interest and still did in their season. But more and more, news items, photos and stories about those remarkable men and the machines they flew in captured my imagination. There were stories of a monster airship in Germany and of Americans flying great distances, and A. V. Roe and Sopwith were becoming familiar names in England. Actual scale models, unlike today, would not fly. But a strong, square, thin stick with a framework wing in front and a much smaller one at the back covered in Chinese silk, or preferably in gold-beaters' skin, and powered by several strands of elastic driving a two-bladed propeller would, in certain conditions, fly about a hundred yards or even further with the wind behind them. As we had many large fields at the top of the road, we had great fun with them but invariably returned with them broken or damaged, for repairing, to fly again the following weekend.

I had never seen a real one; I had seen a few balloons drifting slowly in the sky, but one day when I was on Our Beach a curious droning sound attracted my attention and, there out at sea, descending like a bird and making for the beach was my first aeroplane. Actually it was a seaplane and as it touched down on its two large, boat-shaped floats, both Dad and I started to run to its place of landing on the beach opposite Chalkwell Avenue. A crowd collected from nowhere, all excited and inspecting this modern wonder. It was mostly canvas, wood and wire, with red, white and blue colouring much in evidence. But what attracted my attention particularly were the words in large letters right along the canvas fuselage: 'Wake Up England'. The pilot was the well-known English aviator Graham White, and he was soon the centre of the crowd, but my interest was the machine, so what was discussed I don't know. Later he did several adjustments to the engine, the reason I think for landing, turned it round and roared off out to sea again and away. It was the most exciting thing that had happened to me since my trip in Dad's boat from Gravesend and even now I relish the memory.

But it was not all happy memories that year. Coming home from school one dinner time I found my Auntie Polly trying to console my mother, who was weeping in a manner I had never before witnessed. She rarely, if ever, showed her innermost feelings to us or the outside world, but it was obvious something very shattering had happened.

On the table, bearing an African stamp, lay an envelope and an opened letter. Auntie shooed us out and said we needn't go to school for the rest of the day. Dad came home and the door shut, and after what seemed a very long time we were called back in. For once very silent and with fear in our hearts we listened as Auntie told us Mother's elder and much-loved brother William had been killed in an accident, and once again Mother burst into tears as though her heart would break. He and Thomas were the only kin she had left and she loved them both with a deep affection. When things eventually became more settled Auntie read us the letter telling how he had died an unexpected and painful death.

Demobbed at the finish of the Boer War, in which both brothers served in a section known as 'Kitchener's Light Horse', they both took part in the Battle of the Modder River. It was reputed that the massacre was so great that the river flowed red with blood, but both survived. After many adventures, one of which, the story is told, was their escape from capture by a party of Boers, they were given food and shelter and were hidden in safety by a farming family. Their daughter and William were greatly attracted to each other, although she was of Boer descent. Suffice to say that William decided after the war to go back to Africa and renew the acquaintance, and he did in fact marry her.

Thomas went back to his trade of bricklayer and when my brother Harold met him in Johannesburg many years later he told him how, in the late November of the year he returned from Africa, he was 'topping out' a tall factory chimney of a cement works in Kent. It was bitterly cold and wispy snowflakes blew around in the icy wind. At last the finishing brick was neatly laid in place and the last bit of cement carefully smoothed. He stood up, looked at his mate and deliberately flung his trowel down the open shaft of the newly completed chimney.

'That's the last brick I'll lay in England,' he said, and promptly went home, booked his passage, packed his bags and left to join his brother in Africa. He never returned. I met him and Auntie Olive, his wife, in Cape Town in 1950. He loved soldiering and served in the Boer War, the 1914-18 War, in East Africa, and in spite of his age, in Abyssinia in the Second World War. He met his brother on arrival in Cape Town and joined with him in the Cape Police Force.

But with adventure in their blood, they decided that there were greater opportunities to be found by those who were prepared to seek them, not the least gold and diamonds which were being discovered in increasing numbers. They eventually found themselves, and William's wife Blanche (Tom was still unmarried) in a remote place in Northern Transvaal named Bandolier Kop, and here they settled. Whether this was because it was here that William's wife gave birth to their first born I don't know, but I was told he was born in a tent with lions and hyenas prowling around, when Mother read out Auntie Blanche's letters to us. From all accounts the site was on the only existing road to the north, and the waggon trains, like those in early American history – in fact the whole set-up must have been similar – had to pass this way. No food, water or accommodation was to be found for many, many miles either way. There was that rare and necessary commodity, water, there, so they built what they called in their letters a 'hotel'. I prefer to think of it more as a 'saloon', like those in films of 'Westerns'.

It was, judging from their enthusiastic letters, a success from the start. Later it was decided to extend their business by building a series of smaller stores even further on the road, which they did. This in turn necessitated overnight and even longer journeys on horseback to supervise, replenish and generally attend to their management. These stores were also a great success and the brothers, after several years, were well on the way to becoming very wealthy and highly respected citizens of the small but increasing township that had grown around them. Uncle Will was now able to indulge in his pet hobby of breeding Great Danes. This turned out to be not only a hobby but a financial success also, so with everything going so well and the future so bright, no one was prepared for the tragedy to come.

William, the older brother, was returning from visiting the furthest store and had been absent for several days. He was riding a young, newly acquired pony and had welcomed the opportunity of testing its merits. No doubt glad to be back home, William rode straight to the front entrance and proceeded to dismount, but hardly had he got one foot out of the stirrup than the Great Danes, overjoyed at their master's return, dashed out and leaped up to greet him. The terrified pony took fright, dragging my uncle still with one foot firmly caught in the stirrup for three quarters of a mile back over the rough track he had just traversed, followed almost immediately by his wife and others who had witnessed this appalling accident. He lived for about half an hour but never regained consciousness.

This was the news carried to Mother in the letter and I never realised until then what grief and pain one suffered, as Mother did, at the loss of a loved one. Of course, as is natural with children, he was just a romantic relative whom we had never seen and we soon forgot, but had he lived and continued to prosper it is possible our lives might have been very different as he was already considering the possibilities of at least some of us joining him. But it wasn't to be and Thomas, his brother, then decided to marry and carry on alone. His story was, if not so tragic, equally interesting and while I realise that these stories have nothing whatsoever to do with The Beach or Old Leigh, they do have connections remotely with the family and for that reason I record them.

Thomas, happy-go-lucky, lovable, but perhaps less reliable and not so business-like, carried on, retaining the business and the twenty-seven thousand morgens of land rented at a nominal sum per morgen from the Government, which was anxious to develop it. I don't know what constitutes a morgen [one morgen = two acres] but on any scale it must have been an awful lot. Here and there on it were outcrops of a type of black rock and, when a party of geologists stayed for a few days at the hotel, Tom asked them if they would take samples and analyse them, more out of curiosity than for any other reason.

In due course a letter arrived from Cape Town giving a report on them and bearing the news that it was a mineral known as 'corundum', the basic material used for grinding and polishing and the manufacture of emery or carborundum wheels etc. Its commercial value was not particularly high at that time but it was suggested that he should mine a quantity and send it to England by ship to see if it would find a market which, after consideration, he did. It was shipped to the London docks, put into a warehouse and offered for sale, but all attempts to find a customer failed and, after nine months of mounting storage charges and expense, it was agreed that it be dumped in the Thames and the project abandoned.

Several months passed. The clouds of the First World War loomed. The making of armaments and the materials for their construction and destruction became a number one priority, and among these corundum. The warehouse and agent were contacted, only to be told that this now valuable shipment was at the bottom of the Thames and no longer available. Urgent telegrams passed back and forth. Could he supply more shipments? The makeshift mine was restarted and, with its outdated and somewhat crude machinery, was in a short time turning out 400 tons per month and shipping it to England.

But the demand grew and grew. [By 1917] America was now involved and wanted huge quantities. It was at this stage he was approached through the Minister of Mines by one of the big mining combines. They were run in the main by a group of financiers, whose politics and scruples were successfully hidden by their position and wealth, and where precious metals and diamonds had killed any morals that they might have once had. It was proposed by them that they take over, provide new machinery and make him Company Secretary and Director, and a rosy picture of a marvellous future and wealth untold was presented to him.

I am even now not quite sure just what happened, but first of all the old machinery was removed. New, modern, and up-to-date replacement machinery was on its way and was still 'on its way' nine months later without arriving. In the meantime, nothing was proceeding. Orders were unfulfilled and lost and, worse, he was still under some obscure clause responsible for keeping the firm operating with his own money. In fact he was caught in a carefully set trap with no escape except bankruptcy. By the end of that year he had lost everything. He left Bandolier Kop accompanied by his wife with little more than the clothes they stood in and went to Johannesburg. This, of course, would never have happened had William lived. (The new machinery arrived a fortnight afterwards and the financial syndicate took over.)

In Jo'burg, living in one room, he found a job. After all those years he once again turned to his old trade of bricklayer and I remember he told me how, of the five men taken on by the firm, in the morning he was the only one retained. He worked for this firm until joining the African Forces in East Africa and returned to them when the War ended. He become one of their most trusted foremen and later, when in charge of the construction of a brass foundry, was asked if he would work for them in the capacity of General Manager and Secretary when it was completed. This he did and eventually became a Director and was able to enjoy a very good standard of living until the end of his days in Jo'burg. My auntie stuck by him all through, but I felt that she never forgave him, as she had maintained all through that what he had done was completely against her advice and wishes. I have not heard from her for two years, so I fear that something has happened, as she never really got over Uncle's death around 1960.

Mother now had only one close relation left after Uncle Will's death; that was Uncle Tom, but he was far away in Africa. But we were surrounded by both uncles and aunts on Dad's side and this chronicle would not be complete without reference to them.

Uncle Harry never went to work after his return from Australia but had a small income from property in Cranleigh Drive. When he left school Grandfather apprenticed him and Uncle Will to a large firm of haberdashers in London, where they 'lived in'. I have a small notebook which he kept in those far off days around the early 1880s, and in which he had copied the firm's rules and stipulations of employment. I apologise for their length in recording them, but felt they might be of interest and throw some light on conditions prevailing with shop assistants at that period. They can be ignored if one so wishes.

PETER ROBINSON LTD.
RULES, REGULATIONS & FINES OF THIS ESTABLISHMENT

'All persons entering upon service in this establishment are requested to read the rules before commencing business, and anyone not intending to obey them in every respect is requested not to remain as they will be fully enforced.

Rule 1   That the shop be opened at 8 o'clock and that assistants and apprentices be present at the hour appointed and attend their proper duties.   FINE 3d

Rule 2   Fifteen minutes is allowed for breakfast and tea. Young ladies thirty minutes for dinner and dressing, young men twenty minutes, and assistants must not go to meals out of proper order or leave the department without the correct number at the counter.   FINE 3d

Rule 3   That young men wear black or dark coloured coats and black ties and that they do not take off their coats while serving. Young ladies to wear black dresses, made or looped to clear the ground, and white linen collars. *Coloured bows or ribbons* strictly forbidden.   FINE 3d

Rule 4   Talking to each other while serving, or speaking to another customer unless strictly on business, gossiping, standing in groups or lounging about in an unbusinesslike manner.   FINE 3d

Rule 5   That all remnants be measured at the time of the sale. That all dress goods be cut from the outside of the piece and no length to be cut unless measured up without consent. In all cases regular goods must be shown before introducing remnants.
                                                                FINE 3d

Rule 6   For giving wrong measure, omitting goods sold from parcels. For enclosing goods not sold or charged or selling goods at different prices to those marked.   FINE 3d

Rule 7   For not marking the length and price on goods at the time of sale or not defacing the make of goods out after being measured.   FINE 1d

Rule 8   For not putting goods in their respective places after showing them.   FINE 3d

Rule 9   That articles and money found in the shop be at once taken to the desk and tapers only to be used for lighting the gas.
                                                                FINE 3d

Rule 10   Great care must be taken in serving ribbons, gloves, etc. and not more than two boxes to be shown at the one time and then not to be left open while procuring other articles. Such carelessness often proves the cause of great loss to the firm. FINE 3d

Rule 11   That goods sold out be at once put on order and if wanted immediately, entered in the special book.   FINE 2d

Rule 12   For leaving the premises during business hours, remaining out after 11 o'clock Saturday, and Thursday 12 o'clock or sleeping out without consent.   FINE 2/6d

Second offence: Dismissal

Rule 13   Care and economy in the use of paper, string, pins, etc., none of which must be thrown about or left on the counters or floors but when done with placed in their proper receptacle.

FINE 1d

Rule 14   All P.M'.s must be signed at the time of sale by the shopwalker or the price will be forfeited.

Rule 15   That assistants in each department to be held responsible for all goods being carefully covered at night.   FINE 3d

Rule 16   For sending or taking out to show any goods without having them entered. For not making them returnable. When brought back goods and money to be checked by the shopwalker each way.   FINE 3d

Rule 17   Any goods to be sent for from a customer's house, which have already been allowed for, must be entered to the customer until they are returned and the length of all goods must be carefully ascertained before they are sent out.   FINE 3d

Rule 18   In every case of exchange a fresh duplicate must be made for the goods sold and credit given thereon whether differing in price or not.   FINE 3d

Rule 19   For omitting to enter checks in the index, indistinct duplicates, losing check book or not putting department on small book.   FINE 1d

Rule 20   No one is allowed to cut patterns or take back goods without consulting the shopwalker.   FINE 2d

Rule 21   Receiving cash from customers without marking the amount on the duplicate in full as a check in giving change or taking wrong change from the desk.   FINE 2d

If presented to the customer as right change   6d extra
Wrong bills   FINE 6d

Rule 22   For not calling the attention of the shopwalker in every case of a customer not being properly suited or for passing a bill or duplicate without having it examined or altering the same without the signature of the shopwalker. FINE 3d

Rule 23   In all cases when goods are to be paid for on delivery the duplicate must be passed into the desk with the customer's name and address written thereon. A bill must be made of any two articles or one if the amount is 6d or over. FINE 2d

Rule 24   For filling up an address label as paid, entered 'on approval' when it is not, or vice verse. FINE 6d

Rule 25   If the sale of any article is lost through the one who keeps the stock not knowing the same thoroughly. FINE 2d

Rule 26   All goods must be laid in rotation on the counter at the time of making the bill, so as not to cause needless trouble to the shopwalker at the time. FINE 2d

Rule 27   For standing on chairs or counters. FINE 3d

Rule 28   For leaving useless lengths of any goods or less than 1½ yards of ribbon. FINE 3d

Rule 29   No defect in a piece of goods to be concealed from a customer and the word *warranted* to be avoided. FINE 3d

Rule 30   Ten shillings to be given to any assistant detecting a thief in the establishment, under any circumstances.

Rule 31   That no assistant or apprentice to take parcels or goods from the shop, and all goods wanted by assistants must be purchased before 11 o'clock of the one appointed to serve by the shopwalker and sent by him into the house. FINE 6d

Rule 32   Any goods asked for by a customer from door or windows should be readily and pleasantly taken out and all customers treated in a respectful manner not showing more favour to one than another. FINE 3d

Rule 33   Drawers and boxes to be taken before a customer and in all cases goods must be cut off before the customer only.

FINE 3d

Rule 34   That assistants endeavour politely to obtain payment for goods at the time of sale and if this is not accomplished, explain to the customer that the terms of the house being cash at the time of purchase or on delivery of the goods, the porter will wait for the money when the parcel is presented and that credit be not promised even for a day without the consent of the Governor.

Rule 35   No notice *given or required* in case of leaving.

In presenting this copy of rules and regulations I seek to offer a guide to a uniform and persevering habit. The penalties attached to the rules are intended to make them more impressive and to secure attention to important items of duty which otherwise get neglected or carelessly overlooked. In every case these rules will be strictly carried out and fines stopped.

Signed: Peter Robinson.'

There is no mention of the wage Uncle Harry received; it must have been very small and the fines, while laughable today, quite large by comparison.

There is among a mass of oddments a note mentioning his leaving Peter Robinson's on July 20th, 1888 and arriving in Adelaide, Australia, on September 20th, 1888, but no details of the ship he went on or any reference to employment. A number of medical recipes, a note on selling fifteen gold shares for £114 and a selection of names and addresses leave no clue, but he must have done reasonably well, as on his return he lived a quiet and retired life, with whist drives and his garden his only interests. I have heard Dad tell Mother he also left some land in Adelaide, with instructions for its sale, with a friend or agent and never got any replies to his letters or knew what happened to it. If this was so, it must have become very valuable to someone. He was, unlike Auntie Polly, somewhat impatient with us children but was a good uncle, and I remember him as a quiet, intelligent and pleasant man.

Auntie Polly (Mary Ann) we all loved. My father's older (but not eldest) sister was a second mother to us all and kept Dad strictly in his place – the only one who could – and to a much lesser degree Uncle Harry, to whom she was both sister and housekeeper and carried out both roles admirably. The story is told in the family of how she was engaged to a young man in the Government Service whom the authorities decided was needed in India and he asked her to marry and accompany him. It was a frightening decision to make on her part. She had probably never left Leigh, other than perhaps short visits to friends; India was a mysterious and disease-ridden country in the eyes of her family, so a week before embarkation the young man left for Southampton giving her several days to make a decision. I dread to think of the agony and mental strain caused her, but after three days her affections won and she decided to go. She wrote, gave him her love, time of arrival and other details and, to expedite matters, entrusted the letter to a friend to take and post in London next morning to make sure of its early arrival. She waited for a telegram, for a letter. A week, a fortnight passed without a word and she knew he had sailed. It was a month later the friend, shame-faced, confessed he had just found her letter in his pocket.

So Auntie's dreams of marriage were lost but it never soured her, as the story writers would have us believe, and of all the aunts and uncles we loved her the best and her loss was our gain. She was deeply interested in her own family's past and inherited much of the contents of her old home to which she, as a spinster daughter, was generally accepted as entitled. She had some diaries, note-books – including Charlotte's – and a marvellous photo album of all the great aunts and early members of the family, which she gave me. Unfortunately, to my extreme frustration, while I knew them all by name from two family Bibles (one dated 1805), I had no means of identifying them individually.

She was a goldmine of information on Old Leigh, and it is my greatest regret that I didn't heed her more and learn as much as she could have told me. She did try so hard, and some of it still remains with me. But with so much to fill my time, our business, the boat, but worse still the lack of enthusiasm to enquire more deeply into the wealth of knowledge she possessed, it now grieves me and is sufficient punishment in itself, and I warn others, do not let these chances pass. More particularly, when she offered to buy Uncle Fred's blacksmith shop on his decease and give it to Harold and me to keep it in the family, in whose possession it had been for over two hundred years, for some reason we refused it. How I wish I had accepted. It would have been a marvellous showpiece for Old Leigh but I lacked the foresight and sense to realize it.

When Uncle Harry died he left his property, mostly small hous-es in Cranleigh Drive, to her and later, in 1944 when she departed this life at 89 years through an accident, she left us all one each. The new house we built for her in Station Road is still in my broth-er Vincent's possession. All the rest have been disposed of. So not only did she look after us in life but provided considerable help to us all when she passed on, and her loss hurt as much as our own parents. God bless her.

Three houses down the road from us lived Aunt Louisa and Uncle Brand and their son, Cousin 'Bill' until 1909, when they moved into a large new house that Dad helped to build just across the field in Elm Road. Aunt Louisa was a great dispenser of 'Garibaldi' biscuits, a real luxury, and also slices of bread thickly spread with butter and sugar, which we didn't get at home. In her house we had wonderful Christmas parties, complete with Uncle's magic lantern showing 'Dick Turpin's Ride to York' as a special treat. November 5th was also a great time with them and fairy lights were hung in the trees, and fireworks, sparklers and rockets were let off in great numbers. They were good and kind to us all and gave us those extra luxuries that our parents, with so many of us, couldn't afford. When Uncle retired he spent most of his time sawing up railway sleepers and chopping them into firewood. The large shed at the bottom of their garden was still full of bundles twenty years after he died.

The Risbys lived opposite, all, except the two eldest, around our ages. Elijah, their father, married Dad's eldest brother's daughter, Ada Maria Joscelyne, and such was the gap between the elder brother Frederick and Dad, combined with Dad's late marriage, that Dad was only five years older than his niece, and she was married with children before Dad married. They had eight children; the last six were our playmates and companions until we left school and went our separate ways. Until then I expect we spent as much time in each other's houses as our own, even after the disastrous bath night in the episode described later.

Next door to them lived Humphrey Risby, Elijah's brother, with two children, Madge and Humphrey, two more we counted as family, and just across in Elm Road lived John Risby, another brother. So all in all we were surrounded by family and relatives and there were constant comings and goings between us until time and circumstances divided us up.

Uncle Will, apprenticed to haberdashery in London like Uncle Harry, remained in London. Whether he was at Peter Robinson's also I don't know, but later he became shopwalker and then buyer for the then famous London drapers 'Spencer, Turner and Baldwin' until he retired. Being a bachelor like Uncle Harry, he also went to live with his widowed sister, Aunt Emma, and her two spinster daughters, Lily and Edith, in Park Street, Southend, where

Dad's father had built six small terrace houses (one for each of his children) as he was not only a blacksmith but also dabbled in property. He was a good uncle and left most of his estate to the two daughters, as being spinsters and too old for marriage, they would need support, and there was little or no help from the State in those days. They were kindly and sweet-natured and dedicated their later lives to their mother, who lived to the age of one hundred and one.

I remember calling one day around 1961 and seeing Aunt Emma in the front downstairs room sitting in a large armchair, dressed in black, with a mass of white lace around her shoulders. She had a tiny, colourless, porcelain face, merging into equally colourless white hair in a topknot, but alert bright eyes of someone half her age. She wouldn't be quietened until she fully understood exactly who I was and that I was 'Arthur's boy' and all about me and the rest of the family, that she seemed to have forgotten had passed on long before. I was glad I went, as she died soon after, and left me wondering why I had neglected her for so long. But somehow I never made that little extra effort when I should have.

But Uncle Will didn't entirely forget us either. For several years before he died he would take us up to the Post Office and buy each of us a War Bond, which increased in value every year. It was this small legacy that laid the foundation of my future and helped me start building in partnership with my brother Harold when I finally left the beach, so I have every reason to remember him with gratitude, although we saw much less of him than our other uncles.

Uncle Fred, the oldest brother, inherited his father's blacksmith's business. He was the last of a long line of blacksmiths going back to at least the 1600s. While it was hinted that in his youth he had been rather a rebel, when I remember him he was a kindly old bearded giant in the true traditions of a village blacksmith. Such was the difference in age between him and Dad that he always seemed in my eyes very old. When I was a small child, Dad was a frequent visitor to the old blacksmith shop in Leigh Hill, opposite the bottom of Church Hill, and nothing delighted me more than to pump the huge bellows behind the forge. I never did quite get over the wonder of what appeared to be a bed of lifeless ash suddenly awaken into a red hot heap of fire. But I was terrified when he hammered white hot metal on his anvil and sparks flew everywhere, lighting up the dim interior, while he stood in his leather apron in the midst of them, seemingly without fear or harm.

As he grew much older, Uncle Fred packed up the black-smithing and turned to selling second-hand books and junk at the smithy, the ideal setting. Later still, as his mind began to wander, he insisted that some of his brass junk was 'gold', and often members of his family were called on to bring him back from as far afield as London, where he would try to sell his 'gold'. He was completely harmless and very lovable, but he required looking after, so Auntie Ada (his daughter) had him to live with them and he spent his last years sitting mostly on a seat by 'The Elms' until one day, crossing Elm Road for home, he was knocked down by a car and killed. He was well over ninety but physically he was still a strong and healthy man and could have lived like his older sister Emma to be a hundred. He was the 'tradesman' of the family and as such commanded respect, and his skill was unquestioned. He was liked by the Leigh folk, that alone a passport to his qualities, and had considerable standing among them, but was not so 'edu-cated' and 'gentlemanly' as his two brothers, William and Henry, from their London connections. Dad was the odd one out – he didn't fit in anywhere – but of them all I think his life was the most interesting, even though it was the hardest in later years.

What persuaded Dad and his relations to leave the 'Old Town', where their roots had been for so long, I have often wondered. I think the most likely explanation was Grandfather's legacy to each of them of £100. Except for Uncle Fred, who still had the black-smith's shop and lived in Church Hill, they no longer had any ties or reasons to remain there. Dad's building experience in Hadleigh might have helped, but I suspect the main reason was that plots in this rural area were cheap. Large tracts of farmland, particularly Leigh Hall Farm (which was the Manor House for Leigh), were bought by wealthy land companies, laid out in estates, divided into plots and auctioned off, usually at the Grand Hotel, Leigh. Prices averaged about £35, paid in four instalments over four years. It was the custom of these companies to provide free meals and, more particularly free beer, probably of a quality unknown today, to those attending the sale. Many of them had made the journey from London, apart from local builders. Having got potential buyers in a jovial or even intoxicated mood, they would proceed with the sale, usually around 2.30 p.m. The result of this was a very rapid growth of a new town at the top of the hill, and Dad and my uncles and aunts were amongst the earliest ones to migrate the short distance from the Old Town.

There were, of course, a very limited number of builders in Leigh and most of these were known as 'jobbing builders'. They did anything from plumbing, fencing, painting and the thousand and one repairs that property requires, and one or two of them saw the prospects this era presented. It was mostly speculative building, so costs had to be cut to a minimum. Competition was rife and the houses they built were poor by today's standards, but in spite of this most of them are still standing and, with modernisation, good for a long time to come.

As these houses were the work of just a few builders, they seemed to develop into two fairly distinct types, and others just copied them, price being the over-riding factor. There were a large number of very small terraced houses with quite a lot of stonework and ornamental carving which, unlike the houses in industrial areas, gave them a bit of individual character, and long, narrow, three-bedroomed family houses, still with ornamental stonework in front around the bay and front door. Those that built them in some cases became very wealthy men, and many are the tales told of the methods and tricks some of them resorted to to save money in their construction.

It would take too long to tell of all the stories I have heard of one builder in particular, an uneducated and illiterate man, who became extremely rich by this means. He was accosted one day by a more honest builder and chided for the poor quality and bad workmanship of his houses, only to ask:

'What's the difference?'

The good builder replied, 'I've got satisfied customers and a good name. That's a lot more than you have.'

'Maybe,' said the other, 'And where's it got you? You've got your satisfied customers and you've got your good name. But I've got a fortune!'

Among the many other tales told of the chicanery of this particular builder was when he was showing some prospective customers around and they queried the thickness and sound resistance of the wall dividing the pair of houses he was constructing. He assured them with all the confidence and guile he possessed that the wall was completely soundproof. He called his foreman, who was standing by, listening, and said:

'Go next door, Bill, and see if you can hear me when I shout.' After a suitable interval, with his clients awaiting results, he called out in a loud voice, 'Can you hear me, Bill?' thinking the foreman was as artful as he was and had 'cottoned on' to his deception. He had, but there was not, as expected, complete silence from the other side but a voice coming through the wall loud and clear:

'No Guv, I can't hear a sound. Shout louder.' A disaster for the sale, and it would seem builders haven't changed much either since then.

Fortunately it was not necessary in Dad's case to buy a house. His experience in building the Hadleigh house served him well and, as I have previously mentioned, he started building for his relations and later himself in what was then the outskirts of Leigh. Whether he anticipated it or not, he chose to build one of the larger standard type for his future family and our home, and perhaps a brief description of it would not be amiss.

There were no 'lounges', sitting rooms or dining rooms, they had never been invented in our time or type of home. We had a 'front room', which was used only on special occasions, a very long, dark passage, then a 'drawing room'. A puzzling word I connected entirely with painting and drawing and, because we did neither, assumed that was the reason it was empty except for storing tents, costumes.and towels etc. through the winter and potatoes when necessary. Then there was the kitchen, where all eight of us lived, ate and kept warm, and did most of the cooking and baking on a cast iron monstrosity called a 'Kitchener'. Next came the scullery with its brick-built 'copper' in the corner, a large larder and large, shallow, yellow earthenware sink behind the one small window and later completed with the bath we installed. Beyond the scullery was the 'closet' (the word 'toilet' was unknown then), but it did have a cistern that flushed and was indoors, something considered very modern and up-to-date. And on the first floor, three quite large bedrooms, so we were not cramped for space.

The garden was not particularly large and Dad's big corrugated iron shed took up quite a lot of the bottom end, a workshop-cum-store. Five-gallon drums of linseed oil, turps, white lead and putty, tins of various pigments for colouring paint (he mixed all his own paint), thinners, dryers and strainers, his large wooden bench and basic tools, an ancient bicycle that I never saw him use, and a vast collection of rubbish that 'will come in useful one day' filled it and only just gave him room to work. A narrow passage by the shed and a gate led to 'the meadow', a large fenced piece of ground fronting on Station Road (which was still unmade). The meadow was owned jointly by Dad and his brothers Uncle Will and Uncle Harry and sister Auntie Polly who, only living next door but one, also had a gate opening on it. They had no special use for it, so until Uncle started to cultivate his part because of the war, it was an additional playground. Mother had all her chickens and their houses on it, and I my aviary, which I had now been forced to give up because of the shortage and expense of bird seed. I let its occupants go free, which pleased Uncle Harry and Auntie, because they were always against keeping birds in captivity.

Auntie Polly, although Dad was her favourite, never minced her words and when talking of him in his youth called him unreasonable, thoughtless and irresponsible. But she would never hear a word against him from others, maybe because she had done her share to spoil him.

As I have mentioned previously, his early carefree life and lack of discipline or regular employment, unlike his brothers, didn't help and one of the many ways it showed itself was that he completely ignored normal mealtimes. The tide, or whatever job he was doing, controlled them when he was a bachelor. His diet usually consisted of half a loaf and butter, with either shrimps, winkles or fish which he had caught or got from mates, or cheese, and he thrived on it. But when he married, it was a constant source of irritation and annoyance to Mother. Time and time again she prepared lovely meals – and with her boarding house and hotel experience they were the best – only to be burnt by waiting or never eaten, because either the tide or job had interfered. She finally lost heart and didn't bother, perhaps not an unmixed blessing, as it prepared her for life on the beach later, when our meals were controlled in much the same way by the tides.

One thing puzzles me. In spite of his not bothering with meals in general, Dad had his fads also. He didn't like giving up butter but it was so expensive that when margarine came on the market he reluctantly accepted it but insisted that it had to be 'Maypole' margarine. As the only shop that kept it at that time was the 'Maypole Stores' in Southend, every week he would make the journey to buy it, and also at the same time buy sausages from Byatts in the High Street, as these were the only ones he would eat. Meat was the same, the only acceptable was from Cotgroves, the butcher in Leigh Hill, nearly opposite the blacksmith's shop (now a house), so Mother, or more often Dad, bought it from there.

Then one day a new butcher's shop, 'Eastmans', opened in Leigh Broadway selling New Zealand lamb, the first foreign meat to come to Leigh, and in the window she saw this lovely piece of meat, considerably cheaper. She was tempted and bought it. As soon as she got it home the doubts began to creep in. Would he know the difference? The more she thought about it, the more worried she became. I think she would have taken it back if it had been possible but there was no way out except to cook it for the Sunday dinner and hope for the best. As it turned out it was one of the nicest joints Dad had ever tasted and he was delighted with it. Mother had been too frightened to tell him where it had come from and even more frightened when he said:

'That was a fine piece of meat. I'll tell Cotgrove next time I see him and try to get another bit like it.' Mother said nothing but lived in fear for some weeks after and never bought any more from 'Eastmans' in spite of his praise. And he never did know.

But the tables were turned a short while after, and Dad became the guilty one, but this time the deception did not remain hidden. It happened because Dad was just as difficult with his underclothes as food. He wouldn't buy them anywhere except at what was then called an 'in and out' shop, 'Heddles' in Milton Road, Southend (now an inn). He decided he wanted some shirts and, although it was quite late in the evening – it was winter – it was part of the fun to see all the bright gaslit shops in Southend, so as a special treat I was taken with him. We duly arrived by tram at the

'Cricketers Inn', walked the hundred yards or so to our destination and, for reasons of his own, he left me outside.

I waited and waited, but he didn't come out. Hopping from one foot to the other with a call of nature increasingly asserting itself, I still waited, I don't know how long, but it seemed an awful long time to me. I was getting more and more into a panic; I thought I had lost him. Taking a peep inside the shop, all was quiet. It had two doors, one each end (in and out). I looked in the second door – no sign of Dad. I was very young, no more than seven, if that. Now I was terrified; I *had* lost him. My mind had one thought and one only – to get home. It was dark, it was cold, and the shadows cast by the flickering gas light looked sinister and full of menace, and never once had I been out so late on my own.

As the minutes went by, so my fears increased. In complete panic I started to run up the road and found 'The Cricketers' (not the one that stands there now, but a dilapidated old place). I saw the tram lines stretching in both directions along the London Road (then mostly not built on, and quite rural), and I had no idea where I really was. But I did know from which direction I had come in the tram, so I reasoned if I followed the tram lines, I would reach Leigh Church some time and I knew my way home from there. Again I started to run: how long it took I'll never know, but I never stopped until the ivy-clad St. Clement's stood at the end of the tram-track. Panting with fear and exhaustion, I continued to run down Elm Road, a nightmare in itself with its huge rustling elm trees that lined it making it even darker than the night around, and at last was home, banging on the front door. It was opened by Mother. I fell in, I couldn't speak. Breathless, sobbing and perspiring I gradually recovered and blurted out my story. I had lost Dad.

Some little while later, a frantic banging on the front door heralded Dad's arrival. He was also in a state of shame and fright but greatly relieved to find me at home and equally mystified as to how I had got there as he had made the journey by tram after searching for me, but even so it showed how fast I had covered the distance.

In a very guilty and shamefaced manner he told the truth. He had bought his shirts and feeling the need for his usual pint had slipped out of the other door up to 'The Cricketers' for a quick glass of beer, quietening his conscience that I would be safer outside the shop than the inn. He had met an old pal, one glass led to another, the time slipped by so quickly. Suddenly he realized the time and that I was with him. Going back to 'Heddles' he could find me nowhere, and equally terrified as I had been but for different reasons, he rushed around searching and calling for me. Having failed in this, he had started for home on the tram, fear in his heart both from conscience and more how to tell Mother. On his way he had also called in at the Police Station in Leigh Hall Road and told them I was missing, and this just about saved him from Mother's fury. He saw it coming and, rushing for the front door with the excuse that he must at once notify the police that I was found, made his escape. Mother had somewhat calmed down when, much later, a very contrite and chastened Dad came back and said he was sorry. But it was several days before the atmosphere returned to normal.

I sometimes think when writing these stories how trivial and insignificant they are, and not even worth recording, but that was mostly how our lives were – and don't say I didn't warn you.'

The author, and daughter Clare, in 1961

This colour postcard of 'The Bathers' Corner', dates from around 1909
– the year it became 'Joscelyne's Beach'

Judging by the heavy clothes, it is a chilly day on Joscelyne's Beach.
This picture dates from 1914-15

The author's father – 'Dad' – is on the left. The child in front of
'the Shed' is probably the author's younger brother, Harold. Circa 1914

Row-boats and lines of changing tents grace this picture postcard

It's back-breaking work digging sand barricades on Joscelyne's Beach

The End of the Road

It was, I think, in the spring of 1910 when an unusual happening occurred and broke the monotony of our normally uneventful lives. Although it had little or nothing to do with the beach it is possibly worth recording, although so commonplace today that I expect many will think otherwise. My Uncle Brand acquired a motor car, then a rare and expensive 'toy' seldom seen, much less owned by those around us.

It caused quite a sensation. It wasn't new, an 'Oldsmobile' bought in 1904 by his wealthy elder brother, and now replaced by a new and later model. It was passed down to him either as a gift or at an advantageous price, I am not sure which. A shed was built in the back meadow to house it and we all, aunts, uncles, friends and neighbours, awaited the appointed day and time of its arrival which, strange to say, really happened. It had come all the way from London under its own power until it reached 'Bread and Cheese Hill' at Thundersley but refused to face the climb up the hill. However, with help and its crew pushing behind, it eventually got to the top and once there resumed its journey until it arrived at Station Road, which was then unmade. Spitting fire and smoke, it got about halfway to our field and finally packed up, but there were so many of us to greet it that it was carried almost bodily to its new home, where it was the admiration and wonder of those around.

The following day Uncle Brand, Uncle Harry, Dad, my cousin and I assembled, and Uncle Brand mystified me by pouring what seemed like water from a bottle onto his hand, instructing me to watch it. 'I'll make it disappear,' he said, and sure enough it did slowly go. It was my first introduction to petrol.

With much pushing and shoving we got the 'monster' out of the shed and into the field, but it refused to go. There were, of course, no garages, no mechanics and very few that understood the workings of a car in a locality such as ours. But we were particularly fortunate that in an oil and hardware shop, 'Cardwells', some distance down the 'London Road', was a young man who not only stocked petrol but had some knowledge of mechanics, and he was called on to help us.

It was only a small matter of adjusting the coil and accumulator, and with a series of loud bangs it started. To our great joy we all had a trip round and round the field with Uncle Brand driving. Everyone was delighted and arrangements were made for my uncles and cousin to go for a run on the roads in the afternoon. So with the engine still running and all of us pushing, we negotiated the bumps and cart ruts of Station Road and left it, with me guarding it, until after lunch.

Strangely enough, I had taken it for granted that I should go also, but when the time came Uncle Harry decided he would like to go and there wasn't room for me. The car started with surprisingly little trouble and was soon chugging along the London Road towards the little wooden toll house that stood on the corner of Eastwood Lane, which was then a narrow, rough road bordered by a ditch and hedge as it wandered through grass meadows to Prittle Brook, over a wooden bridge and through cornfields to the sharp turn at the top.

I was heartbroken at being left behind and Mother, seeing how upset I was, suggested that to make up for the disappointment she would take me to Hill's Pond to fish. Previously, when out with Dad, I had seen quite a nice pond just on the further corner of Eastwood Lane and the London Road. I asked to go there instead, hoping to catch newts, which I rated more interesting than fish at that particular time. Mother agreed and in due course we arrived at our destination, but it seemed that disappointment was the 'order of the day' and I never even saw a newt, much less caught one. Mother, realizing my continued disappointment, suggested that although it was now a very long way, we should go to Hill's Pond after all and be satisfied with 'tiddlers'. So, making the best of a bad job, we started down Eastwood Lane.

A hundred yards or so on our journey, with the lane stretching almost in a straight line up the hill, I became aware of an object in the far distance, advancing with gathering speed. It came silently towards us and I recognised Uncle's car, with two perspiring and weary figures running beside it and my cousin in the driving seat, helping to steer.

When they reached us they had a sorry tale to tell. It had broken down just past the 'Woodcutters Inn' and nothing they could do would persuade it to start again. They had pushed it from there to the top of the lane, a hard and relentless task over the rough, uneven road. And the hill had been equally cruel, as they dared not lose speed, to get up as far as possible on the rise beyond the brook. Neither uncle was particularly strong or athletic, and both were getting on in age, and it hadn't improved their tempers either.

We left them struggling once more to overcome the slope to the London Road and, as I looked back, it was surprising what an unholy satisfaction I derived from it. I had a feeling that somehow justice had been done and, what was more, *seen* to have been done. In fact I was so satisfied, that when Mother suggested that it was still a long way to Hill's Pond, I was quite in agreement with her. It occurred to me that maybe if we turned back we might even be in time to see them pushing it home, which I did, with the joy and satisfaction that small boys derive from such happenings. (Quite plainly my attendance at Sunday School had been of little benefit to me!) As far as I remember it never went out again, except to be pushed round to Uncle's big new shed in their new house in Elm Road. A vital part had broken and spares were almost impossible to obtain, so there it stayed.

But my Uncle's first unhappy experience of these new mechanical wonders did not prevent him from buying a second-hand 'James' motor cycle and side-car combination offered by a friend a little later. This was far more successful, until a few weeks before the First World War (1914-18) it in turn became a victim of 'Bread and Cheese Hill' and broke some small part in the gearbox. With the coming of the war and no petrol for pleasure available, it was never repaired, the side-car was disposed of, and the 'James' dumped alongside the 'Oldsmobile'. My uncle died, my cousin had no interest in mechanical things, so there they remained until the spring of 1938, with another world war looming.

Then, with a fortnight's holiday ahead of him, my cousin asked me to help clear out the amalgamation of rubbish and household bits and pieces collected over the many years which, with the hundreds of bundles of firewood his father had chopped when retired, filled nearly the whole of this very large corrugated iron shed. This was a legacy of those days when nothing was *ever* thrown away, a treasure trove of bygones now, but of little value at that time.

Eventually, underneath it all we unearthed both car and motor cycle, rusty and covered in cobwebs and dust. Dragging them out into the light of day and with the combined efforts of a neighbour, we pushed the old car up to the breaker's yard, then just opposite 'The Elms', and gave it to them.

The 'James' was to follow. Rusty and dirty, with nearly a quarter of a century's neglect, it looked a sad sight, but out of curiosity rather than anything else, I propped it up off its flattened tyres onto the rear stand and pulled the back wheel round, with my other hand on the sparking plug. To my amazement and surprise I received a severe electrical shock. It was evident that its ancient magneto was still working perfectly after all these years.

I asked my cousin, 'Have you got any petrol?'

'No,' he replied, then as an afterthought, 'only in a bottle in the shed for cleaning purposes.'

'Can I have some?' I enquired. He walked over and brought a small bottle. Filling the carburettor and dropping a spoonful or so through the sparking plug hole, we pushed it down the lawn a few yards and to our unbelieving eyes and ears the engine started and ran until the petrol was exhausted.

A little later another neighbour brought us a cup of tea and, looking at it, said, 'What do you reckon to do with that old thing?'

My cousin answered, 'it's not such an "old thing", it goes.'

'Pull the other leg, that'll never go,' he said with a laugh.

'Put your hand on the cylinder,' I suggested. He promptly bent down and did so. Touching it, he jumped back with amazement.

'It's bl***y hot, it's burnt me!'

'Yes,' said my cousin, 'I told you, it goes.'

I have never ceased to wonder how, after over twenty years lying useless, this could have happened, and I doubt I would have believed it if I had not actually witnessed it and knew it to be true. My cousin offered it to me. 'Did I want it?' I hesitated, then decided it was of little use, so it joined the other relic of bygone days, the 'Oldsmobile', at the car breaker's.

Both had served their purpose but I cannot help feeling unhappy now that I was partly responsible for the old car's destruction, apart from the motor cycle. It had made me miserable when it first arrived and equally, if not more unhappy, when I look back at such a valuable piece of mechanical history we so thoughtlessly destroyed. What joy it would have given to those who cherish them, irrespective of their monetary value today.

Once again I have wandered 'off course'. All this is a long way from Joscelyne's Beach and the newly built Chalkwell Bridge and the new 'Grosvenor Tea Rooms' and residence just beyond. Mr. Davis, the owner, had previously had a large wooden hut at the corner where the then unmade Chalkwell Avenue and new promenade met, surrounded by the Chalkwell Fields. He supplied teas and light refreshments during the summer months from it, and on the beach opposite he owned a collection of bathing huts on wheels and was a well-known and respected pioneer of this foreshore.

Appointed in charge of these bathing huts was Dad's old friend and companion 'Hictor'. Tall, strong and bearded with a short clay pipe more or less a permanent feature, he was a typical Leighman, kindly, simple in his wants with a streak of common sense. He also had perhaps a share of artfulness that had its advantages when those who only saw the simplicity of his nature tried to take advantage of it. He made the double journey each day from his home at the bottom of Church Hill in Leigh to Chalkwell and the bathing machines. When these were first installed it was considered right and proper that the walk from the machine to the water was somehow indecent for ladies and had to be avoided. So the complete hut on wheels was pulled right to the water's edge, and gradually winched back as the tide came in and the system reversed as the tide receded.

This system was no longer in use. The human body in a bathing costume no longer merited its previous attractions, not that there was much to be seen of its contents in the bathing costumes in use at that time. So the huts were drawn up above the tide line and remained stationary, and an enormous amount of work was saved, something I imagine not lost on 'Hictor' when considering the job. He only worked the tides for some five hours and was paid, I think, £1 per week, but had ample time for his other pursuits and opportunities should they arise, as they did with surprising frequency.

When the tide was filling 'Crowstone Gut' and creeping over the mud flats and he had a half-hour to spare, he would drop in sometimes for a pipe of 'baccer' and a chat. I was very fond of him. He treated me as an equal, not like so many, as a child, and I counted myself as having every right to listen or join in the conversation. This particular morning I saw him coming, told Dad and got out the beer crates, as I knew he was early for the tide and the empty beer crates were an invitation. Seeing Dad and me seated and a third seat ready was sufficient encouragement. He sat down, produced a battered tin tobacco box from his right-hand coat pocket, carefully unwrapped his most prized possession, a large silver watch, consulted it, wrapped it up again in its piece of sail cloth and returned it. Next he dived into his left-hand pocket and produced an identical tin filled with tobacco and carefully and methodically proceeded to fill his pipe, at the same time remarking how difficult it was when offered a pipe of 'baccer' to fill in the correct amount instead of stuffing it so full it wouldn't draw.

Having at last got it going to his satisfaction, he looked out to sea, sighed and quite suddenly said, 'Aye, it was last Monday on the early morning tide, as I fust seed her and a trimmer little craft I ain't clapped me eyes on this twenty year or more. She come down to where I was a'standing, and smiling all over, and sez she to me, "Attendant, have you a nice and proper costume, a towel, and suitable cubicle I can hire," all hoity toity like. And I sez, "Yes Sister, I can fix you up right and proper with all them things." She looks at me a bit sharpish like an' sez, "Sister? I'm not your sister." "Ho yus you are," sez I. "Nonsense," sez she. "I've never seed you afore in my life." "Maybe so," sez I. "But ain't you ever looked in The Good Book and seed as how we all 'ave the one Father?" "Oh," sez she, "I see wot you mean," and she pulls out her purse and gives me half a crown and sez I can keep the change. Then she sez, "You are a good man and I am sorry, of course we'm all brothers and sisters all over the the world, even them poor savages in Africa." But why she mentioned them I can't think, them being sich a unnatshural colour an' all.'

He paused a moment for reflection; he was clearly puzzled, then as if talking to himself said, 'Never had a sister of mine wot was black and, come ter think on it, never knows as anybody else in Leigh fer that matter as did.' At that he got up to go but I could see he was still turning over in his mind this new aspect and how the one Father had produced the two colours, and I was glad I hadn't mentioned Chinese and Red Indians to further complicate matters.

On another occasion he told how, when beach combing along the tide line, he got into conversation with a lady sitting on the beach and sez she, 'Boatman, I've bin sitten nearby that pile o' weed and now I want ta scratch all over. Tell me,' sez she, 'are there fleas in that seaweed?' and I sez, 'Yes Ma'am, lots an' lots,' and then she sez, 'if there be anything I do dislike it's fleas. Don't you Boatman?' an' I sez, 'No Ma'am, they's all God's critters and put on the earth for His purpose, but it's the way as they git their living I don't abide 'cause they gits their living off others, and don't work for theyselves.'

One of his favourite stories was about the visitor to Old Leigh who had never seen the sea before. He walked onto Bell Wharf when the tide was fully in and was amazed at the vast expanse of water. He approached one of the ancients sitting on a bench, passed the time of day and remarked, 'What an enormous pond you've got here. I've never seen so much water in my life.'

'Aye,' sez the old salt, 'And it's "wunnerful" good for they rheumatics and sichlike.'

'Ho,' sez the visitor, 'My sister 'as them something chronic,' and at that the old man picked up the bottle he'd just finished an sez:

'I have the sole rights of selling this 'ere medical water for a shilling a bottle, and he straight away ups and sells a bottleful to 'im. I s'pose seeing the bottle makes the stranger thirsty, cos he walks back along and finds the "Smack" and there 'e stays till closing time, then he finds 'is way back to Bell Wharf and the tide's all gone. The old man was still there, so he goes up to him and sez, "Ain't you sold out quick, it's a good job as how I got that bottleful when I did".' And I still remember that grin and chuckle that lit 'Hictor's' face every time he told it.

Another of his tales was when he was rowing a family of visitors around Leigh. At that time the creek was marked by a line of 'withys' or small trees stuck into the banks at close intervals for those using it to find the deep water, when the banks were just covered. Passing these 'withys' the visitors enquired their use. '"They's winkle trees," sez I. "Winkle trees, never heerd tell of 'em," sez he, so I rows over and there, like wot I knew was some winkles a-climbing up them stalks, like it's a natchual thing they allus do. So I showed them a-climbing up them trees and tells 'em how every night they climbs up to be safe from the crabs wot eat 'em, and how we comes out with a basin and catches 'em when the tide goes out. An' they sez, wot a pity as they was only down for the day, as they would have loved ter bring the kids tonight and catch some. I don't think as how they ever twigged I was only pulling their legs for fun,' and once again he would chuckle and give his sly grin.

Simple stories, having perhaps no place in today's sophistica-tion, but told when Old Leigh, in spite of the progress and expan-sion on the top of the hill, was much the same as it had ever been. Quite a number of the locals had been born before the railway came through in 1854 and the close-knit village life remained ingrained in them. Intermarriage among most of the families made for a clannish community that rejected strangers. The Osbornes, Knoakes, Cotgroves, Turnidges, Thomsons, Brewers, Fords and Deals, and in lesser degree Joscelynes and many others I could name, made up the bulk of the inhabitants and it was said that it was at least forty years before a family of 'furriners' were generally accepted as belonging.

With so many families of the same name it was usual to distinguish them by nicknames. Chaser, Tarpot, Snowball, Biller, Snappy are just a very few I call to mind. In conversation, when discussing a family, this was the means of identifying a particular member. This was invariably followed by a long discourse on exactly who his father and mother and relatives were, and their further relationship with most of the other families, and the other ramifications that were involved in that particular branch. In such a society one would expect family feuds to have developed. If they did I never heard of them but perhaps I was too young to know. It would seem that the villagers' resentment was more concentrated on strangers and I remember my father telling me that when the rail-way first came, the rougher element would pick a fight or knock off the top hats of a visitor they didn't approve of.

This brings to mind that there seemed to be a curious form of password that distinguished those having business or connected with Old Leigh that has puzzled me for a very long time. So, often as a small child walking with my Dad into the Old Town High

Street, we were greeted by, 'Wot'cher (what cheer) Joscelyne, which way does the bull run?'. The correct answer, showing you were acceptable or belonged was, 'Same as Southend lifeboat, "om-ards".' For many of these later years I have tried to find the reason for this peculiar greeting and answer, and a while back I asked a very old Leighman if he knew.

His story was that a certain Leigh fisherman – he told me, but I forget his name – was taking a basket of fish to his sister in Rochford. As was the custom, he was walking almost direct across the farmland and fields that at that time stretched from Leigh to his destination, thus saving the longer journey by road. When he was halfway across 'Dobbins Field' (near Leigh Hall Farm), he was chased by a ferocious bull. His fish scattered, he suffered the indig-nity of being tossed into the thorny hedge surrounding the field. With the bull still snorting and threatening, he was forced to fight his way through bush and thorn, until bruised and battered he scrambled to safety into the next field, and there a young calf was quietly grazing. Cutting a thick stick from the hedge, the fisher-man, still seething with anger and the loss of his fish, attacked the little animal, chasing and beating it with his stick and gave it a severe thrashing. Hoping its cries would be heard by the bull, he shouted, 'Now go an' tell yer old father that's for wot 'e did ter me, the old "varmint".'

The scene, witnessed by one of the farm labourers, was quick-ly told and no doubt embellished in Leigh, and later to the Southend fishermen, whose rivalry and strong dislike of the Leighmen was well known. It was seized on immediately and the story used to make a laughing stock of any Leigh man that strayed in their path. The catch-phrase developed, 'Wot'cher,' then the sur-name followed by, 'Which way does the bull run,' much to the anger and annoyance of the inhabitants of Leigh, as in their eyes it seemed to infer that they were all as simple and cruel as the one actually involved.

Some time later that same winter a severe gale developed and a large ship was driven ashore on the Maplin Sands. This presented a great chance of salvage, and hardly had the distress rockets been fired than both Leigh and Southend boats were, in spite of the gale, ready to take advantage of what they regarded as a heaven-sent chance of extra cash and salvage. A bawley from Leigh, under the shelter of the marshes and protected from the heavy seas, was quickly underway and battling the huge waves. But the Southend boat, although a lifeboat, had no such protection. Huge waves were breaking on the Southend shore – there was no pier then – and the lifeboat was driven back time and again. The crew and their helpers fought hard to launch it but each time it was washed back and at last the attempt was abandoned. The Leigh bawley reached the stranded ship, secured the anchors and claimed the salvage. The Southend men never lived their failure down. Should one of them ever refer to the 'bull', the answer came short and fast – 'Same as Southend lifeboat, "om'ards",' (or more correctly 'homewards').

This was the story told to me, but how it became a password in Leigh is still not completely explained, and recently I have heard two more vague versions of this legend – one that a bull was let loose at a football match between Southend and Leigh fishermen, because Leigh was losing, and secondly a tale of a bull let loose in Old Leigh High Street at a regatta by Southend men. I still hope that one day I might learn the answer. The difference between truth and fiction is so hard to define. How much truth there is in the following story, not of Leigh but the adjoining village of Hadleigh, I don't know, but it is perhaps worth recording, as it was an old friend and Leighman that told it to me.

The story goes that the bailiff for a wealthy local landlord living in the district was returning one winter's evening down 'Bread and Cheese Hill' with the rents, collected quarterly. It was thickly wooded, very dark and lonely. His horse reached a certain spot nearly halfway, stopped and in spite of every effort refused to go forward another inch. Urging, cajoling, whipping was no use, it just reared up and eventually took matters in hand and bolted back up the hill. Its rider, realizing he would never get home the way he wished, turned up the lane (now Kenneth Road) and continued by way of Thundersley Church and eventually came back to the London Road in the region of 'Tarpots', the horse showing no further tantrums. Next day a shallow [empty] grave was discovered just below in the woodland where the horse had refused to go the night before and later two vagrants were caught and confessed it was their intention to waylay, rob and bury the bailiff. I have a vague feeling I have heard other versions of this story, not necessarily in this area. As I have previously remarked, where truth ends and fiction starts is difficult to define.

Having once again wandered down 'side streets', I must return to The Beach. I think I mentioned that both my father and I were members of the Southend Amateur Angling Society. (There was at that time no Leigh Society.) The competitions were held mostly during the summer months. This was convenient in some respects to Dad as his fishing parties on the 'A. J. Soper' were most in demand during the winter, but now the beach was so busy during the season it became more and more of a problem for us to take part, although we now had Mr. Tye, and my uncle would sometimes help out. But Mother was the chief support and helped and encouraged us to enter in all the important events.

By his skill and experience of fishing Dad had won many prizes and twice won the silver cup, the highest award, and this year he surpassed himself. Not only did he win the cup for a third time, which made it his for keeps, but I, the youngest member of the Club, won 'The Shield', the next most prized award. No doubt his local knowledge and, more particularly, the 'Old Wreck' contributed much to our success, and it became quite a normal thing for other anglers to follow and anchor within a stone's throw of where we were fishing. Even so, we still had the best catches and got the most awards. One day just before the competition started we were approached by two committee members and politely but firmly asked if they could examine our boats and bags. They turned out everything and even had the floorboards up, but of course found nothing. They apologised and very much regretted the necessity of their actions but said they had received an anonymous letter stating my Dad caught or bought fish the day or night before, and added them to his competition catch, a thing he would never do.

But the jealousy increased and, while he had many good friends among the members, certain others brought pressure to bear on the committee to define Dad's real status as an amateur. He did not get his living as a fisherman or professional but did get a livelihood to some extent by catering for angling parties and selling bait. When he had joined he had classed himself as a decorator, but now things had changed. Fishing and angling had to be defined.

The committee couldn't agree and there the matter stayed until the following year, but a certain element had been active during that winter. Invitations to whist drives and club dinners were lost or delayed. It was plain an undercurrent of bad feeling was creeping in, so when Dad returned my shield, which was held yearly and a tiny replica added to it with the winner's name, he finally handed in his resignation, and with it most of his enthusiasm, and we left the Club. But with the ever-increasing demands of the Beach, maybe once again his decision was made for him.

Two other events, commonplace in this era but of considerable importance at that time, occurred that winter. We changed from the yellow glow of the paraffin lamp and the tiny night light to the incandescent white of gas. No cooker, just light. Cookers were distrusted and expensive but the light was an instant success and we wondered how we had managed before and were greatly impressed by the wonders of science.

But even more revolutionary, we installed a fixed bath to replace the large old zinc one that had served for so many years, either in the scullery or in front of the kitchen range. Water was heated in the large built-in copper in the scullery and bailed out in a bucket into the bath, and cold water added to suit. This was a normal mode of life among many families and even if the more modern properties now going up did set a small room aside for future use as a bathroom, few were installed.

My Uncle 'Risby' was a plumber and had recently made a small bedroom upstairs into one of these new-fangled luxuries, complete with a fearsome looking geyser that made almost human noises of suffering and spurted steam and water. This filled us children with joy to watch, when as a really special treat the four oldest of us were invited to try it. Half-full of lovely warm water, it seemed the equivalent to a swimming pool. It would hold us all at once and after the first novelty of just sitting in it and splashing each other, we found the added delight of sliding at the sloping end from the rim into the water. In fact its possibilities seemed unending. Water splashed and flowed all around and we had the time of our lives, so much so that I even remember it to this day, but with considerable shame and sorrow as well at our bad behaviour. When the water began to flow through the ceiling beneath we were hurriedly sent home and were never asked again.

But it sowed the seed and convinced Dad that we also should have a bath. Not a luxurious one in a room set apart; we couldn't spare or consider that. A bath was a bath anywhere, so it was decided that it should be fixed in the scullery immediately adjoining the copper, thus avoiding the need for both the buying and fixing of a geyser. The waste pipe was carried along the corner of the floor through the wall to the sink gully outside, so although it was necessary to fill the bath from the copper with boiling water, cold water could by means of a hose be carried to it and, with the removal of the waste plug, the wet and back-aching job of emptying it avoided. The whole was encased in a wooden box with a hinged lid and all in all the finished product was in our eyes equally satisfactory to the one across the road. In fact, as I informed my cousins, it was better, because with the copper going full blast it was much, much warmer in winter than theirs. To this they would retaliate by pointing out they didn't need a copper with such a lovely geyser, a point I wouldn't admit mattered, but secretly envied for the strange noises it made. But geyser or not, it was an unqualified success, a forerunner of the era to come and a very considerable improvement in our lives.

Other than these two highlights in our very ordinary existence, little else disturbed our way of life. School filled five days: on Saturdays, as members of the school football team, we were taken by tram to the 'Cricketers Inn' and marched through West Street and the village of Prittlewell past a tiny fish and chips shop. There my companions introduced me to that most delicious and previously unknown delicacy of two pen'orth of fish and chips, with the added incentive of salt and vinegar free. In Leigh, with its fresh fish, such a shop would probably be unthinkable and heresy, so it was an added treat, and we would then continue on to Jones's Memorial Ground. After the game we spent any surplus pocket money on a halfpenny 'Kalee Bonker', which was amazing value for money, and a glass of raspberry cordial, and home again.

Sunday was usually '*A. J. Soper*'s' day and so our lives went by. When the snow came – and we seemed to have a lot more then – all sorts of wooden contraptions were knocked together to toboggan on the cliffs. These were favourite, but roads from Leigh Broadway to the cliff top were all in use and, other than a horse and cart occasionally, free from traffic. The winters never dragged.

I was building up a nice collection of stamps and cigarette cards, which developed into their own specialised games, and very considerable numbers were lost or won by the throw of one card. And, of course, there in the background were the beach, and rock shifting, and Dad's cronies.

But in the early spring following, a disturbing little incident occurred, perhaps hardly worth mentioning now, but in those days something almost unheard of. Dad still owned the Hadleigh house and its tenant was a middle-aged gentleman, I think of German ancestry, and his wife. He was one of the kindest and nicest of men I knew and, when I used to walk with Dad to Hadleigh to collect the rent, there was always a cake and sixpence for me. His wife, an invalid for many years, was dying of tuberculosis and pitifully ill, so on the plot adjoining he had at very great cost erected a large hexagon-shaped summer-house with wide doors and large windows. The whole complete structure pivoted on a central pin, allowing the entrance to follow the sun in its orbit, and for the most part here she lived and he prepared her meals and looked after her with devotion and love until she passed away. The summer-house remained, and one of my special privileges was being allowed to spin it round and round and jump on it as it revolved, repeating the performance each time it slowed down. His pet hobby was breeding pigeons and it was he who started my own ambition to keep birds by giving me a pair, but of this later.

It was breakfast time some time afterwards when Dad called Mother's attention to a column in the *Southend Standard*. I was, of course, too young to understand its full implications and no explanations were forthcoming from my parents, but I gathered from their conversation it concerned our tenant. Later I got hold of the paper and found the article. It left little doubt; it gave the name and address of the Hadleigh house and it seemed he was concerned in some offence with a young local van driver. Knowing nothing of homosexuality, and no one would even explain what he had done wrong, I was greatly puzzled and deeply aggrieved for him when later he was sentenced to nine months in prison. The mystery surrounding it and the sadness of this nice kind man, after all he had suffered, hurt me deeply. The house was re-let, but the trip to Hadleigh never had much appeal after that. We never heard of him again but I dread to think what prison life, to such a man, did to him.

Generally speaking we enjoyed good health, considering the prevailing conditions. The newer properties being built had both main drainage and piped water, but in the older houses conditions remained primitive and unhygienic, but were accepted. We were the fortunate ones, but in spite of that we had all the usual childish sicknesses and illness – whooping cough, measles, chicken-pox and scarlet fever. The doctor's advice usually was, 'Put them all together and get it over with. What can't be cured must be endured.' That was his favourite expression, so we used to end up in one bedroom with a sheet soaked in Jeyes fluid covering the doorway and, in the case of measles, all blinds drawn, until we got better. When I say 'we', I am referring to the rest of the children, as curiously enough, although I was in close contact I didn't, to everybody's surprise, catch any of these illnesses.

Every year a doctor and nurse would come to North Street and other local schools and we were lined up class by class to be examined. We were checked for 'nits' in the hair, something that was accepted as likely, and usually at weekends Mother would 'go over' us with a nit comb and rub paraffin oil into our scalps. As most of the boys had their heads shaved like convicts, but for a tiny fringe, it wasn't too bad, but with the girls' long hair that was fashionable it took a great deal of both time and patience. In any case, they were re-infected once back at school by those whose parents did not bother. Dirt and lice were also part of the examination, and lastly we were told to open our mouths and say 'aah'.

The two previous years I had returned home with a letter stating I had 'adenoids'. It gave me no inconvenience; possibly it might even have helped in my immunity to the other illnesses, and Dad had done nothing about it. But this letter was severe in its criticism and pointed out the longer it was left the more serious it became and should be attended to immediately. This frightened Dad into action. He made arrangements with old Doctor Day who lived in Dalby House, a lovely residence no longer there in the middle of the Broadway on the south side.

I remember the operation so well, as it was just before Christmas. The kitchen table was moved into the front room, rarely used except for visitors and Christmas. A large fire was lit and my bed brought down and put in a corner. The kitchen range was stoked up and the big iron saucepans Mother used to cook the Christmas pudding filled with water. In due course the doctor arrived in his horse and trap. A clean sheet was laid on the table and something like a drinking glass stuffed with cotton wool and a hole in the bottom was brought out of his bag. I was laid on the table, the open end of the glass was put over nose and mouth, and I was told to count to ten as the doctor dropped a liquid through the little hole onto the cotton wool. I remember reaching eight with difficulty and no more. When I came to for a moment there seemed to be blood everywhere, then I went back to sleep.

When I next awoke I seemed in pain all over. I had terrible ear-ache. My throat and body seemed on fire and no matter how I tried I could find no relief. I will not dwell on the following six weeks but I shall never forget them. To add to my misery it was Christmas and the New Year and I missed out on both. The doctor's account, if I remember rightly, was £5 5s.

The ear-ache was, I think, the worst. There were no pain-killing drugs except alcohol for adults, so I was treated with the only remedy known, olive oil dripped into the ear and a bag of salt or a quarry tile wrapped in a bit of woollen blanket warmed in the oven and applied to the ear. The other aches had to take care of themselves. I lost a lot of schooling but eventually recovered. We have come a long way since then. The same operation today would probably be almost painless and I should have been back at school in a week.

It might be of interest, while on the subject of medicine, to mention a few of the remedies used in Leigh in those days. Whether we had spots or not, in the spring we were given brimstone and treacle to cure them if we had them or stop them if we hadn't, and to clear the blood. It was a concoction of sulphur and Lyle's golden syrup stirred into a thick paste. A dessert spoonful was given each day for at least a fortnight. Most medicines worked on the principle that the worse it tasted, the more good it did you, but this was quite the exception; the syrup made it quite pleasant to take and cancelled out the sulphur. Lyle's syrup came in a large tin with a curious picture in an oval frame stamped on it, a dead lion smothered in flies and 'bluebottles', and the strange quotation underneath 'Out of the strong came forth sweetness' (I think taken from the Bible). But I found it very difficult to understand how one reconciled the purity of the syrup with something so unpleasant as a dead lion providing a meal for flies.

For coughs and colds, ipecacuanha wine or Owbridge's tonic was in general use, but a more effective cure in our home was Russian tallow, a dreadful smelling fat obtained from Uncle Brand's tallow chandler's factory in London. This was stuffed up the nose, a large wad smeared on brown paper and stuck on the chest, and the sufferer was put to bed. The evil smelling cure was almost worse than the cold, but it worked wonders and next morning we were nearly always better, which was understandable, as no self-respecting cold could live with it. Perhaps now, thoroughly refined, it is the basis of medicaments that are so popular both for coughs and colds and aches and pains. There were also poultices of various plant leaves, but we placed our faith for aches and sprains in the Old Leigh remedy, Rum, – there was plenty available (duty free). Castille soap – the only soap that would dissolve in it – and the whites of eggs were all mixed and shaken into a thick liquid and kept in a large bottle in the larder. It lasted a long time and for some magical reason worked wonders when rubbed vigorously into the body. It was greatly valued as a sure cure in our household.

Rheumatism and arthritis were extremely prevalent in Old Leigh. The dampness of their houses and their occupations caused many of the older inhabitants to suffer badly from these painful illnesses, but the relief if not the cure was on their doorstep. The bladder seaweed clinging to the rocks on the sea wall was collected and put into a large zinc bath full of hot water and left overnight. This resulted in a thick, glutinous, red-brown jelly, which I was told was pure iodine and sea salt. With added hot water, one lay and soaked in it. It gave great relief and even now could give comfort to those willing to go to the trouble of preparing it.

Whooping cough caused great distress and was very prevalent. Sulphur candles were in great demand but here again a curious remedy was at hand in Old Leigh for those infected – flounder's blood. When this fish had its tail cut off, a dark thick blood dripped from its backbone. This, placed in a saucer with a lump of sugar, which absorbed the blood, was given as a sweet, and I can confirm from personal knowledge that in one case it worked, or appeared to do so.

One of Mother's customers on the Beach had a little girl suffering very badly from whooping cough. Few of this generation can realise now how distressing and frightening it was. A child would struggle to breathe until blue in the face and then whoop in a way almost as if it was going to die, and the mother of this particular child was desperate after weeks of misery. My mother mentioned she had heard of this old-time cure but knew little other than that, to which the child's mother said she was now at her wits end and would try anything. So that afternoon I was sent to catch a flounder.

They were plentiful and could be caught almost anywhere a few hundred yards off the beach, and in a short while I returned with two. The ritual of the cutting and turning the sugar bright red was carried out and it was taken, after very considerable persuasion. I was not surprised when, twenty minutes or so later, the child was violently sick – it had made me feel sick just looking at it – but from then on there seemed a marked improvement. I can only say that three days later she brought the child to see us and she was completely better. It could, of course, have been pure chance and the child would have got better naturally in any case. But with no medical knowledge I have a quaint theory of my own. Was it just possible that the bacteria germs were attracted by the pure blood and were absorbed by the sickness that followed? Probably a lot of nonsense and I hesitated before expressing it as I searched for an explanation in my own mind, and was loath to accept even what I knew to have actually happened.

Another remedy in great demand in Leigh was Dutch drops. These I have no personal experience of, but I think they were a cure-all for most common illnesses. I have a vague idea that they were imported from Holland and sold in Mr. Frank Bridge's shop next to the 'Smack Inn'. This was not, as one would suppose, a chemist's, but a shop full of leather sea-boots, oilskins and sou'westers, thick heavy canvas smocks and guernseys (not jerseys or sweaters as they are now known) hanging from the ceiling, and an odd assortment of miscellaneous articles and food on shelves and counter, in fact an Aladdin's Cave of useful treasure.

And while I am on this subject of cures, one other incident I recall was how my father through his trade as decorator contracted what was called 'red lead poisoning', a type of eczema. His hand and arm became covered in large weeping wounds and sores which completely incapacitated him for months. Doctor Day couldn't find a cure, so Dad went to Southend Hospital and it seemed they couldn't either. So it went on, and he was in despair, when by chance someone suggested he might try 'Melrose Cream'. This was a thick yellow ointment sold in twopenny tins. It acted immediately and for a few pence he was soon completely cured.

When John Joscelyne came to Leigh in 1780, both typhoid and the ague were commonplace. The latter illness was mostly confined to the low-lying marshlands surrounding Essex villages, and was attributed to the damp and sea mists they were subject to, but these were only partly the cause. In recent years it has been found that these conditions encouraged a type of malaria and these marshes were in fact a breeding ground for the mosquitoes that caused this sickness, and even in recent years I read of them being found around Rochford.

Typhoid was a killer, and the Church registers record the death of three of John's children, aged three, four and nine. Even sadder, three cousins, Lavinia, Elizabeth and Martha, who were staying with them, all died of this sickness within ten days of each other. But this was a not unusual tragedy in those times and its cause not far to find at that period. They had no fresh water, other than that caught in butts from the roofs of their cottages. These old oaken casks or butts started life holding liquids far more potent than water, but no doubt became very foul and smelly. I remember Aunt Polly telling me how it was customary to put a piece of floating wood and a frog in them to, as she expressed it, 'keep the water fresh' by eating the mosquito larvae and little red wriggly worms that infested this 'fresh' water.

Aunt Polly also told me of the time when she was about twelve years old in a particularly dry summer, when the newly installed well and all other sources in the Old Town dried up. She and her sisters had to walk to Dobbin's well with a milk-maid's yoke and two buckets. These were filled at the cost of a halfpenny each and carried back from near Leigh Hall Farm down Leigh Hill to their home behind the blacksmith's shop. Is it remotely possible that could have been the origin of the rhyme 'Jack and Jill'?

Added to the water problem, sanitary hygiene was non-existent. A hole was dug in the ground at the bottom of the garden under cover of a small hut, which I assume had to be rebuilt on another spot when it became unusable. A liberal coating of lime was the only disinfectant used, so it was no wonder epidemics and sickness were prevalent. It is surprising anyone in Leigh ever reached a ripe old age, but they did, as many early photos show. It would seem that these 'privys' not only served the one purpose, either. Once I remember my Dad reminiscing with an old friend, recalling how an uncle of his not only blew the hut apart but lost both hand and eyesight making gun-powder for his fowling piece. Then he added as an afterthought, 'I suppose in some ways it was for the best. The press gangs didn't bother him afterwards' – a form of danger ever present in Leigh at the time.

But enough of the past and back to the Beach. The spring of 1914 found Dad full of hope and enthusiasm. We now had four rowing boats and the 'A. J. Soper', more tents, more bathing costumes and towels, and more help from Mr. Tye, whose health had improved beyond all expectations. We had a prolonged session of rock clearing, and the underwater danger to both boats and bathers was very much reduced in the immediate vicinity of the Beach. The future looked bright.

Only two small incidents other than routine occurred, as far as I remember. I built my longed-for aviary. Previously I had made a pigeon loft to accommodate the pair of pigeons given me by our tenant at Hadleigh. It was a somewhat crude affair and no doubt the reason why a cat gained entry, killed one and allowed the other to escape while I was at school.

Broken-hearted I promised myself never to keep any more birds, only to break this vow when a boy living in the road offered me a number of wild birds he had caught during the winter, mostly greenfinches and chaffinches, but also two blackbirds and a thrush. As he had clipped their wings it was cruel and useless to turn them loose. They were confined in small cages, uncared for and a sorry sight. It left me no alternative. All my love of birds came back and I decided to do a deal with him. A large collection of stamps and cigarette cards changed hands and the birds were brought home. Mother wouldn't have them indoors, so they were installed in an empty chicken house at the bottom of the garden while I enlarged it with a wire-netting addition to allow plenty of flight room when they could fly. I still remember walking to Hadleigh to buy the small-meshed wire netting I needed, as they were the only shop that stocked this size. The seven yards I bought cost seven shillings, the equivalent now of about thirty-five new pence, but it had taken weeks of saving and I had a hard struggle back, it was so heavy.

Dad saw how keen I was and helped me build quite a nice aviary and shortly afterwards the birds were released into it. They gradually acquired the feathers and strength to fly in better conditions and my dream had materialized.

The second event concerned the Beach. Dad, to his surprise and annoyance, got a rate demand for the shed – not much, I think about £1 10s., but enough to make him very angry. He went to the Rates Office and had a row with them but they insisted he was liable as it was a business. Then one of his regular cronies came up with a bright idea. If it was fitted with wheels it became a movable object and, even better, it could possibly be classed as a bathing machine, being on the beach. So four small iron wheels of about one-foot diameter were fitted. Of course, they were useless as far as moving it was concerned; as it was they sank up to their axles in the sand, but it had the desired effect. The Council accepted it was on wheels and did not investigate. We never received another rate demand and maybe somewhere deep in the archives of the Rates Office a bathing machine is recorded on Joscelyne's Beach.

That year, 1914, was a momentous one, not only for England but for most of the world. War clouds were gathering. Dad got very patriotic and excited. Bad feeling was running high against the few local people of German extraction, even if only their name sounded German. One in particular I well remember was a kind old gentleman and local estate agent, Gustave Selighson, a little man with a pointed beard and moustache much like the pictures of the hated Kaiser Wilhelm. He still had a slight German accent but had been many years in England and his family had grown up in Leigh, and until then were generally accepted by the Leigh folk. We would often meet him outside his shop near Leigh Church and chat for a while, but the moment war was declared the windows of his home in London Road were broken by stone-throwing locals and it was unsafe for him to go out. He was interned soon after, the feeling was running so high in the country.

On the actual day war was declared it was the most important holiday week of the year. The cinder path and beaches were crowded with a mass of people and the weather was marvellous. When the news broke that Britain had declared war on Germany a complete hysteria seemed to sweep through the people. It is impossible to describe the atmosphere. Wild patriotism mixed with anger at the audacity of the Germans to question England's power. The disturbance of that holy of holies, the British Bank Holiday, and the underlying fear of the few who realized the sufferings the war brought with it, were all mixed up. But most of all was the patriotism that swept through the crowds and the complete certainty that 'we would show 'em', and the equal conviction it would be all over and won by Christmas, until history proved otherwise.

Confident of early victory, a wave of patriotism, much flag-waving and the calling up of the 'Territorials' gave an air of excitement. There was the amazing and unbelievable march of the German army through France until stopped at the Battle of Mons by the 'Old Contemptibles' (This was what they had been previously called by the German Emperor Kaiser Wilhelm). There was also the strange story of the Angel of Mons, which a number of troops were convinced they saw hovering over the battlefield defending our small army. Everything had a curious mediaeval touch. The War filled the daily papers but had little effect on our lives. We were all sure it would soon be over, so we settled down to wait for this happy event and, for my part, I almost dismissed it.

My mind was still occupied with model aeroplanes, stamps, cigarette cards, butterflies and birds' eggs. I now had my aviary with bullfinches, chaffinches, greenfinches, goldfinches and redpolls and nearly all my very limited pocket money went on birdseed. With feathered creatures much in mind, I decided I would like some baby chicks to give to Mother. It was autumn and there were then none available. This did not deter me; I would rather hatch my own. Completely unaware of the fact that cockerels were an essential part in the scheme of things, and we only had hens (after Mother was actually attacked by a cockerel), I commenced to put my plan into action.

First I had to have some eggs. This was easy, I always collected them after school for Mum, and to her surprise and dismay for some unaccountable reason the hens stopped laying. I would bring in one or two, the others went into a large box filled with hay in a disused chicken house. When I had about eighteen, her hens, much to her relief, returned to normal laying. My next problem was a supply of heat, which I knew to be necessary, and fortunately that was at hand and in fact had prompted the idea in the first place. In my father's work shed was a large metal bin filled with 'lump lime', something that dissolved in water and mixed with sand made lime mortar for building. The fascinating part was that, during the process of mixing the lime and water, the chemical reaction generated a very considerable amount of heat, which lasted for quite a long time. So here was the supply of warmth, with little expense or danger. Having secured a small quantity of lime in a bucket, and adding water, I carefully put my large wooden box of eggs on it and covered the lot with old socks. Each day after school I would carefully renew the heat supply, keeping the whole operation a complete secret, no easy task with brothers and sisters, until I could present Mum with her baby chicks.

Of course, it was quite impracticable and went on for weeks until I finally lost hope and gave up. But I failed to remove the objects of my experiment and Dad suddenly decided to clear out this shed. Picking up the box of hay, not realizing its contents, he threw it out. An appalling smell filled the air. A bucket of lime and a spent pile of used lime in the corner under a sack revealed the whole sorry story and the consequences were very disastrous to me. Dad was very angry in spite of my protests that I was only doing it for Mother.

Christmas Day [1914] came along, bright and warm for the time of year and Dad, as was his custom, took me round to visit the aunts and uncles all living near to wish them the compliments of the season. This was celebrated at each stop in appropriate manner, so that Mother's efforts for Christmas Dinner were usually wasted on him, but not on us.

We had just left Uncle Brand's when the unusual sound of an aeroplane, followed closely by another, passed overhead. They were quite low and my knowledge of planes made me realize the leading one was a 'Taube', a German plane, followed by an English machine. The pilot could be plainly seen leaning over the cockpit with either a gun or revolver, as he tried to draw level with the leading plane. It was all in slow motion, compared with present speeds, and I was jumping with excitement. The war was real after all. They disappeared towards the south-east. I never read of it in the papers afterwards but it made my Christmas and gave Dad a shock. I think brought home to him that it might be next Christmas at least before the war would be over.

But the routine of normal living went on. Shopping was more difficult for Mum and food supplies getting short, so Dad started digging his garden and two allotments in Elm Road and filling them mostly with potatoes. The war seemed at a stalemate with no signs of it ending, and so we entered the spring and summer of 1915.

I can't remember exactly, but I think it was late May when, soundly asleep in our beds, we children were awakened by a general uproar. Mum and Dad were rushing around and we were pulled out of bed. Flickering lights licked the walls of our bedroom, and looking out of the window into the back garden a bright bonfire was raging. Beyond at regular intervals in a straight line, similar other bonfires were lighting up the fields and meadows that divided the few houses dotted around in them.

Rushing to the front bedroom windows, I saw Dad struggling with his ladder, putting it up to the front bedroom window of 'The Browns' opposite, where smoke was pouring out and they were all gathered shouting for help. Dad got them down while other neighbours attacked the source of the fire – an incendiary bomb which had gone through the roof and landed at the foot of the staircase making it impossible to get out, other than by the way they were rescued. It was put out with buckets of water but the staircase was completely destroyed. The other fires were left to go out themselves.

Our house by chance escaped, as it was in the space between the bombs. All incendiaries weighed about 50 lbs. each and were, it seemed, dropped in a stick of six at the one time. Further down the London Road another similar lot had fallen all in fields, missing houses, almost as though Providence had ordained that they did as little damage as possible. But it was our first experience of bombing by 'Zeppelins' from the sky and, while exciting, was also very terrifying, in comparison just as frightening as our later experiences, when the damage and danger was so much greater. It all happened about 3 a.m., but we didn't go back to bed and as soon as it was light I joined my pals up the street to search for bits of bombs for mementoes of this auspicious occasion.

From then onwards we dreaded the dark nights as the 'Zeps' began to come over in increasing numbers. The only warnings we had were from the street wardens. Dad took his turn, armed with the old bird-scaring rattles and later bells, shouting 'Take cover at once', which in our case was under the staircase. The two elderly ladies, the Misses Harvey from next door, joined us, so with Mother and the six of us as well wedged in, it was pretty crowded to say the least. To make our peace with the Lord, whom we seldom thought of otherwise, but were wondering if we should all need at these times, we sang hymns at the top of our voices to drown the sound of failing bombs or gunfire. But next morning, with the coming of daylight, all our fears would be forgotten until nightfall again.

It became a regular thing to be awakened from sleep, rushed down the stairs and bundled into the stairs' cupboard, while Dad took his wooden rattle and patrolled the street, but as time went on we only took shelter when they were very near or overhead. One night I well remember being by the back door, looking up, and there in a break in the clouds and silhouetted against the sky was this cigar-like shape right above me. It appeared quite stationary and no sound came from it. The most likely explanation was that it was dropping an observation capsule, a torpedo-like body of metal containing a crewman lowered on a steel cable – sometimes as long as 1,500 ft. – through the clouds to pinpoint its position, and seen on this occasion through the clouds thinning for a moment. But it left them very vulnerable and was, I think, later discontinued.

There seemed at the time no adequate defence against the 'Zeps' and London became their regular target. Our planes could not fly high enough to reach them, even in the unlikely event of finding them. And anti-aircraft fire didn't in most cases, against an invisible enemy, seem to be effective, although one was brought down by this means at Gt. Wigborough in Essex. We became almost reconciled to accepting them as part of a war that wasn't quite what we expected. German technology in air, sea and land, it seemed, was far in advance of ours, and only now were we waking up to reality. At last the Government realized it and found an answer.

As usual the night was dark and the now-imposed 'black-out' made it even darker. The rattles and bells warned once again of the presence of raiders as they passed overhead at intervals on the way to London. We awaited their return with some apprehension as – if for some reason they didn't unload their dangerous cargo on London – Southend, Leigh and Westcliff offered the best alternative. It seemed no different to any other raid as I looked out in the garden, when suddenly a ball of fire like a big red moon appeared in the sky, slowly, it seemed very slowly, falling to earth well beyond Hadleigh. For some moments all was quiet; even the distant gunfire ceased, then an ever-increasing sound that came from nowhere or anywhere in particular filled the night. It broke in a roar of human cheers; it seemed in those silent streets the whole population had been watching and waiting for this night. When a short time later, in another raid, the same thing was repeated at Cufley near London, we knew an answer had been found, or so we thought.

The first one fell at Gt. Burstead, near Billericay: it was, I think, a Thursday night, in any case Saturday was very close and two other boys and I decided to cycle there to see the remains. Suffice to say, of the journey I had no idea it was so far away, but we eventually got there. Guarded by soldiers, the airship sat in a field, a monster of tangled framework and latticed aluminium, bent and broken on grass burnt black with heat. It was surprising how few onlookers were there looking at it. But some were being taken by one of its guardians on an unofficial tour to an impression in the soft ground. It was reputed to have been made by the body of one of the crew as he jumped from the blazing airship. The 'guide' had casually remarked he made no charge for this service but cigarettes or small gratuities were most acceptable. A brisk trade was also going on in the background for bits and pieces of aluminium framework and oddments by another resourceful tommy. I invested the whole five shillings I had taken with me and secured quite a quantity to bring home. These later were exchanged for those things that were dear to a boy's heart in transactions with my school companions.

No one expressed the slightest sorrow at the terrible fate of the crew, but I believe they were buried with military honours in Gt. Burstead churchyard and later, after the war ended, were transferred to their homeland.

It was plain now that the faster, high-flying and better armed 'Sopwith Pups', which superseded the old Avro, but more particularly the invention of the phosphorus bullet, which ignited the gas-filled Zeppelins, were a disaster for the enemy. The most they had was perhaps a dozen or so. Nine, I think, was the largest number they ever sent at one time, the risk and loss-rate being too high to pay, so the raids ceased. There was, of course, no possible comparison with the terrible destruction and constant raids both night and day of the Second World War. The raids only took place when the weather conditions suited, but it was the first time in history old folk, women and children in England became victims of this new type of ruthless war, which was equally terrifying and frightening as the raids that came later.

Apart from the upset during the actual raids, life continued with perhaps less disturbance in this little corner of Essex than in the big cities. Our hobbies, school, model aeroplanes and a very active interest in and knowledge of real planes filled our time. Dad worked two or three hours a day on his allotments and filled them mostly with potatoes, as food was getting short and going 'on ration'.

The summer came and, with it, the holiday makers and visitors, maybe not so many – men on leave or wounded, others to get a break from London – and the locals. So all in all our life, certainly as far as we children and our friends were concerned, went on as usual. We, in particular, had no very close relatives involved and Dad was too old for military service. The Beach continued to provide a living, the autumn came with a bumper crop of potatoes and vegetables to see us through the winter, and the chickens were laying, but their corn was very expensive. Dad still went fishing, so we didn't go short except for meat and, although we took it all for granted, I suppose we were much luckier and better off than many others, particularly those in London who had none of these advantages and all the suffering. We even had fuel for our fire from driftwood Dad collected. Now coal was getting scarce, and when we were sent home from school during the very cold spells because they had no coal for heating, it was regarded as an extra holiday and almost welcomed.

We were free from Zeppelins, but not for long. It was plain to both sides that aerial warfare had an extremely important part to play in winning the war, and that we were no longer an island, sheltering behind our sea power. Both England and Germany were now desperately engaged in developing a giant bombing plane, giant by the standard of that time. The German 'Gotha' was said to be a replica of a prototype 'Handley Page' that was being designed and built in England, and by a traitorous act had been stolen and landed in Germany for them to copy. How true this was I don't know. With official secrecy, all sorts of rumours and half-truths flourished, but there is now doubt. They were almost identical in appearance but far more efficient in performance than the 'Zeps'.

So after a short lull the old misery of sleepless nights returned but this time it was the moonlight that brought them, faster, more in number and with heavier loads and more powerful bombs. The bright nights became even more to be dreaded than the dark and clouded skies of the earlier times.

Going to bed I would look out of the bedroom window and see the world bathed in moonlight and I would lie there, waiting, as I knew they were coming. The first warning was the dogs. Almost all the families around us had dogs and there were many of them, not cosseted as today, but in kennels or roaming outside. Long before the dreaded double-beat throb of the twin engines were heard the dogs started, first one then others joining the chorus in competition. Some howled, others set up a constant barking. Then faintly, but ever increasingly, there was the sound of many engines. They would, with luck, pass overhead and, such is human frailty, we would give thanks with little thought to those on the receiving end of their evil mission. To the accompaniment of anti-aircraft guns we would once again all dive under the stairs until their engines and the sound of gunfire faded into the distance. We knew that we had now almost exactly one hour before they would once again pass overhead on the journey back.

It was no good going back to bed; the nights were bright with moonlight, sometimes almost as light as day, so with my pals and a collection of small brothers and sisters, we started taking our model aeroplanes to the fields at the top of Cranleigh Drive where we lived, until the faint beat of engines and gunfire in the distance sent us scuttling back to the doubtful safety of our hide-out. It was a mixture of fun and fear that seemed to disappear with the light of day, and strangely enough was almost forgotten until the next moonlit night or nights. Occasionally, for some unknown reason, they would drop a few bombs on the town, so we never felt safe or free from danger, but local damage was small in comparison to London. However, the constant expectation that we might receive their full attention this or next time was always there.

As the winter closed in we welcomed, as we had never done before, the winter gales, leaden skies, rain beating on our windows, or the icy blasts and bitter cold of the north winds, as we sat huddled around the old cast iron 'Kitchener' that served both to cook our meals and keep us warm and did neither efficiently. I was old enough now to realize that while we sat there almost in comfort, knowing we could sleep in peace, those self-same conditions were bringing misery and death to the seamen bringing vital food and supplies to us, but we could do little or nothing about it. We went to bed early with a stone ginger beer bottle filled with hot water to keep warm and save fuel in the knowledge that our night would not be disturbed or sleep broken, but always aware we had been only granted temporary remission.

As we approached the spring [of 1916], Dad once again got busy with his allotments. He had added a third one, all in Elm Road, which was at that time living up to its name. Huge elms lined both sides of the road, except here and there, with breaks for side roads or a few houses, from Rectory Grove to 'The Elms' – which was originally 'Ellen Elms Farm' before being converted to a public house.

One evening we were playing football on the grass in its forecourt when the sound of an aeroplane engine came out of the gathering dusk and an 'Avro' suddenly appeared very low overhead. Passing over, it seemed to land at the top of Elmsleigh

Drive. An aeroplane was still a rarity, even more so on the ground, so all of us, big and little alike, started off to find it.

When we reached the top of Elmsleigh Drive there was no sign of it, so we continued running and I, with the few others left, eventually reached Eastwoodbury Church, still without finding it. The night was now very dark, we had run all the way there and now we ran with the fear of the consequences all the way back. I dropped inside the back door, out of breath, tired and frightened, to be sent immediately to bed with no supper and a promise of punishment to come next morning. This, fortunately, in the usual rush of breakfast and getting off to school, didn't materialise.

Later we realized that had we gone on a little further we would have found it safe and well, the forerunner of many others and the beginning of Rochford Aerodrome. It would later become a regular Saturday journey to see the comings and goings of our planes as it became an established airfield. On the west side was a narrow footpath between Eastwoodbury Church and a thick hedge that acted as a boundary for the new aerodrome. A soldier with a rifle guarded this footpath at the entrance, but we were allowed to go through and, some hundred or so yards beyond, was a gap in this hedge through which I could see the fuselage of an old 'Avro' plane. Just inside, about forty yards in front of it, was a bank of earth, so I guessed that it was a machine gun practising machine. The plane was obviously past use otherwise; stripped of wings and engine it sat there dilapidated and alone. But it had something I dearly wanted, the large red, white and blue roundel that adorned its canvas side, and I determined to possess it, satisfying my conscience that the plane was no more use with or without it.

So one evening after school I set off, my penknife sharpened on Dad's grindstone, and on arrival boldly walked past the sentry at the gate of the footpath. I had timed it for dusk. With my heart pounding almost loud enough to hear, I slipped through the hole in the hedge, ran in the deepening shadows to the plane and cut out a large canvas square with the coveted roundel in the centre and slipped back through the gap in the hedge. I had brought a bag, but the canvas was far too stiff to fold, and I had to get past the sentry at the entrance. For a moment I panicked and thought of leaving it, but in no way now I had it in my possession could I contemplate such a disaster. Stripping off my coat and jersey, I wrapped it tightly round my body twice and put back my clothes. It was so stiff I could hardly walk naturally but taking courage in both hands and walking like an automaton stiff and straight, and swinging my arms backwards and forwards like a soldier on parade, I reached the guardian at the gate. With an exaggerated military salute I passed through. He looked at me in a puzzled and curious way – I think he was wondering but couldn't quite make up his mind whether I was being polite or taking the 'mickey' out of him – and let me pass. Once across the road and hidden by the hedge opposite I took to my heels until I was out of sight, undressed, removed my precious spoils and arrived home once again late and in trouble. Fortunately this time Dad was still enjoying his pint in the 'Smack' so I got away with 'straight to bed and no supper' again.

I framed my treasure. It was the envy of my friends and it hung in splendour on my bedroom wall until it was unceremoniously dumped in Dad's shed. I have often speculated on what might have happened if that sentry had been more alert and I had been caught, or even the possibility that as an intruder in the airfield I could have been shot at and questioned afterwards, that is, providing I had been alive to answer. It was a foolhardy thing to do, but try telling a twelve-year-old boy that!

Our playgrounds were the fields at the top of the road, but in the short evenings we played in the street in front of the house. There was little or no danger, even a horse and cart was unusual. An occasional cyclist would pass but the street was a safe and easy alternative to the back garden. Mother had warned us of tramps and gipsies, who had the reputation for stealing little children, and Mother told us in all seriousness that the stolen children had their faces and hands rubbed with walnut juice to make them like gipsies and unrecognisable to their parents. But we seldom saw them, except when they came round with home-made wooden clothes pegs or wicker baskets full of blackberries to sell for jam making.

My Dad spoke of the time when they had an encampment on the field in which we now played, just opposite 'The Elms'. It seems that smallpox had broken out among them, and the Leigh folk, who at the best of times counted them as thieves and vagabonds, fearing that the epidemic would spread got an order from the magistrates to have them removed. The one constable Leigh possessed was powerless on his own to carry out the order, so recruited the Leigh fishermen. Armed with boat hooks and various weapons and dearly loving a fight, they marched onto the encampment. At first there was considerable resistance and a few black eyes and broken noses. But realising they had little chance, the gipsies harnessed their horses to the caravans and were personally escorted by the victorious Leighmen to the Eastwood site in Bell House Lane, as being far enough from Leigh to escape the sickness. Even many years later, one day when I was out with Dad we went a long way round to avoid passing near their camp for fear of attack, but they didn't trouble us now and we rarely saw a tramp, as there was little for them in Leigh or Southend.

The only other fear was the 'onion men', Brettons who came over every autumn with shipments of 'home grown', big, round onions. A half a dozen or so lodged in the barn that at that time stood just behind 'The Elms', a legacy of its farming days, where they slept in the straw and fended for themselves, speaking only sufficient English to barter a price for their wares. They also brought their bicycles, which they overloaded with big strings of onions to sell to the local housewives. It took a long time to reach agreement on price and almost developed into a game of skill.

In Dad's eyes the danger was not for us children but for the women folk. He was firmly convinced the Brettons were less interested in selling their wares than in seducing the innocent wives of Leighmen, a view shared by many others in the Old Town. They were young, many darkly handsome and attractive. The bargaining took a long time; a friendly cup of tea wasn't amiss and above all they were romantically different. It didn't take long for the sturdy fishermen of Leigh to recognise it, but they could do little other than sigh with relief when the onion men had sold out and gone back after a period of about three weeks or more. (And now I come to think of it, there were one or two dark, handsome children around in school – maybe just a coincidence.)

Onion men, gipsies and tramps played no part in our thoughts and we children, both girls and boys, wandered abroad without fear. We knew most of the people around. They were all, by and large, decent honest folk to be feared only if we 'scrumped' their fruit or chased their chickens. Of course, we knew Germans were evil. It was rumoured lately they were even dropping poisoned sweets for children to pick up. To a lesser degree there were black men with bones through their ears who lived on islands with palm trees and had big iron pots they cooked missionaries in, but these had to be forgiven as they knew no better, according to my Sunday School teacher.

But as both Germans and black men lived so far away it didn't matter. We were playing quite happily with no fear or thought of anything other than the game of rounders in the street in front of our own home, when this shabbily dressed man, a stranger to us, walked up the road. He came to a halt, leaned against the tree which served as a rounders stop, and stood watching us for quite a while. My twin sisters and I were playing, otherwise we were alone. Suddenly, when my sister Lily arrived at the tree, he got hold of her by the left hand and said what a pretty little girl she was and that, if she would come with him, he would buy her some sweets at the sweet shop at the top of the road. Without question and with complete innocence she started off up the street, holding his hand.

While I knew nothing of the possible consequences that could happen, a desperate fear, and instinct that it should not be, swept over me. I ran after them, now some twenty yards or more further on, shouting, 'Come back, come back, you mustn't go.' Neither of them took the slightest notice, in fact Lily was as equally determined to go as he was to take her. Catching up I grabbed her right hand. He was still holding her left hand and I started to tug her away but the two of them pulling together was far too much to struggle against and I was rapidly being pulled along. I fell over but would not let go. I rolled over on my back with both hands gripping my sister's hand. She was now stretched between us and screaming for all she was worth. I was still being dragged along, and we had now reached Harry Bolton's house, my special pal who lived about fifty yards higher up the road.

By this time my other sister had alerted my mother, who now came running and shouting towards us, and two local men were coming down on the other pavement. The man now relinquished his hold on my sister, Mother grabbed her, and we ran and dragged her home. Running up our side entrance we slammed and bolted the side gate, thinking it was all over, but to our astonishment and fear a heavy banging on the gate showed that the stranger had followed us back and was now trying to get in. Mother was terrified. Gathering us all together, we fled down the back garden, along the path at the back and into the back of Uncle Harry and Auntie Polly's house.

Uncle armed himself with a heavy stick and, with me at a safe distance behind, went back. Seeing a man coming, the intruder then made off. Uncle never chased him like I thought he should have done, neither did we tell the policeman as we should also have done, but as Mother said afterwards, 'Thank goodness your Dad wasn't here, he'd have killed him.' I truly believe he would have, as he had an uncontrollable and violent temper if anyone other than he ever threatened or laid hands on us. Whether the stranger was drunk, mental or just evil I don't know. I constantly watched out for him but never saw him again.

I was duly praised for my efforts in saving my sister from being 'taken away' and from conversations overheard with neighbours even something much more terrible could have happened to her. This I assumed, rightly or wrongly, was that she might have been killed. My curiosity and enquiries were met with Mother's stock reply when she didn't want to answer anything, 'Ask no questions and you'll hear no lies.' So I concluded I was right in my previous assumption, but the incident sowed the first seeds of suspicion in my mind that it wasn't only Germans to be feared or who were dangerous to children.

However, the Sunday papers were now filled with the stories of deep caves in Germany where they were boiling down the bodies of the thousands of soldiers killed in action on the Western Front for fat to turn into margarine. This was an infamous lie for propaganda but believed by many, particularly as photographs of huge cauldrons with fires under them appeared with the articles to give further proof of the authenticity of the stories. My mind again connected them with savages and missionaries, so when I found a perfectly good crate of New Zealand butter floating ashore, in spite of the fact that we hadn't tasted butter for a very long time, we were frightened to eat it in case it had been poisoned and dropped by the enemy. In reality it was probably part of the cargo of one of the many merchant ships being sunk by mine and submarine all around our shores, and in some parts a rich harvest was being reaped by longshoremen.

I remember one early morning walking along the cinder path to the Beach and seeing a nearly submerged cabin trunk just visible among the floating seaweed. It was too heavy to pull up the beach when I secured it, but the tide was ebbing fast and I was soon able to get at it. I don't know what I expected to find as I hammered away at the locks with a heavy stone, but well recollect the disappointment I felt when it was finally opened and I found it to be full of saturated woman's clothing, blouses, dresses, skirts and other bits and pieces of a female wardrobe. To me it was a dead loss, but I selected a couple of lace and net dresses as suitable for making fishing and butterfly nets etc. and left the rest.

When I eventually arrived home I showed Mother the dresses and told her of my find. Her reaction was immediate and angry: 'You silly child, these dresses are most expensive and beautiful and I expect the rest were like them.' Stopping only to take off her apron, she rushed me back to where I had left my find. It was still there but empty, someone else had taken the lot. Mother's disappointment was sad to see. With clothes now almost unobtainable, particularly of the quality of those I had found, I had thrown away something of value, but worse, something that it would have delighted Mother's heart just to possess, in this period of drabness and scarcity, through thoughtlessness and ignorance.

These, other than driftwood and timber, were the only 'finds' I remember but the 'shrimpers' had a windfall one day. A ship was sunk lower down the estuary. Sides of meat and huge bunches of bananas floated from her, and abandoning their fishing, they set about salvaging all they could collect. Loaded with their spoils they landed at 'Bell Wharf'. The news spread like wildfire in the Old Town. Bananas and lumps of precious meat were changing hands and soon the news got 'up the hill', where the local greengrocer, Mr. Palmer, dispensed his wares. He lost no time in arriving with transport and, shortly afterwards, fully loaded with what must have seemed heaven-sent treasure (we hadn't seen a banana for months), he was about to start his journey back when the Devil appeared disguised as a customs' officer. He confiscated the lot and any stray bits around, until the necessary salvage claims were lodged and forms filled in to conform with the regulations, a process that would take far too long to fight with such perishable goods.

I don't know how it was ultimately settled but there were no signs of extra meat or bananas in the local shops. However, it was not a complete loss as far as I was concerned, as several bawleys had held back a few bunches of bananas and had strung them up on the lower part of their port or starboard shrouds to ripen, as they were very green. A few went missing as I passed when wandering towards evening across the mud, satisfying my conscience that they had only found them too.

It has struck me since that, in spite of going regularly to Sunday School, nature had endowed me with a most amenable and accommodating conscience in those boyhood years. I have often queried in my mind just how much 'the wee small voice' of conscience is an inborn product of human nature and how much was due to the environment and age we lived in. I remember how I caught and caged wild birds in an aviary or stole their eggs, yet at that time I had no particular qualms in so doing, although I deeply regretted it in later years. Our parents and even teachers knew we did these things but never once do I remember being told it was wrong. But I do recollect a lecture from my headmaster for not wearing a hat or cap to school, an insignificant matter of no importance in comparison.

So, neglecting our usual Saturday trip to the aerodrome, I would search the trees, hedges and undergrowth within the limits of walking distance in the early spring for birds' eggs to add to my collection, or baby birds to rear by hand, but rarely successfully. Thrushes, blackbirds, all the finches, whitethroats, linnets, rooks, jays and magpies all fell victims to my craze, but in fairness to myself, I took none from the more common birds if I had specimens already and only one or two from the scarcer ones if they had swapping value.

Canvey Island was my very special hunting ground and one I kept to myself, or a very favoured companion. Going by train to Benfleet, I would try to time it for when the tide was out and I could cross the Benfleet Creek without paying the ferry. On the other side was a rough road sloping into the creek but raised above the marshland on either side. It extended about 150 yards to Waterside Farm which, other than a Dutch cottage further on still, was the only inhabited building around. But before the farm was reached I turned left onto the sea wall which led to one of the even more wild and remote parts that was general on Canvey. A mile or more along the sea wall, which was skirted on the inner side the whole way with a dyke, between the wall and dyke, sloe and hawthorn bushes grew in profusion. It was a place where the rarer birds, pipits and warblers nested, and later it was my hunting ground also for the caterpillars of the rare 'Oak Egger' and lappet moths which abounded there. Searching through this undergrowth, which usually compensated for the scratches and cuts received, I found a yellowhammer's nest with four eggs.

Leaving the sea wall I walked across a field that had a large wide dyke on the further side against another sea wall and remember this as a momentous occasion. I had hardly started through the deep grass of the field when a redshank flew up between my feet leaving a nest with four eggs, a prize indeed. A few yards further on the same thing happened; this time a skylark and four more valuable eggs.

Continuing on, it again happened with a lapwing. It seemed almost unbelievable but still my luck continued and, by the edge of the dyke, a wild duck sprang up dragging one wing. It flapped painfully along the ground, to all appearances seriously injured, and I automatically gave chase. By strange chance it managed to keep just ahead until about a hundred yards from where we started and then, to my surprise, suddenly soared into the air squawking loudly and I realized I was the victim of a trick. I retraced my steps and found its nest. There were a dozen eggs in it but I restrained my greed and also out of admiration for her efforts only took four. It never occurred to me that wild ducks' eggs would have made a welcome addition to Mother's problems of rationing.

Continuing on, I waded deep into the thick reeds that filled the dyke, nearly up to my waist in water but with my boots and clothes still on. I searched the reeds and found a moorhen's nest with sixteen eggs. Taking four, I waded on and discovered what I thought were old and disused moorhen's nests. Disappointed, I passed them by until one caught my attention, covered with wet bits of reed and weed and floating almost under water. I decided to have a closer look and there, under a top layer securely hidden, were four dirty brown eggs. The nest was that of the 'dabchick' and these were added to my haul.

I now knew the secret of the apparently empty, deserted nests I had previously found and learned how, both with the wild duck and the 'dabchick', nature tried to protect her own, but unfortunately not against the human animal. I found several nests, all skilfully hidden under a covering of camouflage, and took one egg from each, amazed that it was possible eggs could hatch almost under water as these were. I had been up to my waist in water for more than an hour – I was cold but more than satisfied with the results.

Enough was enough, and just as a matter of interest, during the whole time I never saw another human being in sight, such was the isolation of Canvey, so with the incoming tide at the ferry crossing in mind, I decided to return home, saturated trousers, stockings and boots drying on me as I walked. Arriving at Benfleet Station I called at the little café by the entrance for a hot cup of tea and a bun and caught the train home, my clothes by now quite dry and with a box full of treasures in sawdust and not even a well-deserved cold or chill afterwards.

It might appear that I have recorded this particular trip in unnecessary detail, but apart from the excitement of that memorable day, it emphasises the abundance of wild birds that had their habitat on Canvey. Though in retrospect I deeply regret it, the eggs I took made little difference in comparison to the deadly toll that our modern insecticides took some forty years later, or the oil slicks of the present day. My collection grew and among it were many rare eggs bought or exchanged. I kept it until just before World War Two, when I gave it to a teacher friend and it was taken to Chalkwell Hall School and, I think, later to my old school, North Street. I have no knowledge of what happened to it afterwards. If it is still in existence it might help this later generation to see eggs of species no longer found in the Essex countryside or even England. Did I hear that 'small wee voice' say, 'There he goes again, just easing his conscience?'

The air raids continued intermittently and the war dragged on. It was stalemate; in spite of censorship, reports of huge losses of both men and equipment in France filled the daily papers, and accusations of tragic mistakes by both politicians and generals disturbed and frightened the public, who now realized that they were fighting a dangerous and determined enemy, and the optimism of the past was a fallacy. Our losses at sea were mounting in alarming numbers and in the air it was the same. Many things were short or unobtainable, profiteering was rife and I remember out of the many scandals that rocked the nation one in which a large firm of jam makers had obtained a monopoly to supply strawberry jam to the British army. On analysis, the jam was found to be strawberry-flavoured apple, with manufactured wooden pips. I think it must have been the wooden pips that intrigued me and remained in my memory, but all these things added to the despondency of the nation.

Shoes were almost unobtainable, so Dad patched and mended our old ones until they were unwearable, then he bought us wooden-soled clogs which we hated but had to wear. Meat and oranges we missed most of all. Sometimes the butcher got a consignment of whale meat which was 'off ration'. Mother would queue for long periods to get some, a wasted effort as we disliked its cod liver oil flavour and wouldn't eat it. Very occasionally a few oranges came in. The news would spread like wildfire but the controlling factor was the distance one lived from the shop and even after a long wait they were all gone.

We did have a bit of luck one day. Mother was at the grocer's when a consignment of what was called 'glucose' came in. It was a dirty brown sugarish collection of lumps and supposed to be for sweetening tea and other things. We were warned that it was to be used sparingly as it could be harmful. Mother got 2 lbs. It tasted horrible in tea but eaten like a piece of toffee it wasn't so bad, and in spite of the warning, had no unpleasant results as far as I know.

Then one day amid great excitement a large wooden box arrived from Africa. Mother recognised Uncle Tom's writing and we lost no time in prising it open. It was filled with what we afterwards found out to be 'pemmican', sun-dried strips of meat, used in Africa. They were like hard pieces of old leather wrapped around a bone and we, and the now-assembled neighbours, were all puzzled and wondering what the stuff was and what should be done with it. No one had seen anything like it; there was no

115

letter or instructions. Those followed months later, long after it had gone.

One neighbour suggested perhaps it should be planted in the garden, another that it was for soling boots, but Mother decided it should be boiled. We tried boiling, frying and steaming it, but it remained so tough it was uneatable. We didn't know what to do with it. We gave some to Auntie Polly and Uncle and they had no better results and at last we threw it out for the chickens. They loved it and with commendable perseverance pecked and pecked until there was nothing left. It solved our problem and they had the lot.

But in spite of the gloom and difficulties ours and other parents suffered, it made surprisingly little difference to us or the other children in the street. We adapted to conditions and continued to accept them without question. Admittedly we in particular, as I have said previously, were more fortunate than many. Our standard of living had never been particularly good. Going without anything other than warmth, clothing and filling food was no hardship and we had all these necessities at hand provided by Dad, and even some clothing and boots from my cousin.

He was slightly older and bigger than me and an only child, so the need of passing down did not arise and instead they were passed on to me and then down the line in our family. Being quite well off, the quality was the best. My cousin's clothes were not allowed to have the repeated wear that ours required and his shoes were never really worn out like ours, and this brings one particular occurrence to mind. His mother, my auntie, passed on one of his 'special' suits, a light speckled blue and green Norfolk jacket. I can only liken it to those associated with Sherlock Holmes of detective fame, belted at the waist. It had four large buttoned pockets and large bone buttons between two long pleats down the front. A waistcoat of the same material was added, all buttons, and knickerbocker trousers with little straps around the bottoms, and to top it off a white stiff starched collar, bow-tie and button boots, all very suitable for parties in the best places. The whole 'ensemble' was too big for me, the jacket hung almost to my knees and the trousers did up nearer my ankles than knees. but there was a special occasion at school, so with various adjustments I was told I had got to wear it.

With deep foreboding I reached school and all my fears were justified. I must have looked a curious sight; certainly my school mates thought so. Had I been in rags I doubt it would have warranted a passing glance, but this creation was like an apparition from another world, in our plebeian school. A crowd gathered around me, sarcastic and snide remarks were thrown at me and my life made a misery with that cruel skill school children are capable of.

I was relieved to get into my classroom. It was safe there; we had a man teacher who kept strict discipline and I liked him. When I walked in and took my allotted seat he gazed at me with a mixture of wonder, curiosity and surprise, no doubt justified after the rough treatment outside. Several times I caught his eyes on me and a faint smile crossing his face, but I had no inkling of what was to come, when he called me out and handed over the registers, instructing me to collect the other classroom registers and give them to the headmaster. It was in the normal way a much-prized job only given to a special few, and I was not one of them.

It was evident that he thought the opportunity too good to pass by and thought he would share me with the rest of the school, with little consideration for my feelings. I could do nothing about it. As I entered each classroom a murmur or suppressed titter of laughter filled the background, quickly suppressed by the teacher, who was trying at the same time to control the broad grin or sly smile on his own face.

With growing misery and a very strong inclination to run home I visited all the classrooms and eventually arrived at our headmaster's office. A little, active, grey-headed man, old Mr. Thatcher was held by us all in awe. He rarely if ever smiled; the cares of North Street weighed heavily on his shoulders, and when I knocked and entered a look of astonished surprise, but followed by a gentle smile, covered his face. He spoke to me kindly, asked after my parents and kept me in conversation for a few minutes, something I had never known before, and thanked me for returning the registers. I was overwhelmed with his kindness and understanding and reassured that at least the headmaster was my friend, if no one else was.

I stayed in during playtime; I couldn't face my classmates outside and waited behind at twelve o'clock when it was time to go home. A great mistake, I should have rushed out first and got away. As it was, most of my classmates and, it seemed, half the school were waiting and as soon as I appeared a chorus of, 'Where did you get that suit, that collar and that tie?' a parody on a popular song of the time, greeted me. I was surrounded and tried to fight my way through and was soon at the bottom of a heap of yelling youngsters. Fortunately for me my teacher, perhaps expecting it, came out and dispersed the crowd and escorted me to the school gates, where I took to my heels and ran home in tears. Mother was down on the beach, so running straight up the stairs I tore the offending suit and collar off, stamped on them and threw them out of sight under the bed. I never wore them again, and donned my old clothes.

The 'important person' and the original cause of my being 'dressed up' arrived in the afternoon and we were all lined up to receive him and his speech. I was in the front line in my old blue jersey and still older short trousers and crinkled stockings. His glance fell on me and passed me by without notice and I was left wondering just what effect it would have had on him if it had been that morning instead. It was a humiliating experience but it taught me a lesson. I never called after 'Henery' or 'Daddy Watson', two local characters whose lives were made equally miserable by us children, again, and once back in my old clothes I was accepted and things returned to normal.

With the opposing armies dug in and at stalemate in France, unable to bomb the civilian population of England into submission, our enemy decided to try their only alternative, to starve us out. This was a very real threat; our losses of merchant shipping and crews at sea were enormous and increasing week by week as the blockading German submarines took their toll, and at that time there was no efficient means of stopping them. Oil, machinery, corn and all the essentials to living and fighting were being sent to the bottom of the sea and, most dangerous of all, our food supplies. The farmers and others did their best but tractors, chemical fertilizers and modern methods of producing food were almost unknown and the possibility of starvation, like the sieges of the old castles, looked like being repeated and we would have to give in.

Dad, always fiercely protective of us, frustrated through age – he was now fifty – from being actively involved, turned his attention to our survival. From seven o'clock until about ten in the morning he worked and extended his allotments to almost double their length. He would then walk to the beach, collect and saw wood, go fishing or do other jobs, then go back again to his allotments in the evenings if it were light enough. But most surprising of all, he gave up drink. No longer did his footsteps lead him each evening to 'The Smack', his cronies and his pints of ale, although he had been a steady and heavy drinker all his life, as were a great many of his companions in the Old Town. It pleased us all and delighted Mother. His excuse was that the war-time beer was no longer fit to drink, but I think the urgency of the times and the worry that we would all be without food unless he provided it was the real reason.

And he was not alone in this fear. The school authorities now planned that the older boys should dig up the field between the school boundary wall and Pall Mall, quite a large area, and turn it into allotments. At first it was two days a week during school hours, until all those who wished had a nice well-dug patch of ground, and it was surprising how many did when it was learned that under a teacher's supervision every Friday was to be given to planting and tending them. So with time off for the cold spells and now more for gardening, a very welcome break from actual lessons was appreciated by most of us, and as far as I know our education didn't in any way suffer. We all learned to read and write and add up accurately, something there seems some reason to doubt at the present day.

We were allowed to work on the allotments in our free time if we wished, so I found another activity to add to my already other numerous interests, and the close companionship with Dad was further eroded. In today's language I wanted to 'do my own thing'. Vincent, my younger brother, took my place to some extent, but all the conditions and freedom I experienced with Dad no longer existed in these war-torn days, so he had little of the close and intimate contact that had been my fortunate lot. Vincent had only just got over rheumatic fever, which left him with a weak heart, so he was unable to do the things I had done. I still went with Dad with his fishing parties in the 'A. J. Soper' but more frequently dug my

119

own bait and went fishing on my own in the Tub Boat as a proof of my independence. At times I even took a customer with me, on the promise that I kept this side of the creek so Dad could keep an eye on me.

This one particular morning Dad was still on his allotment but he gave me permission to go out fishing on my own. I was getting the Tub Boat ready on the beach when a friend and customer of my father, Mr. Young, a retired and elderly gentleman who dearly loved a few hours' fishing, came to chat. Finding I was off to fish for a couple of hours or so, he asked if he could come with me. I didn't really want him; he was very heavy and awkward and moved in a dinghy with difficulty and stiffness, but on the other hand he was generous to a fault and I knew I would be well rewarded. I had plenty of bait and a spare line so I saw no reason to refuse and off we went.

From the beginning I knew it was wrong; his weight in the stern completely out-balanced my weight on the front seat. Like a seesaw, my end was up and his down, which stopped me from using the oars efficiently, they were too high out of the water. But assisted with a now freshening 'offshore' wind behind us, it wasn't too bad and I anchored opposite the beach, just this side of Leigh Creek, about a quarter of a mile from the shore. Normally it was quite a good place to fish for flounders and I nearly always caught enough for our tea, but today they just didn't bite and all we did was feed the crabs. With growing impatience and disappointment my passenger suggested we go to 'Marsh End', a bank of hard sand extending from Canvey Point to the low way. It had about eight feet of water over it at high tide and was a favourite and prolific fishing ground for Dad and me, but it was a mile further out.

I knew from the start it was foolish and I shouldn't do it and if I had been on my own I would never even have considered it. But we had caught no fish and I felt somehow my reputation was at stake as a good fisherman and I really wanted Mr. Young to catch some, so completely against my better judgement we started off. The same wind that so kindly helped us before continued with increasing force. The further we were from the shore, the faster we went. I hardly needed to row now; with the wind and waves behind us we skipped along at a rare pace and it seemed no time before we passed the line of moored bawleys that identified the Ray

Channel and a few hundred yards beyond reached our chosen ground.

With the wind and waves behind and urging us on it hadn't been too bad, but now at anchor with high tide and a freshening wind we were being tossed around like a cork in a basin and I could see Mr. Young was already regretting coming. He wasn't alone; I was now realizing my own foolhardiness and wondering what to do. I had no Dad with me now to help me and, even worse, I had the responsibility of this old and frightened man as well. Every time the bow rose to meet the waves, so the stern, with its almost unmovable ballast, sank deep in the water and occasionally water lapped over the gunwale and transom, each time adding weight aft and increasing the danger of sinking stern first.

Had it been a larger boat it wouldn't have mattered; had I been alone it wouldn't have mattered. Had it been any other dinghy of the same length other than the Tub Boat we would have surely sunk and even now I wasn't sure we would not. Seeing the danger I asked Mr. Young to ease himself slowly forward off the back seat and sit on the floorboards. This he did; it was a miserable, uncomfortable position with water sloshing around him, and I moved right forward as a counter balance. The dinghy was rising easier now and for quite a while we lay at anchor. The tide was ebbing and I thought maybe, if I could row to one of the bawleys in the Ray and tie up, we would be safer. Hauling up the anchor I took to the oars but the only progress I made was backwards. I struggled with every inch of my strength to row against the current, but with the wind and now fast-ebbing tide, I lost ground and was rapidly being swept out into the fairway and even greater danger, so over went the anchor again and I had lost another hundred yards.

All that was left now was to ride it out until the tide left us high and dry. I saw two boats in the distance and waved frantically. They just waved back and were soon gone. My only hope now was that some fishermen would come into the Ray and hear my call for help from the sandbank. Poor old Mr. Young. He sat in water nodding and half asleep, on the verge of seasickness, a picture of abject misery and discomfort, but I could do little for him. I was equally wet and miserable and there we sat and waited, pitching and tossing around waiting for the tide to go out.

Every so often, I tried the depth of water to see how long it still had to be, and this time found it was only waist deep. Suddenly an idea came to me: if I got overboard I could now push the dinghy to the Ray and once there by luck even get across to the opposite bank, although Leigh Creek was still an obstacle to be faced, if I ever got there.

With all these 'ifs' in mind, I slipped overboard to my waist in water. Sometimes I pushed, at other times I pulled. It was a fight every inch of the way, but it worked and it became a race to reach the Ray before the tide, now running out fast, beat me to it. And through it all poor Mr. Young just sat there helpless and unable to do anything. Slowly but surely I was winning, the bawleys were getting nearer, the water was less and less, but it was easier for me all the time. Then it started to deepen and I knew I had reached the channel bank. I could get no further; the sandbank behind me was now rapidly uncovering and as the depth of water dropped I eased the dinghy further into the Ray. Soon both banks were well above water, and the narrowing stretch of water between, protected from the wind, became calm.

Perhaps now I could reach the other bank. Mr. Young now looked really ill and it was essential I got help, so I started to row. But the fast-running ebb was taking me as fast sideways as I was going forward and I finished at the mouth of Leigh Creek, at its junction with the Ray, some quarter of a mile further down. Here, of course, the tide was against me and, unlike the sandbank, the creek was full of shallows and pockets of deep water. Nevertheless, I got overboard again determined to try and push the dinghy against the current as far as possible up the creek. Tired out, soaking wet and fighting a losing battle, I had no choice to do otherwise.

Mr. Young had completely lost interest in everything. He was sitting on the floorboards with the back seat holding him from failing over, in a sort of sleep, when in the distance I saw Dad coming, running and walking in rushes across the mud, and when he finally reached me he was hopping mad. I had never seen him so angry. He used no physical violence – he never did on us – but his fury lashed me almost as much. He ordered me ashore and took over the oars, and his anger showed itself even in the mad strength of his rowing. He pulled against the current and up the creek to the hard patch of shingle that joined the ridge of hard sand and pebbles off the Crowstone, and now forms the hardway opposite Chalkwell Avenue. I didn't know if he meant I was to go right ashore or to the creek bank, but I followed along the bank crying my eyes out, tired and weary with my exertions. I had just about 'had it' without this added upset.

Reaching the spot where he landed I found him struggling to get my passenger ashore, no easy task. I rushed to help. His anger had subsided. I moored the Tub Boat and between us we struggled and half-carried Mr. Young ashore to the Crowstone, something that would have proved completely impossible on my own, even if I had succeeded in reaching access to the shore in the shape of the hardway. He was now recovering his circulation, and movement was returning, and with the help of a kindly stranger we got to the comfort of the shed and 'put the kettle on'. There were no phones, cars or taxis readily available as now, in those days, so after resting and warming up I went to Mr. Young's house nearby and his two sons who lived with him got their father home, put him to bed and called a doctor. It seems that while I was away the old gentleman had taken the full blame for what had happened and was full of praise for my efforts to get back. He insisted I had saved his life and considerably altered Dad's temper and outlook. He even seemed a little proud of the way I had got out of the mess that I should never have got into in the first place.

I was only thirteen at the time. It was a frightening lesson, that could easily have ended in both of us being drowned or Mr. Young not surviving the strain. It should never have happened except for two reasons: first and foremost I should not have disobeyed Dad's orders, and secondly, in lesser degree, it was chance and circumstances that he had not been there to watch me. He had worked late on his allotment and when he did arrive on the beach I was where I should have been, this side of the creek. He was doubtful of the weather but reassured by seeing I had someone with me, not knowing it was Mr. Young. He reasoned that even if we couldn't row back it was a short walk over the mud as soon as the tide left, so he returned home for dinner. He didn't hurry back and was not unduly worried that I had not returned home and it wasn't until he arrived back, with the tide nearly out, that with no signs of either boat or me around he became deeply worried.

Searching the seascape, he saw the only likely answer in a small and very distant dinghy well beyond the Ray. It was too late and too shallow to launch a boat, so he started to wade and slosh through water and mud and reached the creek, which at this time was pouring out so fast and so deep it was impossible to cross. Being so much nearer he could see I was now on the edge of the Ray channel and was being swept by the tide to the creek entrance. He made his way towards it, arriving at almost the same time as me, and from here I have already described what followed.

Several days afterwards, a now fully recovered Mr. Young turned up with a large brown paper parcel and handed it to me. He said it was a present for saving his life (I suppose I should have mentioned I had been equally interested in saving my own, but let it pass). The parcel contained a most expensive and beautifully bound copy of *European Butterflies and Moths* with colour plates of hundreds of species, but all the names were in Latin and the writing so highly technical that it was far beyond me. I doubt I opened it a dozen times and then only to look at the illustrations. It told me nothing about the simpler things that interested me, where to find and feed caterpillars, how to keep the rarer chrysalises and suchlike mundane knowledge, but it looked very imposing on my shelf until many years later when I passed it on to someone who valued its true worth.

Perhaps this interest in moths and butterflies may now be the reason why I still recall how butterflies suddenly at this period became a major concern to the Government, not to conserve, as one might expect, but to destroy them, at least, one particular species. With every ounce of food precious, the great increase in the production of vegetables in fields, allotments and gardens seemed to upset the balance of nature. All at once there was unlimited food for cabbage caterpillars and they increased in vast numbers. These in turn produced equally large numbers of the cabbage white species and other white butterflies, and they again produced millions of eggs, and so the cycle was repeated on an ever-increasing scale.

We had none of the efficient insecticides of today and no satisfactory means to combat them. Their natural enemies, the birds, couldn't cope and other than going over each plant at regular intervals and picking them off by hand and putting them in a jam

124

jar half-filled with salt water, there was no means of destroying them.

The destruction they caused was unbelievable. Rows of cabbages become bare skeletons on stalks with caterpillars crawling all over like ants. They were everywhere, climbing up walls and fences to find places to change into their next stage, and later again into more white butterflies. So the Government, through the schools, declared war on them. They couldn't do much about the caterpillars except beg everyone that could to destroy them, but prizes and certificates were offered to children who in their summer holidays caught the largest number of white butterflies, so a lot of us became butterfly collectors. I caught just over six hundred but some caught more and the prizewinner in our school had eight hundred and fifty. I think it was kept going for another year or more. I left school after the second year, so don't know, but it was quite a serious threat at the time and much added to the work on Dad's and my allotment. I think it is worth recording that the plagues were not entirely confined to Egypt!

Once again it seems that Mother has faded into the background, but while Dad seemed to be doing so much, Mum in a less noticeable way was working just as hard to cope with conditions, mending, darning, patching our clothes. She even had a go at mending and soling our boots and shoes. Standing in queues for both rationed and unrationed goods, and making do with anything available was not easy with seven of us to look after. Fortunately, having no spare rooms, she had no soldiers billeted on her, like Aunt and Uncle and some neighbours, who were paid a small sum for this service, which included board as well as lodging. Meanwhile the air raids continued at intervals with little effect here in Leigh.

With the situation as it was, we had little hope for the summer and the business. The season came round and to our great surprise we started getting busy. There was a steady demand for both tents and rowing boats, which increased well beyond expectation as the summer reached its peak. It seemed that locals and visitors alike, in spite of everything, were going to have their holidays whatever happened, air raids and other inconveniences included. They needed to get away from the monotony and drabness of wartime life, and this ensured that the income our parents so depended on was once again earned for another year.

I think it was this year when, apart from the troops billeted in the town for overseas service, 'Athlone', a large house at the junction of Grand Drive and Grand Parade, was taken over by the military. A searchlight was also installed on the only flat piece of ground on the undercliff side about halfway along the Parade, which then was overgrown, wild and completely free of buildings. In the long, warm, dark summer evenings I used to stop on practice nights watching with a mixture of frustration and envy the large variety of rare and, to me, valuable, moths, attracted and dancing in its powerful rays, and longed to get my hands on them. But with a job to do, the soldiers had no time for small boys, whom they regarded more as a nuisance to be kept at a distance, so I was not welcome.

I also remember that during the dark nights of winter the cinder path was closed and patrolled from Bell Wharf onwards to the beach by soldiers, and permits were issued to those who had legitimate reasons for using it, but even then not after sunset. This restriction was obviously lifted for the summer, and how long it was imposed I don't know; I wasn't around at that time on my own on dark winter nights.

But one occasion I shall not forget was when we had gone fishing. It was after dinner before we started and Dad decided that with such a short afternoon he would only go this side of the Ray on the north bank. So we dropped anchor, much to my disappointment, in a place we had never bothered to fish before. We always had our special spots and this wasn't one. With reluctance and quite sure we were wasting our time, I put my line overboard. It had hardly reached the bottom before I had a bite and caught a large flounder. At the same moment, Dad hooked another and so it continued. It was one of those fishing days one never forgets.

We had no time to put them in our bags. Every moment was precious. We just unhooked them and dropped them on the floorboards. Anything to get our lines baited and back into the water. The floor was covered with wet, slippery fish but we couldn't stop. The night was rapidly closing in, we had to be back before the curfew and we still had to row home. On the other hand, we just couldn't leave them. Darkness came and the tide was ebbing fast.

We had to get back. If we landed on our beach there was a possibility of some trigger-happy or frightened young soldier thinking we were spies or intruders, or the more real danger of Dad losing his permit and being fined.

With a boat full of fish, and as it was now quite dark, we did not know what to do. In the end, Dad decided to row silently to Leigh and the launch-way of 'The Smack', a narrow dark passage that led past the side door of the inn to the creek. This we did, successfully. We packed both our bags full of fish and even then there were lots left to collect next day. Tying up to a ring in the wall, we crept up the alley. Dad went into the side door, had a few words with the landlord, and met me at the front door on the High Street, and no one knew otherwise. It was the only time I think I remember Dad selling his catch, but the weight was too much to drag home and there was still plenty in the boat. So we called at 'Juniper's' and sold him our catch, I think for nine shillings, because being nearly all flounders they didn't sell well, even in wartime. A 'fisherman's tale', but it really happened.

My particular pal was Harry Bolton, who lived a hundred or so yards up the road. We were about the same age and started in the same class at nearly the same time. Having similar interests, it was natural for us to be together and be friends, although not before constant wrestling matches, fights and arguments proved that, physically even though I was no weakling, he was the stronger and always won. This decided, but never quite accepted by me, we settled down to an amicable compromise, and slowly our mutual interests took over and we became very close.

As the war came nearer, his interest in aeroplanes became more and more of an obsession rather than a hobby. Unlike me, who spread my interests over everything that was collectable, he concentrated on anything connected with aircraft and flying. He knew every aircraft that flew of every nationality (actually not many), designed and made model aeroplanes that far outdid my efforts of construction, and most of my knowledge I derived from him.

He developed a type of kite-cum-glider. It was based on the F. E. (Farman Experimental), one of the original 'stick and string' biplanes, which he flew on a long string like a kite. Indeed a similar kite carrying a man for observation over enemy lines was developed early in the war and was used until aeroplanes took over. Harry had success with his smaller models, so decided to make a much larger one of eight or nine-feet wingspan, a truly awesome monster which took quite a while to make. When it was finished we took it to our usual field, fastened it to a long length of strong fishing line and got it airborne.

It took off and flew beautifully and was a complete success. Later we added more and more line and it flew even higher. I can remember seeing it in the air from the school gates, a couple of miles away, looking exactly like a real plane except it was riding about in the sky and not going anywhere. In fact it looked so real that the police tracked it down and under some obscure government regulation that prevented kite-flying in wartime, and the threat of confiscation and fine, it was grounded.

But the seed had been sown. If this was so successful, surely a much bigger one exactly to scale might fly with someone in it – that someone being either of us – and the more he thought about the idea the more he liked it. His enthusiasm caught and carried me with it and we decided that as soon as circumstances allowed we would make it.

Here chance took a hand. I was on the beach; a daylight raid of enemy planes was in progress and I had seen them pass over, dots in the sky surrounded by puffs of anti-aircraft shells, when the sound of an aircraft flying very low with its engine spluttering came from the direction of the Crowstone. I was just in time to see an aeroplane, an 'Avro', land on the water and begin to sink. It had purposely or by chance landed near a man fishing in a small boat and I saw him row over and rescue the pilot. There was quite a crowd – I was one of them – waiting for the dinghy to reach the shore, and the pilot seemed unhurt. Whether he had been shot down or engine trouble was the cause, no one seemed to know, and the pilot was collected soon after by a Royal Flying Corps vehicle. I rowed out later but only the tail of the plane was above water.

The following morning I was down there early to see it and soon afterwards a squad of R. F. C. personnel turned up. It had landed in a particularly soft patch of mud in 'Crowstone Gut'. Fifty yards or so to the east it would have been on the hardway shingle but, as it was, it became a nightmare to those working on it. I was horrified when the corporal in charge took an axe that was in the cockpit and slashed a hole in the petrol tank, allowing its precious contents to gush out. He did the same to the oil tank and the mud become an oily, slimy mess.

They only had short wellingtons and it was evident that they had never been in a like situation, in fact I doubt they had ever seen Southend mud before. The wings were removed, the engine dismantled, wheels and undercarriage, tail and rudder taken off, and as they worked so they sank deeper and deeper and the mud became a quagmire. They even accepted my help, as with my long waders and more experience I helped to get the lighter bits across to the hard patch. Had they been properly equipped with boards and planks etc., it might have helped but, as it was, it slowly became quite impossible to remove the remainder and there was a very real danger of their sinking so far into the morass that they couldn't get out. It would be hard to describe fairly what they looked like. They had long previously discarded their wellingtons and were caked in mud from head to foot and many new words were added to my knowledge of swearing.

Later, another truck arrived with more men, who loaded all the removed parts and took the men away. Just as the corporal left, I asked him what was going to happen to the rest and he replied, 'I dunno, kid. It's yours if yer want the bl***y thing, I've had all I want.' I didn't know whether to interpret this as applying to his personal feelings or whether the remains would be left for me to keep.

I watched over them for several days. In any case, no one could get to it, sitting in a hole of black, syrupy mud. I felt sure now it was abandoned, so decided if possible to salvage it. I secured the aid of the older boys who joined me to help out, and with their dinghy and the Tub Boat we set off on the last of the early morning tide and moored one on either side of the fuselage. When the tide left we got ropes under it and secured it inside by the seats of our dinghies. The petrol and oil tanks that had filled and emptied each tide were now empty and I sealed the axe gash with stuffed rags. It all took time but, when we finished, by laying the floor-boards of my friends' old dinghy on the mud and rotating them we got to the firm ground and went back to the beach until evening and the incoming tide.

Back in the dinghies we waited and, as the tide increased, so they and the wreckage lifted with it. It was not particularly heavy but, even so, the gunwales were nearly submerged and by counter-balancing and careful pushing with the oars, the flood tide brought our prize home. Later, on high tide, with Dad's help as well, we got it ashore on our beach, although how much he approved of it is doubtful.

It is amazing what a number of small boys can do if they really want to, so we got it home to the vacant land next to Harry's house, where in a small shed lived Mrs. Bolton's pet goose, worse by far than any watch-dog. It was the terror both of tradesmen and the children hereabouts. With flapping wings, outstretched neck and a loud hissing it would, for no proper reason, rush out and bite viciously at our buttocks. It was really a menace and we all gave it a wide berth. In fact Mrs. Bolton had so many rows and complaints over it and made so many enemies she was at last forced to fence it in, but she and Harry could do anything with it and it was quite affectionate to them. So with the goose in the same field we knew our acquisition was safe.

Here was the nucleus of the 'glider' we wished to make. Harry accepted automatically that it was his. I suppose, in actual fact, I had this in mind from the beginning and willingly passed owner-ship on. Across the road in Mr. Mills' field was a large empty sta-ble and loft, and on condition we cleaned it up, he agreed to loan us the loft for nothing.

Here was the ideal spacious workshop, and we set to work to make wings, tail-plane and rudder, removing tanks and all surplus weight and other items thought unnecessary. This took every moment of our holidays, spare time and all our pocket money to buy the long lengths of wood needed for the wings. Dad had a huge, rat-eaten cotton spinnaker on the 'A. J. Soper'. He gave it to me and it was just right for wing covering. We had a mass of wire and wire-strainers rescued with the wreck, and our parents, uncles and friends were pestered for suitable timber for struts and other essentials. With the gluepot boiling in the corner, our parents had no problems of our whereabouts, hardly ever saw us, and counted their contribution as well spent!

In the meantime, we wove fantasies of what was going to hap-pen when it was finished, chief among these launching it off the top of the Leigh Cliff on its steepest part. When it was suggested by one of those who hadn't been picked to fly in it that it might come down on the railway lines, he was soon put in place and told, 'Of course it won't, it'll fly over them,' then as an afterthought, 'probably to the creek or the Ray.'

At last it was finished. Unfortunately we had no suitable wheels or undercarriage, but then Harry's other models didn't either and they flew, so the body was fixed to a pair of skids like a sledge, only about six inches above the ground, the Achilles heel as events proved. The parts were brought down from the loft and assembled, screwed, bolted or nailed together on the stable forecourt. It was an object of wonder to all and sundry, especially customers of 'The Elms'. Harry decided that before lumping off the cliffs we would test it, like his model, on a length of rope and make it fly like a kite first.

It was quite an impressive sight with its twenty-foot wing-span, as about twenty of us children dragged and carried it down the then unmade Elmsleigh Drive to the large field that sloped from Blenheim Chase to Prittle Brook. In the centre of this field were two quite big earth mounds. I don't know how they got there or what their purpose was. I have since wondered if they were ancient burial barrows; that's what they looked like. The plan was to take 'the glider' to the top of this field, attach two long lines (pinched clothes lines) to the undercarriage, and with all of us pulling rush down the field and up and over one of the mounds. In theory it would take off and soar into the sky.

It was conceded that it would be better to start with a light-weight first, so my youngest brother Harold, then about seven, was chosen for the honour of being first to fly. Seated in the front seat and almost unable to see over the top, he was given the necessary instructions on just when to pull the lever back to make it rise into the air – this being the exact moment on top of the mound – and slowly push it forward when he wanted to come down. How much he really understood was questionable. With great enthusiasm we started tearing down the field over the mound where it was supposed to 'take off'. Afterwards some said it lifted and glided a few feet, others were equally certain it never left the ground. Certainly it was firmly on the ground when I looked back. But we didn't stop, it was now a race between the two towing teams to the brook, irrespective of our original plan, with the glider bouncing along behind, when suddenly, with a splintering and tearing sound, first one wing and a moment later the other were torn off, the top wings going with them.

We had hit two iron stakes, unnoticeable in the long grass, used for tethering goats. The fuselage with the towing ropes attached continued on, as the wings, connected by masses of wire, pulled off and trailed behind. Months of work and effort destroyed in a moment of time. Harold, shaken but fortunately unhurt, scrambled out of the wreckage thinking it was all his fault for pulling the lever the wrong way and had to be comforted. We all surveyed the sorry mess with a mixture of sorrow or amusement, depending on how deeply one was individually involved.

Collecting all the bits together, it was once again dragged and carried to Mrs. Bolton's adjoining field after the goose was locked up. We were determined that we would rebuild it, but never got round to it; maybe it was a good thing we didn't, and Mrs. Bolton's goose took over the fuselage in preference to its shed and guarded the remains day and night thereafter.

So ended our dream of flying, but Harry continued his mechanical interests and later became involved in the motor cycle races held for several years along the Chalkwell Promenade roadway. He also invented and made a three-wheeler type of car with an Indian motor cycle engine driving a tractor propeller, but it was not entirely satisfactory and the police stopped him using it as they considered it dangerous. Later, he took over some garages and a workshop, but his heart was still with aeroplanes and he went to America and joined a large aircraft company where, until his retirement recently, he held an important executive position. He travelled all over the world for them and when he visits England still calls to see me and chat over old times. Although he has a lovely home on Long Island, New York, he still counts England 'home'. Few boyhood dreams have been so successful and fulfilling as his have been – on reflection perhaps just as well – as there would be an awful lot of train and fire engine drivers around now!

But for all these diversions, the war still went on, the air raids still continued, now sometimes in daylight, and no really effective means of preventing them had been invented. With no early-warning systems like radar, the planes were almost overhead before our combat planes could take off. The slower speed and climbing rate of even our best machines made it difficult to reach them, the raiders flew so high in daylight, and even with searchlights it was pretty hopeless at night. But other than the fear while they were actually overhead, and the inconvenience of the severe rationing of food and clothing, we continued to live our own selfish lives, shutting our eyes to the suffering of those, mostly in London, from the bombing and hunger we had so far escaped.

But it was not all gloom. A more efficient and fairer rationing system was operating generally, a new shake-up of Government ministers and generals gave the country more confidence, and the introduction of women in large numbers into the munition factories increased our output enormously. But most of all the convoy system and other means like 'Q' boats and improved detection and destruction were beginning to take effect, and it seemed at long last we were now overcoming the worst of our fears. But perhaps I am only speaking as I saw it through my eyes with the confidence of youth.

This confidence was somewhat shattered, when one afternoon our headmaster, Mr. Thatcher, called all the school together and announced in solemn tones that our great general, Lord Kitchener, had been lost at sea on a battleship bound for Russia, but he didn't give us the rest of the afternoon off as we felt for some reason he should have done. But later, when a very cold period came just after Christmas, we didn't go to school for three weeks because there was no coal for heating, so I suppose we had no cause to complain.

All I know was that most of us welcomed any chance of not going if we could find any excuse to stop away. I did not actually dislike school, neither did I like it much, and I think I speak for most of the children there. Our teachers were not unduly harsh, or discipline particularly strict, although much more so than today. We respected and feared those in authority and were in awe of our headmaster as being the normal shape of things, but our parents, or most of them, did not much encourage education and were more concerned with us leaving school and getting a job – any job – if it helped the family's income. A few, if they could afford it, did realize a trade was important and their children were then either apprenticed to a tradesman or followed their father's occupation to take over later.

So in the following March, when I would be fourteen, Dad, having no real occupation other than occasional building work and the beach, decided to apprentice me to the engineering trade, which at that time seemed to have the greatest and most promising future, with cars and engines the shape of things to come. A far-sighted and very sensible choice, as things stood, but one I was never given any say in. Fathers and mothers never consulted their children then, and I was told that when I left school I was going to be apprenticed to Mr. Davis, the owner of the Southend Engineering Company in Leigh Old Town, two or three months before my schooldays ended.

Previous to that, the 'powers that be', through the school authorities, decreed that we cultivate more land. So now, on Fridays, the older boys were marched, complete with borrowed forks and spades, to the top of Hadleigh Road – why so far from our school I cannot comprehend – to some vacant land immediately adjoining 'Lapwater Hall', a very lovely and elegant house built of red brick in around 1750. The house is the subject of a story by Arthur Morrison, the author of the one book I never tire of reading, entitled *Cunning Murrell*. Murrell was a local man who was reputed to be deeply involved in witchcraft and who, I have little doubt, was well known to my own grandfather around 1850.

For the full story, one would have to obtain a copy of *Divers Vanities*, a very rare book, long out of print, but briefly for those interested, the tale is told how on the site of an old and dilapidated farmhouse, a certain Gilbert Craddock had the remains demolished and this gracious house built. Bricklayers from Rochford and labour from Leigh were engaged, their wages in part paid in cash and part in beer, a barrel of which was wheeled daily in a barrow from 'The Smack' to the site, and it was surprising what an unduly long time it took to build the house. Craddock, an ill-tempered and much-disliked man, was growing more and more impatient and dissatisfied.

Matters eventually came to a head when the age-old ceremony of 'topping out' on a newly built house arrived. A flag was hoisted on the last completed chimney-stack and a spread prepared for those employed on the job. It was customary for the owner to supply a generous amount of beer to celebrate the occasion. The tables were laid and piled with food and they waited expectantly for the beer, but while the owner appeared, no liquid refreshment arrived. Eventually, becoming more and more impatient, they loudly demanded their 'rights'. Craddock met their demands with abuse and curses, then pointing to the pond adjoining, and beside himself with rage and anger, shouted, 'Beer? Beer'? If you're thirsty, then lap water, like the lazy dogs you are, ye boosy scabs, you swill-pot dogs. If more drink ye must have, then lap water, you'll get no more beer from me.'

From that day on, although Craddock insisted the name of his house was 'Leigh House', it was always known as 'Lapwater' amongst the inhabitants of Leigh, and its nickname spread to the ale houses and inns of the surrounding countryside to show their disapproval of him. In spite of all his efforts it was never known by its real name.

But the story does not end there. After the house was built it was rumoured that he intended to marry and bring his bride, Lady —— to live there, but other than installing an ancient crone as housekeeper, he disappeared for long periods and the house remained hardly used, much to the curiosity of the Leigh folk. The mystery was solved when, one dark and blustery night, a loud knocking on the door was heard by the old woman and, on open-ing it, Gilbert Craddock fell in, bleeding from a gaping gunshot wound in his shoulder and completely exhausted. She bathed the wound while he drank brandy to ease the pain and after a short while said he would stable his horse, which covered in sweat and shivering, stood patiently by the door.

He had hardly left before a party of horsemen drew up and demanded entrance, announcing they were 'Bow Street Runners' and intended to search the house. It proved fruitless; Craddock was nowhere to be found, but next morning his body was found under the culvert that drained into the same pond where he had previously told his workmen to lap water, proof in the eyes of the good folk of Leigh that it was a 'judgement' on him.

He had hidden under the culvert, and loss of blood and exposure had caused his death, after being chased for miles across the Essex marshes and countryside. The mystery of his identity was solved; he was none other than the famous and ill-famed highwayman and scourge of the Essex roads, 'Cutter Lynch'. Those knowledgeable folk in Old Leigh nodded wisely and said, 'I allus knowed as how there war summut queer about 'im, no sooner en I set eyes on 'im,' and the name 'Lapwater' and later 'Lapwater Hall' remained until it was pulled down in the 1930s and a block of flats bearing the name was put in its place.

Surrounded by huge elms, the old house (now inhabited by a respectable family) overlooked our efforts and the pond, still in existence, provided ample water for planting seedlings. Our Friday outing was something to look forward to, as we marched with our forks and spades to our destination. Life was grey and drab, everything was in short supply, but now firmly established on ration cards and the air raids were getting worse.

Enemy aircraft now defied us by coming in daylight, in large numbers with even heavier loads of destruction, but London was their target and here in Leigh we rarely suffered from their visits. Occasionally one or two were brought down by gunfire or our planes, but all in all, they seemed to have it all their own way as, in compact and orderly groups, they passed overhead, dropped their deadly cargo on their destination, and returned.

But in France, with ever-increasing American troops and aid, the news looked more hopeful and optimism began to take over from despair. But to us children it had become a way of life; it had been with us so long. We knew little different and had learned to live with it and were completely adjusted to it. I had no thought of what Fate had in store for the family before the fruits of my labours were harvested.

So as I dug and sowed that early spring, I was far more concerned about my immediate future – my fourteenth birthday – and when that day arrived I had already got a job to go to. It came on a Wednesday, and Dad had already made arrangements for me to start at the 'Southend Engineering Co.' on the following Monday.

I was worried: how did I tell my school teacher I was leaving? I asked Dad. 'Just tell her you are fourteen and you've got a job to go to,' he said. He had little respect for those in authority and even less for higher education, and his wildly patriotic nature convinced him I should be doing far more good turning out shell fuses than being educated or digging for victory. So, with little help, and far less a letter from Dad, I found myself at playtime stopping behind and approaching Mrs. Nicholson.

'I'm fourteen and I've got to leave today,' I blurted out. She looked surprised.

'Have you got a letter for Mr. Thatcher?' she asked.

'No, Dad said it wasn't necessary, and I've got a job to go to on Monday.'

She was a firm but kind teacher and I think she liked me, although I'll never forget how she kept me in until one o'clock trying to get a sum right (and I never did), while she sat at her desk marking papers, when I should have left at mid-day. But this time she was kindness itself. She listened to my request, took me to Mr. Thatcher, and at 10.30 that day I was free from school, a day of gladness and sadness, so mixed I wasn't sure which was which. And the Monday that followed I started my new life.

The workforce consisted of about six boys of various ages, a foreman, Mr. Shaw, a head boy, and Mr. Davis, although he never did any manual work. The machines were all 'set', in other words called for very little skill, and mostly performed one operation only by pulling a lever. Each of us had our own lathe to look after and keep clean. It was a deadly monotonous job and we learnt little or nothing of real engineering. I was supposed to be apprenticed, but as far as I know, no legal papers were signed. However, it probably accounted for the apprentice wages of five shillings per week I received, and when later that year two pretty girls replaced two of the older boys, it added a touch of glamour and excitement and helped to make it less dreary and our behaviour more civilized.

We worked from 8 a.m. until 6 p.m. with an hour for dinner and a quarter of an hour mid-morning. There was, unlike today, no supply of tea or refreshment, and we mostly brought cold tea and sandwiches, but 'Shaw's' the baker, a few doors away, did supply cakes if we could afford them, and old Mrs. Chilcraft sold sweets in her tiny shop opposite, so our basic needs were catered for.

I suppose it was because I was employed at the S. E. Co. that I remember so little of the earlier part of that summer of 1918, other than work, or roaming the fields and hedges in pursuit of my hobbies, and helping Dad and Mother on the beach, bait digging and fishing in the tub boat at weekends and in the evenings.

Except that there was one unpleasant experience, brought about as usual by my own foolishness, and the forerunner of the tragedy to come.

Charley Myers came into my life without invitation. He lived at Thundersley. He didn't go to school with me; he didn't belong to anyone I knew; he was not the son of a customer; but one day he just seemed to be there, on the Beach. At first we thought he belonged to someone in the tents. He sat and talked, first with one and then another of our customers and made himself thoroughly at home, bathing and generally joining in with all and sundry. It wasn't until he climbed into the tub boat with me and asked me to let him row that I became suspicious and by questioning him found that he had decided to adopt us, beach and all on it.

At first I was nonplussed, then annoyed at his cheek. This was followed by a strange admiration at the complete confidence he had in himself and we finished up on the most friendly terms. Mother and Dad fell for his charms and, I must say, he was most willing and helpful and even when I wasn't there helped them all he could. What I had taken for granted for so many years was all new to him, and he both loved and envied me. He had no time for my other interests and hobbies. Boats and the Beach filled his life. We became the very best of pals and most of my spare time on the beach was spent with him that year, but at its end he vanished with no more warning than when he arrived.

He told me little or nothing of his home life but did tell me of a large pond at the bottom of his garden and claimed that he went for trips on it quite often in an ordinary large, round, zinc bath, similar to the one we washed our costumes and towels in. I found this difficult to believe and, as we did have one available, I challenged him to show me if he could. To my astonishment he squeezed himself into it and paddled himself with his hands at a surprising speed, although its rim was only inches above water. Determined not to be outdone, I had a go, only to find I capsized immediately and it took me a great deal of time and practice before I became proficient in this form of travel. It also aroused a spirit of competition in me, because he was so much better at it than me, but I prided myself I could swim and do more tricks in the water than he could and it became quite a challenge between us, to see which of us could better the other.

I well remember that Sunday mid-day; the tide was high and very quiet – a lovely summer's day. The beach had been very busy; the tents and boats were all let, and there was a constant stream of customers. Charley and I normally went in bathing together to lark about and have fun, but this particular day was too busy for us both to be away at the same time and Dad and Mother wanted a bit of lunch, so it was agreed between us that Charley should have his bathe and then 'take over' while I had mine afterwards.

He had his turn when it was about high water, but it was quite a long time later that I was able to have mine, and the tide was now quite low in comparison, but I was determined to have my swim anyhow. On the edge of the tide was Charley. With pride he pointed to a 12 ft. motor dinghy moored some thirty yards off the shore. 'See that boat?' he said. 'Well, I dived and swam underneath it this morning.'

'That's easy, if you can do it, so can I,' was my boastful retort and, my mind completely occupied with the challenge, I swam out and dived under it.

What happened next would be hard to describe in words: the terror and fear I experienced. The falling tide and the considerable extra depth of the motor dinghy had left only about a foot of water beneath its keel. My dive had carried me under it until I was lying spreadeagled with the keel across my back, holding me down. In panic I tried to get up on my knees, but although the boat lifted a little with my efforts, my knees just sank deeper in the sandy mud. Straightening out, I tried clawing my way out but my back seemed firmly wedged under the keel and as I dragged myself along the bottom the boat merely slid sideways on the water. In a complete panic I clawed and dragged myself around on the sea bed. I was now desperate; my breath would no longer hold out. With a supreme effort and the strength that is brought by fear I put both hands on the bottom and forced my way upwards.

By merciful Providence it worked. The boot tilted and dipped on its other bilge and my head came above water. I could now use my knees for extra strength and I exerted all my strength, with one final effort, to rid myself of it. Tilting even further, it slid down my back and I was free. With a mouth full of salt water, a pounding heart and shaking like a leaf, I held onto the gunwale to collect my wits and recover my breath and then waded ashore.

Charley was waiting for me. He had watched the boat as it moved about and thought how clever I was to invent this new trick. He had never realized for one moment the danger I had been in and I could have easily drowned while he looked on. Flattered by this new aspect of it, I decided to think matters over before confiding the facts to him. We walked to 'the shed' to get a glass of fresh water to wash the taste of salt from my mouth. My back hurt, but not badly, it seemed just numb, but as I stood there blood and salt water trickled down my legs.

Mother spotted it; she pulled me round, looked in stunned silence for a moment and burst out, 'Good heavens, child.' What on earth have you done to your back? The skin's all torn off,' and pulling my costume down to the waist, she exclaimed, 'Your back's torn to pieces and smothered in blood.' I realized then. A year's growth of barnacles and the edges of the overlapping planking of the dinghy sliding down my back was far worse than I had thought, but it didn't seem to hurt much until feeling started coming back to my cold body – or perhaps the salt water had deadened it.

Ashamed to tell Mother of my foolishness, I assumed an innocent look and said, 'It doesn't hurt much, perhaps a jellyfish stung me.'

'No jellyfish ever did that,' she said, 'it must have been a shark.' Then she spotted a grin on Charley's face. 'Come on, out with it. What have you two been up to?' And out came the story, not all of it, only as much as was good for her to know – I had dived under a boat but scraped the bottom on coming up. Of the rest I made no mention.

It was near enough true and she accepted it, bathed the damage in fresh water, dried and covered it with zinc or sulphur ointment, and although I suffered severe pain for about a week, it was healed in a fortnight. However, I had to stay away from work, which in its own way compensated somewhat for it. As with previous – and later – times, it would seem my guardian angel was close at hand when needed.

Although the war was still on, the Beach had been sufficiently busy to provide a steady income. The highlight of the year, August Bank Holiday, was due that weekend. However, unlike most of the previous years of sunshine, a summer gale, a prelude to others, hit the beach with a ferocity that wreaked a sad toll of both tents and boats. Pieces of seaweed and rubbish covered the beach, the tents were blown down or ripped to pieces, and many small boats sunk or damaged, among them our own rowing boats.

I was free on the Saturday; it happened overnight, so I helped Dad all I could by baling and recovering floorboards etc., not only of our dinghies but those of other customers also, and Dad surprised me with his strength, for he was not a big, powerful man. By rocking a dinghy back and forth on its keel and getting a surge of water, he would tip it and empty the full contents in one enormous lift, and he excelled himself that day. The gale had gone, to be replaced by bright skies, and he was desperate to get back to normal for the Sunday and Monday holiday. We piled huge piles of seaweed well below high-water mark, in the hope it would at least diminish with the next tide, while Mother struggled with needle and thread to patch and repair the damaged tents as best she could. Some we carried home for more work on her sewing machine and she sat late into the night, while we slept, exhausted by the day's efforts.

The next day, Sunday, at breakfast, Dad complained of feeling unwell and refused his food, but as he was so rarely ill – in fact the only time I ever remember was when he had had 'red lead poisoning' many years before – I don't think we were unduly worried. He insisted that he must get early to the beach to continue our previous day's efforts. Mother and the family followed and we arrived mid-morning. Dad and Mr. Tye had been clearing more weed, the sun was shining and, generally speaking, we were in a fair condition to face the Bank Holiday rush.

But both Mother and I were worried by Dad's looks. His usual brown, sunburned face had given place to a strangely bloodless appearance and his eyes were tired and heavy. He had been sick and was complaining of severe pains in his stomach. He refused his dinner and became so weak that Mother persuaded him, in spite of the increasing number of customers, to go and lie down in Mr. Tye's tent. We coped as best we could and were terribly busy. Dad made one or two attempts to help but had to go back on the rough bed of old tents we had made for him.

Late that afternoon I heard the drone of aircraft and, looking up, saw several aircraft in formation coming in over Southend and a moment later realized they were enemy aircraft. I shouted out, 'Look out, they're Germans,' probably to air my knowledge, rather than to warn of danger. All those nearby rushed around seeking shelter, and others, seeing the excitement, got the message also. Everybody was milling around. We all made for the shelter (which was not an air-raid shelter) under Chalkwell Bridge and were soon squashed flat against the inner wall as more and more panic-stricken people tried to get in. There was little other cover available, and in any case its whole south front was open. No anti-aircraft guns had opened up, but later it was said that our fighter planes had taken off early and had engaged them. A heavy explosion was followed by several more as they dropped their loads and ran for home. It was the worst local raid we had suffered and I think the last. Much damage was done and many people were killed and injured in Southend, but Leigh once again escaped undamaged.

Mother stopped with Dad in the tent and, of course, everybody made for home. Here a problem arose: there was no available transport and Mother was desperately anxious to get Dad home, and he was equally anxious to get there. There was nothing for it but for him to walk. I stopped behind to pack and tidy up, but Mother told me later of that nightmare journey, the many stoppages to rest, how at times she had to half-carry, half-support him, like a helplessly drunken man, until they reached home and bed.

He was worse by morning and in great pain, so I went for Dr. Watson, who lived in Leigh House just by the Church (it is no longer there). He called shortly afterwards and immediately arranged for Dad's removal to Victoria Hospital in Southchurch Road, Southend, and an emergency operation was carried out. We were notified later the operation had been successful. I looked after the beach while Mother visited him next day and came home quite happy that he was well on the road to recovery. Next day was even better; he had had a meal and thoroughly enjoyed it and was sitting up in bed. The third day he didn't seem so well and next morning the hospital notified us he had died in the night, an unexpected and devastating blow. The death certificate said 'Cause of death – strangulated hernia'.

The doctor suggested it could have been caused by lifting a heavy object and I called to mind his strenuous efforts just previously. I had little doubt it was his method of emptying dinghies which was to blame, although later for many years I adopted the same method, without heeding its warning.

It left us all completely numbed, but even then the beach seemed to be the overriding priority: its demands seemed to swamp our grief, it was there still with its customers, its boats, tents and livelihood to be attended to, and Mother was allowed little time for grief. Dad's relations round about were kind, but I think felt an undefined resentment that the Beach interfered with the usual show and length of the mourning customary in the Joscelyne family. Shortly after the funeral, I remember Uncle Harry said to Mother, 'You'll have to give up the beach now for the sake of the children.'

'They are the very reason why I have no intention of doing so. I intend to carry on for their benefit,' was her abrupt answer. And from then on, she became both master and mistress of that tiny corner of seaweed, sand and salt water, 'Joscelyne's Beach'.

I went back to work and she, with the willing help of Mr. Tye, continued as best she could from where Fate had intervened with such finality for the following three weeks or so. Then, once again, gale-force winds hit the beach with a repeat performance of the previous disastrous occasion, again at the weekend. All night, as I lay in bed the windows shook and the wind howled and at daylight I was up and, with my two sisters and younger brother, made my way down to Chalkwell.

I knew exactly what to expect and I wasn't disappointed. We were back to the chaos and destruction of the earlier experience, in fact much worse. I won't go into details of how the four of us and, later, Mother tried to bring some semblance of order back. The tents were our first concern; ripped and sodden, we did what was possible to dry and rescue those few worth saving. The piles of seaweed and wreckage we ignored, our own boats I baled and pulled up, and packed the few unbroken tent poles. Squalls of wind and rain interrupted and hampered our efforts and at last we called it a day and trudged home, pushing in turn our old trolley filled with the few repairable tents left.

Although only the beginning of September, that was the end of the season on the beach and Mother rarely, if at all, visited her domain again that year. The following day, Sunday, with the help of some of the 'regulars', I got our boats up and packed away for the winter, and apart from going down occasionally to check, I continued through that miserable winter to work in the Old Town.

But suddenly I was made to realize I was no longer just a unit in the family and, next to Mother, had now to share it with her and its responsibilities. This was brought home to me, when six weeks or so after Dad's death, Uncle Harry informed me he would dig the potatoes on Dad's three Elm Road allotments, but I would have to barrow them home. A simple enough plan at first sight, and probably leaving one perplexed at even its mention. That is, without seeing the size of the barrow and the crop.

The barrow, a huge wooden affair with an iron tyred, spoked, wooden wheel, weighed, even when empty, almost as much as me, and the crop of potatoes were the best we had ever had, and must have weighed at least three tons, or so it seemed. Each day for a month or more Uncle dug the potatoes and left them to dry, and each evening after work I struggled back and forth until dark with this huge barrow loaded with as many as I could manage and tipped them into an empty chicken house at the bottom of the garden. It seemed unending and remains permanently in my memory, coupled with never-forgotten journeys I made along the London Road to my Lapwater Hall allotment I had given so much effort to in the previous spring. To this day I never cease to wonder how, and sometimes why I did it, particularly as it all turned out a waste of time in the end, because we left them, or most of them, in the chicken run uncovered, and the severe frosts later that winter turned them black, rotten, and uneatable.

My somewhat unorthodox leaving of North Street apparently left no bad feeling towards me, and in early September of that same year Mother received a letter from the Education Authorities, telling her my name had been put forward for an evening class scholarship at the Southend School of Art. Should I wish to take advantage of it, I was to attend with some of my paintings and drawings on a certain date to be interviewed by Mr. Commibere, the headmaster. Mother, flattered perhaps that my work was good enough to receive such an invitation, was anxious that I should take advantage of the offer, and in due course we arrived and my efforts with paint and pencil were examined and accepted. I had the choice of art, but the headmaster suggested that as I was occupied in engineering as a career, it might be more advantageous to take up metalwork, and this I did. At first it was two nights a week but I enjoyed it so much I asked if I could come four nights instead and was allowed to.

From then on, for the following four or five years, I attended as regularly as I could. I don't know how long it was supposed to have been for in the beginning, but each start of the winter term I turned up and nobody seemed either to mind or to say I should-n't, and I honestly believe if circumstances had allowed I could have stayed indefinitely. I made jewellery, copper work, and sever-al enamelled jewel boxes (some I still have), but with my own gas blowpipe and tools at home, it helped me enormously in making metal parts of the model ships and other models I was engaged on at that time.

I learned a great deal and do not regret one moment of the time spent. Just for the record, the School of Art was at that time on the very top floor of Southend Technical School, and was later removed to the rear of that building and housed in a long single-storey corrugated iron building fronting on Dowsett Avenue. Apart from the headmaster, Mr. Commibere, I also remember three other staff, Mr. Taylor, Mr. Thomas and Mr. Horton, and liked them all. Regrettably, both buildings have now been demol-ished, and in their place a car park and open space occupies their site at the top of Southend High Street.

But that memorable year was not over before the most longed for and welcome event of all took place. In early November 'the war ended in victory' and for the world in general a new era had begun. Here in England a 'land fit for heroes' was planned by the politicians who guided our destinies. But apart from the blackout being lifted and the peace of mind brought by the knowledge that there would be no more killing or air raids, and things must of necessity improve, it changed things very little for us or those around.

I continued to work at the Southend Engineering Company throughout that autumn and the long winter following my father's death, and I suppose I should say, being so close to him in life, that it broke my heart and I was never the same afterwards. But in all honesty, after the first few weeks of his not being among us, we settled down to accept it. Such was the now-strong personality of Mother, that she took over the responsibilities of both parents, and life continued much as before. The Hadleigh house was sold to pay death duties and this was sufficient to pay off the mortgages on Dad's other two small properties adjoining in Cranleigh Drive.

There was also a small terrace house in Park Street, Southend, now converted into a little picture-framing shop, that had been left to Dad by his grandfather. The very elderly widow and her son, who lived and worked in it, were always in debt for the rent, and it cost Mother more in repairs than she ever received from it, but she hadn't the heart nor will to turn them out, so it remained a liability, but the rents from the other two helped considerably, and as I have previously said, our needs were small.

With no state help or welfare in those days, she had to sell the 'A. J. Soper', and Dad's beloved 'Minnie' to 'Bob' Deal, who used it for many years afterwards, taking trippers for short rides from the beach adjoining Bell Wharf – not a particularly happy ending for Dad's beloved 'White Elephant'. We kept the Tub Boat and two rowing skiffs, which at that time Mother couldn't sell. My two sisters were sent to 'King Edward's School', which was really a high-class orphanage and considered quite difficult to get into without influence. Uncle Will supplied the influence, but it was a day's journey to visit them and they were desperately unhappy there, so after three or four months Mother took matters into her own hands, defied Uncle's ideas, and paid £20 6s. for their release, which was a severe setback financially. Then, out of the blue, came a letter from Uncle Tom in Africa enclosing a sum of money (Mother never told me how much), and things once again looked brighter and in her capable hands family life continued.

I worked five and a half days a week at the S. E. Co., and four nights a week in the metal-working class. Most of my time was fully occupied and little happened other than two small incidents at work, and building a canoe, which remain in my memory of that winter – and the bitter cold, which led to the first incident.

The War was still on, if I remember correctly. We had no heating at all in the 'works'. It was open, cold, draughty, with concrete floors and was full of cold metal machinery. In the depths of winter it was almost impossible to keep warm, so I made a 'winter warmer' – a large cocoa tin with small holes punched with a nail in each end. This was filled with oily rag or cotton waste, lit and the lid put back on. A string tied round the middle of the cannister allowed it to be swung round fast in a circle occasionally to keep the contents smouldering. It was not too hot to be held in the hand and it really provided a comforting warmth.

It was most successful and, when it came to dinner time – and I usually went home, although it was an awful rush in an hour – I was loath to put it out, but it required draught to keep going, so I had a bright idea. There was, right in the peak of the gable in the front of this building, a small round opening window. I was able to climb up on the heavy 'goods entrance' doors beneath and deposit my portable 'central heating unit' at the bottom of this circular opening, where a steady incoming draught would keep it going until I got back. To make sure it would keep up its temperature I covered it with an old piece of woollen sweater, a cleaning rag, and went home.

When I came back I was surprised to see quite a large crowd gathered outside. A white mist seemed to surround the building, wisps of smoke were coming out of joints in the doors and from the little circular window a steady column of fog-like white mist was curling into the atmosphere. Inside there was pandemonium. Figures were rushing around in a thick blanket of eye-smarting haze trying to locate the source of the fire. The smoke seemed everywhere, but as it was equally distributed it seemed to have no source, neither were there flames to account for or help locate it, yet it was getting worse all the time. The foreman and the others were rushing around with fire extinguishers but could find nowhere to use them, and this was the state of affairs when I arrived. I joined in the general melée. Some suggested opening the big doors to clear the smoke; others said no, it would fan the combustion into flames, while others wanted to send for the fire brigade. While this argument was going on, suddenly a horrifying thought came to me – my 'winter warmer'.

With increasing fear of the consequences and the sure knowledge I had found the culprit, I climbed, once again, up to the little window and there, a dull, red-glowing heap of smouldering wool and the end of a red hot cocoa tin, generating an overpowering quantity of smoke, lay the cause of our troubles. With a steel rule I had in my overalls pocket, I gave the whole glowing mass a push out of the window, where it fell at the feet of the onlookers outside, burst into flames and was quickly stamped out.

At first I was acclaimed as the saviour of the situation. The doors were flung open and the smoke and onlookers quickly dispersed. Then questions began to be asked. How had I found it? What led me to climb up to the little window when no one else had even thought of it or its possibilities? It was no good; I thought of denying it, of knowing nothing about it, but knew no one would believe me and I would be branded a liar, as well as foolish, so I made a clean breast of it.

Fortunately the 'guvnor', Mr. Davis, was away and I had only the foreman to deal with. He was one of the nicest of men and even at that time dying of T. B., and should never have been at work, but his skill was so badly needed in the war effort. I admired and respected him, and he in turn had a soft spot for me and, what was more, had a deep sympathy with us all in the cold, miserable conditions existing both in our work and lives, so with a formal 'ticking off' for the sake of discipline the episode ended and was soon forgotten.

The second small incident could perhaps have been more serious. The eldest and biggest boy, accepted as in charge of the rest of us, all younger boys, was a darkly handsome fellow of doubtful ancestry. He was a bully at heart, who delighted in bossing us around, but was careful to keep in with those in authority and was generally disliked by most of us. His Christian name was Rupert – I never knew his surname.

Part of my job was to wash the shell fuse fittings we were making in 'naphtha' to remove all traces of oil or grease before they were processed by a shellac lacquer to make them rustproof. I doubt many of this generation know what naphtha is, and I am not sure of its origin myself, but it was like a very refined type of paraffin or maybe a less refined petrol. It was used a great deal by market traders to light up their stalls at night, where its bright naked flame issuing from the nozzle of a container hanging from a pole blew around in the breeze and lit up their wares. Like petrol and paraffin, it was a spirit and, like them also, it dissolved both oil and grease. So it was not only a source of light but a valuable cleaning agent, and it was in this capacity that I was in a tiny alcove at the back of the works with a large bowl of naphtha on the bench in front of me, carefully washing each component and putting them aside to dry.

Suddenly and without warning I felt a heavy hand round the back of my neck, forcing my face down towards the bowl full of liquid. My reaction was to place both hands on the bench and resist with all my strength, but with ever-increasing pressure from the bigger and stronger form behind me, my head was slowly but surely being forced down, nearer and nearer to the naphtha. I resisted with all my strength, but the pressure still increased and suddenly my resistance went, it could no longer take the strain and my face and head disappeared in the bowl.

The liquid at once penetrated my eyes and I screamed in pain, only to get a mouthful of burning spirit. It penetrated up my nose and into my ears and burnt my face before I felt the hand leave my neck and release me. A very frightened Rupert stood behind me as I continued to cry out in agony. Soon I was surrounded by others and the foreman, Mr. Shaw, took matters in hand by leading me to the wash house and burying my head in a large bucket of water, twice, and telling me to try to open my eyes under water to wash them out. Eventually the worst of the pain went, leaving my eyes bloodshot and swollen, but very painful for several days after and I was told I could stay at home until they were better.

Rupert was not sacked, but told that there wouldn't be a 'next time' and he was always as nice as his nature would let him be to me afterwards. I don't think he even meant to actually push my face into the bowl, only just to frighten me, pretending he would, and I am not sure who got the greatest fright when his attempt misfired. But it taught him a lesson and stopped his bullying.

All aboard in the author's dinghy. Among the customers are some of
Lady Dorothy Moore's children

This is it – part of the 200 yards of triangular beach leased from the
London, Tilbury and Southend Railway for 39 years

Before the days of Chalkwell Station and the shore footpath, a 'cinder path'
linked Old Leigh with Joscelyne's Beach. Judging from this photo, it was busy

'Joscelyne's Beach' says this postcard. The author is standing in a row-boat.
Almost hidden among the trees are the long-vanished Bungalow Tea-Rooms

It's time for a breather, as a train chugs past what
would later be Chalkwell station

1962. Locals still know it as 'Joscelyne's Beach', even though it was taken away
fourteen years earlier. The caption reads 'The Beach, Westcliff-on-Sea'

The Birds and Bees

1918, I think, was also the year I built a canoe and learnt the facts of life.

Some years previously two young men, one a tall, dark youth, the other, in contrast, small, blond and fair-skinned, arrived on the Beach struggling with a very large canoe between them. I think, other than pictures of Indian canoes, it was the first real one I had seen. About sixteen or seventeen feet long, it was made of canvas stretched over a beautifully moulded wooden framework. From the bow it was half-decked to about amidships, making a small but useful cabin with sufficient room for them both to sleep in, or store their equipment and food from the elements. In my eyes it was perfection and the envy and ambition to have or make one like it was born that very moment I saw it.

They asked Dad, could he look after and store it on the Beach for them? A spot was chosen at the back of the tents, a price agreed for weekly storage, and there for most of that summer it filled me with envy and longing. Every Saturday they would arrive with their sleeping bags and a large cardboard and wooden box filled with 'lovely grub', cakes, tinned fruit of all descriptions and other luxuries, apart from the usual foods and drink. They would paddle off into the unknown, or more possibly the creeks and inlets of Canvey and the marshlands of Benfleet and Pitsea, arriving on the last of the tide or as late as possible on the Sunday.

That they were extremely fond of each other there was little doubt. That they enjoyed every minute of their weekend, there was even less doubt. They called me 'young un' and I was their willing slave, particularly when rewarded from their box of luxuries. It was a fine summer and they rarely missed a weekend. September came and they departed as they came and I never saw them again. But the desire to build and own a similar canoe remained with me. It was some four years after that, circumstances, in the shape of an old shop blind of heavy canvas given to me, decided that it was now the time to put my ambition into practice and build the canoe of my dreams.

So, late that summer, with my friend Harry Bolton, I made my way to Taylor's timber yard in Leigh Hall Road. Old Mr. Taylor served us and I still call to mind how I started to select the long, thin strips of timber, free of knots and holes. He watched me as I carefully inspected each length and laid it aside until I had the requisite number. I then proceeded to do the same with the timber I needed for the keel, ribs and stem and stern-posts etc., all as knot-free and clean of damage as possible. All this took quite a time, but at last I had it all assembled, ready to carry away. Mr. Taylor stood there, saying nothing, and booking it down on a piece of paper.

Harry and I collected it; I stood ready to pay and start for home, when Mr. Taylor looked up from his writing and said, 'Now you can put it all back again. When you go to a greengrocer's shop, you don't pick out the best apples or oranges and leave the rubbish for someone else.' As there was no choice we had to take what we were given, and I got the message.

Every weekend found me at work on its construction. It was as near as I remembered the same, but smaller, about eleven or twelve feet long and with about three-feet beam (far too little, I found out later). I suppose for a youngster with little or no experience it was a reasonable job and did resemble to some extent the model it was based on, but the proportions were all wrong, as I found out later. However, I was quite proud of it when it was at last finished, a week before Christmas, after the greatest difficulties in getting boiled oil and paint to make the canvas watertight, owing to the war.

I just couldn't wait to try it out, so on the following Saturday (the day before Christmas) Harry Bolton and I, with two other boys, started off, carrying it in turn down the then unmade Elmsleigh Drive to the brook, up the field past Hill's Farm to Hill's Pond, a very large, deep pond, some hundred and fifty yards across, originally a sandpit, which now lies somewhere under the concrete of Woodleigh Avenue or nearby. It was a boys' paradise, filled with sticklebacks and frog spawn, and both a bathing and watering place for the gipsies and their horses camped in Bell House Lane nearby, and many were the hours I spent around it. It was a wet, cold and miserable day as we struggled through the mud, pools and cart tracks that led past the farm, but our exertions kept us warm, and full of enthusiasm we eventually arrived. It was agreed that we should all have turns in it, me first.

The sides of the canoe were too high for me to sit on the floor to paddle it (my first mistake), so I had taken a large wooden box to sit on to give me the necessary height. It slid into the water and floated like a cork. I took my seat on the box and eager hands gave it a push, and with complete confidence I leaned to one side, dipping my paddle into the water to make a spectacular and fast getaway. I immediately capsized and found myself in the pond and the canoe half-full of water. It was only a short distance from the bank and shallow, so I dragged it back and we emptied it. Not an auspicious start.

I realized that seated on the box it was top-heavy and needed ballast, so we filled the box with earth and stones, replaced it, and tried again, this time seated on the floor. It worked – only just – but with care and some difficulty in paddling we all in turn had trips around the pond. However, it was evident it still needed more ballast to be a success, and it was then I found what I thought was the perfect answer.

Several times in the middle of the pond I had noticed, just floating above the surface, the top of a large lump of waterlogged timber, so paddling over to it, I was able to edge it gently to the bank. It weighed little or nothing in the water. It turned out to be an old railway sleeper, saturated from months of immersion, greasy and slimy. It was difficult to lift but the ideal ballast we needed, so substituting the box of stones with this new form of ballast, we tried again. This time it really worked and we all had turns getting up quite good speeds and having a marvellous time.

Not content with paddling, I had also brought with me a long pole, and I found, when it was my turn, that I got even better results by putting the pole on the pond bottom and pushing along, like punting, than with a paddle. This worked fine in the shallows near the bank and I was not watching where I was going and was putting all my strength on the pole. Suddenly there was no bottom, the canoe leaned over, the slimy lump of timber slid to the side, and once again I was in the water. With the heavy great lump of timber in it, the canoe was slowly sinking as it filled with water. I swam to the bank and watched it go down, but not quite. A quantity of air trapped under the fore-deck kept its bows just above water in the centre of the pond.

Soaking wet and shivering, I stood and watched, hoping the slight breeze would ease it towards the bank. My companions threw bits of stick at it but it didn't help, and then informed me they were going home. It hurt, especially as they had just as many turns as I had, and I told them so, with little effect, such being the frailties of boys, and they promptly put their threat into practice and ran off.

Sitting disconsolately, wet to the skin, with the early winter evening closing in, alone and on the verge of tears, I sat there on the bank, gazing at the little bit of my canoe just showing above water in the middle of this huge pond.

For some while, getting colder all the time, I waited, hoping against hope that by some miracle it would float within reach. I even offered up a silent prayer, hoping that, being the day before Christmas, it might help, but no gentle breeze stirred the waters in answer.

But maybe I am misjudging – perhaps it was heard. Somehow I found myself thinking, 'God helps them that help themselves,' and I realized if I wanted my canoe back there was only one way – swim out to it and drag it back. After all, I could get no wetter or colder, so throwing off my jacket I waded, then swam to it and started to retrieve it. It was quite an effort to drag and push the nearly sunken canoe to the bank, float the waterlogged sleeper out and tip it sideways, to empty the water, as I eased it up the bank and finally emptied it. But at least I had got it back.

But I was little or no better off. It still had to be got home, a mile or more. I valued it too much to leave it in the hopes of getting help next day, so once again I sat in saturated clothes, miserable, tired, very cold, hungry and alone, and a more lonely place on an approaching Christmas Eve would have been difficult to even conceive.

I had not seen a soul since my companions had left me and I was, added to all my other woes, getting frightened. What was going to happen if and when I did get home? It was already two or three hours since I should have been home to dinner. Mother would be either worried to death or angry, probably both. There seemed no joy was ever going to come from the hopes and efforts lavished on the canoe I had waited for, worked on and dreamed of for so long, and somehow at that age disappointment or happiness

156

are both so much sharper than when one is older and has learned to cope. I sat down and cried; I'd had enough.

And there I continued to sit, desperate to go home, frightened at what might happen if I left it, frightened if I didn't, and the cold was making me sleepy. Certainly I was quite unaware of the approach or presence of anybody, until a slight noise behind me brought my senses back to reality with a jerk.

Standing some six feet away was a dirty, dark-skinned, black-haired lad with a red handkerchief knotted round his neck. He was a bit bigger and perhaps a little older than me and my first reaction was one of fear. He was a gipsy, one of those outside the pale of decent folk, one to be mistrusted and feared. In fact, other than to buy blackberries or clothes pegs from their womenfolk (no men ever sold these things), to be avoided like the plague, such was the feeling among the Leigh folk of those days and I had grown up with it. But I wasn't going to show him I was frightened, although in truth I was terrified.

He stood there, chewing on a piece of grass stem. We eyed each other warily, neither saying a word. He chewed and spat on the ground. I sat on the canoe and watched him. It was a drama in slow motion and still we said nothing. Obviously it couldn't go on indefinitely but it seemed an age.

Then he, shuffled forwards. I wouldn't give ground; I still sat there looking him in the face. He reached the canoe, looked inside it, shuffled round it curiously, kicked it, removed the piece of grass from his mouth, spat in front of me, kicked the canoe again and with a look of disdain, finally spoke. 'I'd sooner 'ave an 'orse.'

Having never had the necessity of choosing between the merits of canoes and horses, I was placed at a disadvantage and didn't know quite how to reply, so I said, 'Well, you can't go on a pond with a horse.'

He replied, 'Ho yus you can,' which seemed to exhaust the subject, both thinking we had made our point.

Another silence ensued. He chewed and spat and fidgeted. I sat firm, then he burst out, 'What's yer name?'

I said, 'Bill.' It wasn't, but I had no intention of telling him my real name.

'Mine's Zach. Mum says it's Zachariah, but they all calls me Zach. I can write it too, just the three letters. Can you write?'

157

I said, 'Yes.'

'And read?'

I said, 'Yes.' He looked at me with a new interest and perhaps a little respect and I was beginning, if not to actually like him, at least to think he wasn't so bad after all, and was rapidly losing my fear of him. In fact once the barriers were broken I was almost glad of his company. He next asked where I lived and I told him:

'By "The Elms".' He volunteered that he lived in 'Bell 'us Lane' not far away, and had just tethered his father's horse in the next field, which accounted for his presence now.

It was now getting dark and, having reached a reasonable state of understanding between us, I was bold enough to offer him a shilling to help me home with the cause of my troubles – namely the canoe – and he accepted without hesitation. A shilling (or a 'bob', as it was in those days) was a lot of money when it was possible to buy a quarter of broken chocolate for twopence, but it was well worth it to me, so we hoisted it onto our shoulders and started for home.

I have hesitated to go on with my story. It would be so easy and proper to round it off by adding 'and eventually arrived home'. That way it would have eased my conscience of anything others might find offensive in the unpleasant words that follow, if I continue, but by so doing I make this episode incomplete. So with some reluctance I will resume, with apologies to those of my time and age who have not come to terms with this permissive society, or find Mrs. Mary Whitehouse out of date.

Three times that day I had been completely immersed in the icy waters of Hill's Pond and three times soaked to the skin. Now we had the journey home with a canoe that seemed to weigh at least twice as much as when we brought it. We staggered through the cart ruts, pools of dirty water, cow manure and slime that seems part of a farm in the winter and took the track that passed the farmhouse to arrive at the top of Elmsleigh Drive field. Neither of us had spoken. We had been too occupied sliding through the muck, which had now reached well over my knees, and keeping our balance in these difficult conditions, but it was easier going now on the grass.

Suddenly my companion spoke. ''Ave yer ever screwed a gal?' I was completely mystified. I had never even heard the word. My knowledge of it was entirely confined to the carpentry class at school and I think he recognised immediately that when I replied – 'I don't know what you mean' – that I was entirely ignorant of such matters. Of course, I no longer believed babies were found under gooseberry bushes; that story had long been discounted along with Father Christmas. I had heard vague talk, hints that I didn't understand and had a fear that it was both wrong and improper to want to know. It didn't bother me anyhow, and such was the secrecy and silence surrounding all matters of sex that it ranked almost with blasphemy and heresy. It is almost unbelievable in this day and age to imagine the aura of darkness that enveloped it and many twice my age, including males, went into marriage with little or no real knowledge of the subject, at least in homes like ours, and others like us.

Realizing he had knowledge of a subject of which he could see I was entirely ignorant boosted his ego and gave him the confidence that comes with superiority. Here was the chance to show this boy who could read and write he wasn't entirely lacking in knowledge either, and in fact knew more than I did.

I could almost feel the note of one-upmanship as he launched into an explicit and detailed account of this pastime or hobby – I wasn't sure which – and I listened, mystified, horrified, curious, but mostly with a feeling of guilt, either because it was sinful to listen to it or because perhaps I should not have been so ignorant for my age.

As we struggled, changing shoulders, taking frequent rests, past the 'hollow oak' down to Prittle Brook, he continued to elaborate and enlarge on its merits with an inner satisfaction of one who really knew his subject, bringing light to those who lived in darkness – meaning me – although he didn't put it in such nice words but in crude and direct language that shocked and sickened me. Once started, though, it filled the rest of the journey home. I gathered also, his sister shared in these delights with him; he even magnanimously offered to arrange a meeting, for a small remuneration, with this same sister to give me a practical introduction into the delights I could enjoy with her, a thought that if she was as unkempt as her brother filled me with horror. But I must honestly admit it took some of the strain off our struggle and the time passed quicker until we got home. It was now quite dark and the shadows of the street lamps hid the dirt and mud of my home-coming from the neighbours.

We carried our burden up the side path and crept past the light-ed kitchen window. Instinct told me I was 'for it' but I wanted to delay it as long as possible. I whispered to my companion to remain quiet by the back door and went to get the promised shilling that was in my cupboard upstairs in my bedroom.

Unfortunately I had to go through the kitchen first, where Mum and the family were all sitting. As I opened the door, Mother took one look at me – and so she might. My clothes, still wet and covered in mud almost to my waist, with the smell of a farmyard still clinging to me, were just too much.

Jumping up she screamed, 'Don't you come in here in that state, take your filthy clothes off outside,' and with that propelled me to the back door where the gipsy boy was still waiting. She took one look at him (he looked even worse than me), and waited for no explanation. 'Get out of here you dirty boy or I'll fetch a police-man' – a dire threat at that time to any romany. Such was her feroc-ity, he took to his heels and ran in spite of my protestations that I owed him a shilling.

She wouldn't listen. 'Don't you dare bring these dirty boys home with you again,' she said, as though it was a regular habit. Off came my clothes; she never stopped for breath. My dinner was spoilt, she'd been worried to death that something had happened, my clothes were ruined, and most of all I should have known bet-ter at my age, etc. etc., I should surely die of pneumonia – were some of the things I remember and a lot I didn't. I was rushed to bed with an old stone ginger earthenware bottle filled with hot water, while the big iron saucepans we used to cook the Christmas puddings were brought off the scullery shelf and filled with water. The old 'Kitchener' was stoked up till it glowed red hot on top and later, with the room like an oven, I had a hot bath and was sent back to bed.

I had done everything to catch pneumonia but next day – Christmas Day – I showed no ill-effects from my adventures, which was more than I deserved. I think the relief that it was so, helped by the fact it was Christmas, prevented me getting punished as I should have been. I was genuinely sorry that I hadn't been able to pay the promised shilling to the gipsy boy and I never visited him again, in case I met him without it. Not only had he helped me when I was in trouble, but taught me 'the facts of life' in no uncertain manner. I wonder just how many others have learned about 'the birds and bees' soaking wet through, covered in mud and carrying a heavy burden down Elmsleigh Drive on Christmas Eve? Not the best way to learn, but guaranteed to remain in one's memory for life.

And what of the canoe? I lost all interest. I had experienced nothing but trouble from it. I almost wished I'd given it to the gipsy boy until I remembered his remarks on the merits of horses and his marked preference for the same, so it was dumped upside down at the end of the garden with the threat that, should it happen again, it would go on the copper fire, which consumed all our inflammable rubbish. And there it stayed until the summer and my interest awakened in it again.

Mother's old pram was now in honourable retirement in one of the chicken houses, now all empty. Corn was too scarce and expensive and the beach took all her time, so she had stopped keeping chickens. I 'borrowed' the axle and two large wheels from it and made a trolley, loaded the canoe on it and wheeled it down to the Essex Yacht Club's boat, 'The Gipsy'. I filled up two large bags of sand for ballast and paddled it to our beach, where it was installed in the place its illustrious predecessor once occupied and served as a lasting reminder of what it should have looked like. With the sandbags as ballast, it was reasonably safe from capsizing and my friends and I had quite good fun with it, but it was never satisfactory and I had no affection for it. That autumn I brought it home, took off all the fore-deck, cut it down six inches all round, forced out the sides to make more beam and it finished up more like the orthodox Indian canoe. This turned out the next year to be very successful, but in no way resembled my first love, the lovely craft that I so envied and tried to copy, and when a customer on the beach offered me £3 for it, for his children to play with, I accepted it with no regrets.

After the first shock of Dad's sudden death, Mother picked up the threads and started to guide our future with the same strength of character she had previously shown. Nothing much altered in our way of life, other than a visit from an unknown nephew of Aunty Blanche's (Uncle Will's widow in Africa).

161

His visit only lasted a week, after we received a letter completely 'out of the blue' from this relative, stating he was in a transit camp in England, part of the African Expeditionary Force, now awaiting demobilisation and shipment back to Africa. Could he visit us for a week? Mother, delighted to have contact with one of her own family, if only by marriage, wrote immediately and invited him to stay. We were all quite excited at this rare event and waited impatiently for his arrival.

He was in his early twenties, tall, lean, swarthy, with a pencil moustache and black hair plastered down – it looked like it was painted on his head. His beautiful khaki uniform – knee breeches, leather encased shiny buskins finished in equally shiny brown leather shoes, and topped off with a large-brimmed, Mounties'-type hat – made him a sight to behold, and he beguiled us with tales of his war adventures in Afrikaaner accents.

He ate us out of house and home and all our rations, stopped in bed until late in the morning, sat in front of the 'Kitchener' – Mother's only source of cooking – piling on our precious coal with impunity until dinner time, and stayed out long after we had gone to bed. He spoke quite proudly of his conquests with a bunch of land girls (W. L. A.) in Southend, casually mentioning he had given his allotment of civilian rationing tickets, specially issued for such visits, to them, and one night took me to the Southend Hippodrome for a treat. It was, I think, my first visit other than to a pantomime.

We then went to a restaurant just opposite and had an enormous supper of sausages and mash. Later we called at a public house and he brought me out a half pint of beer, something I had never had before in my life. When we got home eventually I wasn't feeling too well. I was up all night, sick and running downstairs to the toilet in turns and in great pain, and stayed in bed all next day.

Mother was getting more angry every day. How she kept her temper with him I don't know, and his departure couldn't come quickly enough for her. Whether he realized it is questionable, and when he did go, he said he'd had a wonderful time, which I think added even more to Mother's feelings. Never once did he offer to take Mother out (and he was so handsome, I know she would have loved it) or even bring her a bunch of flowers to show his gratitude, and it was Aunty Blanche, some months later, who thanked her for having him. It was a pity his manners didn't match his attractive appearance. I suppose it takes all sorts to make a world.

The Christmas that shortly followed his visit was a miserable one. Not only had my canoe been a 'dead loss', it brought home to us all the tragedy of Dad's death and that he had gone from us forever. He loved Christmas and when he was no longer there the whole spirit of the festive season went with him. Mother did her best, but there was rationing and almost everything connected with Christmas was either unobtainable or too expensive, so Mother and I went to Southend a few evenings before the holiday, searching the shops to buy a chicken. We came home with a goose from Garons, where they were auctioning them off, and we had waited two hours for the auction to start. It still had its head and all its feathers on, and we must have been a queer sight as we trudged home at eleven o'clock that night and got off the tram at Leigh Church, its body slung over my shoulder and held by its long neck, and its head and beak swinging back and forth. However, once again it only added to our misfortunes, because when it was cooked for Christmas dinner, it had melted to half its size in grease and was so tough it wasn't worth eating.

But that wasn't the end of our troubles. Early in the New Year a severe frost – as I mentioned previously – turned all our stored potatoes black and rotten, chiefly my own fault as I had never covered them properly. Mother was also finding that Dad's contribution – from fishing and odd decorating and other jobs, supplying firewood and much else – to our income was far more noticeable than we had given credit for. There was no welfare state or outside help, other than for orphans, and the organisations were mostly voluntary (the Salvation Army and Dr. Barnado's being chief among them). So we could turn, if need be, only to relatives; those being nearly all on Dad's side (apart from Uncle Tom in Africa). Mother's new-found independence and pride almost made it impossible to ask them. So she made do and cut out every luxury, and even comfort, for us to survive with reasonable dignity in our small community, never once showing how difficult it was to make 'both ends meet'. My contribution of five shillings per week I earned at work didn't help a lot either, and my sisters Lily and

Rosie were sent for a time to King Edward's School for Girls, better class, but still an orphanage.

As we struggled on through that winter and spring the most important decision of this new chapter in our lives, the renewal of our yearly lease on the beach, was getting ever closer. In her heart Mother had already determined it, while perhaps not admitting it to others. An indication of this did not escape me when at 'Keddies' sale, in Leigh Broadway, later that spring she bought a large roll of light and dark striped material – I think it was called 'ticking', used normally for covering mattresses. About two yards wide, it was terribly heavy to get home and that is why, I think, I remember it so well.

Most of our tents had been destroyed or damaged beyond repair by the previous summer's disastrous storm, so with this material she started making new ones. She only had a small 'Harris' hand-sewing machine and ordinary cotton, and after seeing to the usual daily round, night after night she sat making new tents – I think some ten in all. I bought the eyelets and the tool to fix them from the sailmaker, and rough poles from the timber yard to complete them. So really there was no real decision needed and, if the truth was known, it had been made just after Dad had passed away, to Uncle Harry, as I indicated earlier.

At the end of April 1919 I handed in my notice to the Southend Engineering Co. and picked up the strands of life again on the beach, but this time to help support a family that had previously supported me, with all the responsibilities that went with it.

The first of these was to get a licence as a waterman to hire out the two rowing boots and tub boat we still owned, so I was dressed up in my best clothes and, with Mother, duly presented to Captain Herbert, the pier-master and grand presenter of licences. I fear he was a little shocked when he saw how young I was, and I could see he had strong doubts as to my ability and suitability to have such a licence. They were, after all, entrusting visitors' lives to the judgement of those who possessed them, and they were not easily granted.

He asked me quite a lot of questions. Some answers, I think, satisfied him, and Mother reminded him that my father had held one for many years and explained, now that my father was dead, how necessary it was. The Captain had no knowledge of Dad's passing and was shocked to hear the news. This was, I think, the reason for him withdrawing the reservation he had of my capabilities. He granted me a 2nd class (1st class was for *being in charge* of either sailing or motor boat carrying passengers) waterman's licence to offer rowing boats for hire. He was a kind and good man and it is a pity that so many men with authority lose that understanding and sympathy shown by him. I remember him with gratitude and would like to record his kindness.

As the season approached and the lease was altered and renewed in Mother's name without objection from the Railway Co., I started painting up the shed and our boats. I was surprised and pleased at the encouragement I got from many of Dad's old friends and associates, and how much advice I received from them, mostly helpful. I believe I benefited from it and it pleased them anyway.

The war behind us, a general lightening of the gloom around us and a fine summer all helped to make it a good and prosperous year. Mother and I both worked hard. She was there early and late and our tents were all full, mostly for short periods, so we had an ever-changing mixture of customers. Both of us seemed to develop an uncanny instinct, with a few careful questions, for sorting out the least troublesome ones, to keep the general harmony together. We made mistakes, but as it was usually for short periods only, they were suffered for that time, with reservations for the future.

My greatest problem was Mother's home-made tents. Not only were they highly inflammable, but so flimsy that it meant taking them all down every night and putting them up every morning, some fourteen or more, in case of bad weather or accident destroying them. As it was, Mother was constantly sewing and patching them to keep them usable.

Many of the customers, being anxious to benefit fully from their short holiday, would be there both early and late, so it meant starting very early in the morning and staying very late at night to do this job, as we now had no night watchman. (Mr. Tye had bought one of our rowing boots and worked on his own account.) Our own rowing boats were also in constant demand, so I had little or no time to myself that year. But it was a highly successful year and a great help to the family exchequer, and in fact proved a turning point in our fortunes. From then on we knew we could not only survive but manage our lives and the beach, in spite of the tragedy that had hit us.

The following winter, some of our old customers and a few others who had acquired boats, knowing I should be around, brought them up for storage, so my daily walk to the beach became both a necessity and habit which I never lost even in the depths of winter. But as far as I remember I did little else, except for art school in the evenings, that left any lasting impression. The following year I painted our house, 'did up' the boats, and the summer and winter were much of a repeat of the previous ones. Mother had made a few more tents, this time of bleached calico, which was a little stronger but still required the same treatment as the others. That was also a good year for us and we finished the summer with confidence and success. Mother was now completely dedicated to it and I was quite happy to be an integral part of that dedication. We had survived and were on our way to a brighter future.

The war had been over three or four years. Both Mother's and my side of the business were noticeably overcoming the disastrous war years. The world, while not returning to life as it had been prior to 1914, was nevertheless, with the brilliantly fine summer of 1921, beginning to feel a new era of hope and change, and in a small way we benefited also. Surplus war material of heavy canvas, both for boat covers and tents, became available quite cheaply, and our tents were now being made professionally by Leigh's leading and only sailmaker 'Francy Tunnige' (Francis Turnidge). They could withstand all but the heaviest gales and become permanent fixtures, releasing me from a great deal of work, although I still planed and pointed the bottom of the rough 2 x 2 inch timber that made the four corner poles. The change taking place in the world outside Chalkwell was also affecting our little world, the Beach.

The local residents and those who owned boats moored in and around the vicinity began to take over the tents for the whole summer, unlike previously, when they were let much like board residence to customers on holiday for a week, fortnight or month to coincide with their stay locally. Many of these were regular customers previously and we did our best to fit in the ones we liked or who were the least trouble, fixing extra tents for them, particularly when the neap tides came round and the beach extended that much further.

For many years we held a few spare tents for these customers or perhaps, more accurately, friends, as they had become over the years, and I must say it was much more interesting and exciting when we had a constantly changing population. Not the least of this were the attractive daughters of many of them, which I was the right age to appreciate and my mother to worry about. It was surprising how often it became difficult for Mum to fit these visitors in the following year.

But the 'take over' by the locals suited Mother. It cut down the difficult problem of 'fitting in' the correspondence and overlapping of dates, and preparation of accounts, a department she kept entirely to herself. It was an advantage in every respect. The certainty of a tent being let for the whole summer, namely from the first of June to the end of September, was assured, with – in most cases – the rent in advance, benefited her greatly, compared with the previous system and she realized and encouraged it.

Strangely enough, the tents were far less occupied except, perhaps, for school holidays. Even then, as quite a number did, the locals went elsewhere for their holidays or other diversions, and the tents remained empty far more than occupied. This in turn gave Mother a greater freedom from the care and responsibility which she automatically assumed and there was no doubt; the comfort and wellbeing of her 'people' was her overriding concern, and the Beach – at least for the summer months – her 'kingdom'.

With the responsibility of raising her family since Dad's death, she had fulfilled her earlier promise of confidence and strength of character beyond all expectation. She ruled the Beach and its customers with a kindly but regal hand, and as time went on and the demand grew, picked 'her people' with an uncanny knack. Those who harmoniously fitted into the scheme of things, those whose children and visitors behaved themselves, those who lived in accord with their neighbours and acted properly, but more particularly those with young families, who left the beach early, as she rarely went home until her customers had left and the tents were closed up.

167

She made her own rules:– no more than six to occupy a tent and, should they want visitors, her permission was required. This would perhaps seem autocratic, but her reason was that no one had the right to encroach on their neighbours' adjoining strip of sand. If things were quiet and the tent on one or the other side was unlikely to be used, then she would allow even more, particularly the children's parties on birthdays. No bottles or litter and no dogs. Deep holes dug by children had to be filled in before leaving. There were other rules, but unimportant ones. Strangely enough, her customers accepted without question her despotism, with a little fear but much affection, and the children, for all her firmness with them, were very fond of her. But more, she was respected.

Eventually the same families came back year after year, and any vacancy that did occur was quickly filled from the recommendation of the others. The whole system ran smoothly and surprisingly little discord or disagreement arose, except possibly with the children, and usually this could be overcome by moving the families as far apart as possible. I don't ever remember any serious quarrels or upsets between parents. Whether people were more tolerant and neighbourly than nowadays, or the stress of living was not so difficult, I cannot say, but I somehow doubt whether it would be possible that the same situation could happen in this present day. Certainly, recent society would not now tolerate a private beach kept solely for the benefit of a few privileged people and their families in such a manner. Even then, the rumblings of discontent began to undermine the pleasure and happiness I had in being part of such a pleasant community.

I worked quite hard, both for myself in the spring and for Mother during the summer months, letting out the rowing boats, fixing tents and doing the hundred and one jobs, such as fixing deck-chairs, mending, repairing and maintenance generally, but life was still one long holiday. I was young, healthy and fit, and it was a joy to be alive. I doubt I ever really appreciated how lucky I was. Apart from the ever-watchful eyes of my mother, I was almost as free as my father had been in his youth. I was not tied to office hours or trains and I looked forward to every day that dawned.

I suppose it is natural to remember the sunshine, the happy days that filled my summers and made my life so different and the envy of my friends. The changing mixture of the people I met, mostly well-behaved and very ordinary folk, and the occasional odd characters I have included later, all helped these happy memories and tend to make me forget that like most things it had another side. While we seemed to have such fine summers all the time, when I search my conscience there were gales that lashed and tore our tents and sunk and destroyed many small craft, but more particularly filled our corner with huge piles of seaweed. These, after a few days, if left, became smelly and the haunt of thousands of sand flies and other small creatures. No sooner had I cleared one lot than another arrived.

Immediately the tide started to ebb, I would start throwing the seaweed back with a fork into the sea. It would often take two hours of back-breaking work to remove most of it, and in a bad summer it became a regular chore. But with unemployment, that was leading up to the General Strike, quite a number of my friends were unemployed and available during the day. A chosen few who weren't afraid of hard work were accepted by Mother as necessary help and provided with tea and sandwiches for their labours.

The tents suffered too, even those of strong canvas ripped and tore their fastenings or were blown over, and I had to get busy with sailmaker's awl, needle and twine, repairing and patching ready for the customers next day. Our boats were vulnerable too, and sometimes ours and many others were sunk on their moorings and I spent hours baling and emptying them. But while this was always upsetting to Mother, it never had much effect or spoiled things for me, and my only reason for recording it was to show that my life was not an entirely lazy carefree existence.

On calm days I filled my old dinghy with the children on the beach; as many as could cram in it. Foolish, perhaps, looking back, but we were never far from the shore. When the tide was out we formed parties, both adults and children, and walked across the mud and the hard sands to the Ray, a deep-water channel some mile or so from the beach. This was a very popular pastime in those times, and I well remember on very fine days it would seem that the whole population of Westcliff and Chalkwell beaches had transported itself onto its banks, swimming and generally enjoying themselves on its sandy approaches.

Sand-castle competitions for the children, cricket, and even the raking up of seaweed became fun and I question if any had a happier or more enjoyable youth. To the boat owners moored around, I was regarded as a friend, rather than one who looked after their boats, and I was in some cases free to use them during the week. So while not owning a sailing boat myself, I had the choice and use of one any weekday, and in return I looked after them and baled them out and protected them from wandering children, a satisfactory arrangement for both sides and one which added even more to my enjoyable and carefree existence.

But slowly this happy state began to be eroded. Rightly or wrongly the old system of privilege and class was being gradually but increasingly whittled away and replaced by another, either more fair or unfair system, according to one's inherited beliefs. People, the working classes in particular, no longer accepted the old standards and began to demand equal rights with those who previously claimed privilege, and this began to show even in our little secluded world in this corner of Chalkwell.

My father, although a working man, came from a family who had always been their own masters and self-employed, and also had property in their own right. He had very strong views on where he stood in the social structure and class. He was a deep-dyed Conservative: his outlook was simple – if you owned something it was yours, and if you rented something it was also yours while you paid the rent and kept the contract. If a farmer owned a field he had every right to stop people trespassing, and Dad was fully convinced he had this same right with his beach.

Unfortunately, it was not protected by a thick hedge, or fence and a gate, and there were obscure laws connected with where the boundaries lay in accordance with the state of high tide, etc. In this particular case we did have a clearly defined limit in the shape of something like a granite tombstone, buried for about half its length in the mud and bearing an inscription – 'BOUNDARY MARK L. T. S. R.' (London, Tilbury and Southend Railway).

A tall, thick wooden pole surmounted with a crossbar immediately in front of this dangerous hazard, sticking up some two or three feet out of the sand or mud, served as a warning to mariners and others. These, spaced about two hundred yards apart from Chalkwell to Bell Wharf, clearly defined the Railway Company's ownership and also included the whole of the then Joscelyne's Beach. To Dad's mind he had complete authority to do as he wished with it, and that above all else meant he maintained the right to choose who came on it, or alternatively to ban anyone having no business to be there.

Owing to its originally isolated position, this was easy. Few if any holiday visitors ever wished to use this tiny triangle of sand and pebbles. It was a trap for seaweed, flotsam and jetsam, and most of the rubbish that floated from Leigh. Dangerous rocks lay all around, a menace to boats and bathers, and in contrast, immediately adjoining were the Chalkwell beaches with space and clean sands open to all. So with the large notice erected by the L. T. S. Railway Company informing all and sundry it was their property, and the big white lettering on 'the shed' that 'A. JOSCELYNE WAS GRANTEE OF THIS FORESHORE', in the beginning Dad had little or no difficulty in maintaining the private nature of his investment.

As time went on, and the business grew, visitors and residents in increasing numbers began to find their way to Chalkwell. It became more difficult to prevent families settling on the beach, particularly as we had cleaned and cleared it considerably, and to our surprise it was increasing in size. It seemed not only had it been a trap for rubbish, but extra sand – possibly from the efforts of the sand barges that were more and more frequently removing the sand for brickmaking in ninety-ton loads from the 'Ray' sands – was finding its way to our little corner. These conditions now made it a desirable little spot and it attracted those who wished to be apart from their fellow humans, and although many locals knew it was private, it made the most tempting haven for those that did not.

It also made it very difficult. As in those earlier days, our living depended on letting the tents to bathers and boats for hire. Consequently we were in a great degree dependent on those very people that didn't know, and if we turned them off we lost potential customers. Many, after hiring a tent to bathe or a boat, quite rightly assumed they had every reason for staying afterwards and often arguments ensued.

To some extent the problem resolved itself. On busy days Dad shut his eyes to them, much against his inclination, as it meant a lot ganging up together and refusing to go. At quiet times he mostly let them stay but shooed them up the further end, or they went without question. But some refused and this led to many rows as Dad, although quite small in stature, never minced his words or was frightened of anybody. I vividly remember him 'telling off' the famous boxer 'Bombadier' Wells, who at that time was in training at 'The Elms' in Leigh, for attempting to jump two upturned dinghies and landing on one of them. Fortunately for Dad, 'The Bombadier' was a gentleman and instead of hitting my father, apologised. Dad never, as far as I remember, came to actual blows with these unwanted squatters, but I was always frightened and upset and every time feared the worst.

During the war years fewer and fewer people came on holiday. The Westcliff beaches were less crowded, so the problem eased for a while, but with Dad's death and the war ended, it arose again and, this time, to my increasing dismay, came onto my shoulders.

Mother was equally as convinced of the rightness of our claim, if not more so, as Dad, and having taken over completely, altered our previous arrangements of providing service and bathing facilities for the holiday crowd and casual visitors. As I have previously mentioned, she started letting the tents for short or long periods to those living or staying locally, but mostly to those on holiday, as local residents could, for a small seasonal fee, pitch their own tents anywhere on the Chalkwell beaches.

For a while we used to store some of these tents in a little place built in and under Chalkwell bridge for a small sum per month. The fact that the tents were now occupied most of the day made it more than ever important to keep the fronts clear of unwanted strangers. As we were now using the further end as well, this also had to be kept free of them, and I was constantly back and forth during the busy months moving them off.

I would approach quite politely and point out that the beach was Railway property, and private, and that they were trespassing because it was not public foreshore. For the most part they would leave amicably and sometimes even apologise, but occasionally there were those who became quite abusive, some threatening bodily harm and others just stubbornly refusing to move.

Unfortunately my youth didn't command the respect or authority of an older man. These I would tell: 'I give you a half hour to get off. If in that time you are still here, I will call the police and have you charged for trespass'. It rarely – if ever – failed. No one on holiday wanted that holiday spoilt and it was easier to go than be involved with the police, but quite often they would stop the full half-hour to make their protest.

But the fundamental problem remained, until I found a way that helped very considerably – a simple answer and one I cannot understand I hadn't thought of before. I put up another large board on the sea wall at the further end of the beach stressing the fact that this foreshore was the private property of the London, Tilbury and Southend Railway and let for business purposes, not publicly owned, and trespassers could be prosecuted. How much of this would have stood up in law I don't know; suffice to say both Mother and I believed it. In between my board and the Railway board I put two more, marked 'PRIVATE BEACH. NO TRESPASSERS'. It had a very marked effect and my journeys back and forth were greatly reduced but never completely ended.

As time went on, a growing attitude of defiance to authority and the old values began to become more and more noticeable. Private property was no longer respected as of old. The war had altered many of the younger generation's outlook, and a demand for greater equality was slowly but very surely taking the place of the old concept. It showed itself increasingly in the difficulty I had in keeping the beach clear and I found the only way I could do this was to pounce on the interlopers almost before they settled and move them on. It was fatal to let a family or even a single person get established, as in less than no time several other families were in occupation and they would all gang up together and refuse to move.

Sometimes I would have to call the police, but they had no heart in it, and could do little about it unless I was constantly prepared to press charges and go to Court. It became a never-ending nightmare that hung constantly over me during the summer months, slowly killing all the joy and pleasure I had always associated with the holiday season on the beach. I began to wish the days away until I could return to the quiet peace of the autumn and spring with my regular customers, their boats and companionship, free of the constant unpleasantness and upsets occasioned through the necessity of keeping the beach entirely for our clients' use.

To make matters worse, I was aware of a growing feeling in me that beaches shouldn't be private, a treacherous and traitorous thought that wouldn't go away and added even more difficulty to my very necessary job. I had to do it, as Mother's business depended now entirely on the private nature of it, and our customers would no longer have the benefits of the seclusion, peace and quiet they were paying for and considered their right.

Whenever possible I shouldered this burden – for such it had become – for Mother. Her approach was simple and direct. She, unlike me, had no doubts as to the rightness of her claim and strangers were plainly and bluntly told to 'Get off'. It worked effectively with most, but occasionally led to almost violent reactions. Only the fact she was a woman, or that police action would follow, saved her, but the worst part was the upset and disturbance she caused herself, which sometimes made her quite ill. But 'her beach' and 'her people' always came first in her 'kingdom', so I came to accept it and did all I could to avoid her having to do this miserable job by doing it myself.

Of course, few of the legitimate customers saw or bothered about these upsets; it was part of the service and taken for granted that their way of life on Joscelyne's Beach had to continue, and they were paying for the privilege. The other beaches were free and most times had plenty of room, so they also felt they were right, and maybe at that period were quite justified in so thinking. Mother, right or wrong, was encouraged even more in the rightness of her cause and nothing would have convinced her otherwise. I am not suggesting these upsets happened constantly, although rarely a day passed without the usual 'moving on'. I think the uncertainty of one's reception, never quite knowing what the reaction would be, or the unpleasantness that might follow, grew out of proportion to actual fact. Also, I might have been unduly sensitive and not of the aggressive nature required to handle the situation; after all I was a young boy and usually much more youthful than those I had to order off, and that might have caused resentment.

I have given rather more time to this subject than would seem either necessary or justified, but my own unwanted doubts, and the increasing difficulty of carrying out this very necessary duty, I am sure played an important part in my later decision to leave the beach, something not even contemplated at that time. Reading back, I feel now that perhaps I got this problem out of perspective. The good times still outweighed the one job I hated, but it had a greater impact on me than the many advantages, and the happy days and evenings I somehow took for granted, and certainly did not appreciate as I should have done, but now look back on with so much pleasure.

I was in and out of the water, swimming or teaching others to swim. I had plenty of companionship from the many visitors and the few elderly gentlemen privileged to a seat on our special beer crates just outside the shed door, within handing distance of a cup of tea, and this did on at least two occasions lead to proposals of marriage, but Mother would have none of it. She had a saying, 'I go to bed "Missus" and wake up "Master" and that's how it's going to stay.'

And here maybe a word on beer crates would not be amiss, as they played quite an important part in our business. Made of strong wood, they were almost indestructible and about eighteen inches square. We must have had at least forty of them. Cheap to buy, they served as seats in each tent and the water never harmed them. Two with a board made a most satisfactory bench, both for working on and sitting on in a row for children's parties. They were ideal for propping up boats in the winter, made a strong fulcrum for levering up anything very heavy, and lastly they sometimes had bottles put in them. I don't know what we would have done without them, especially the two or three very special upholstered ones kept in the shed. These had the advantage of being comfortable but not so comfortable that the occupant remained too long. It was usually understood by both Mother and the occupier that about one hour or less was the allotted time and those that stayed much longer (except in unusual circumstances) weren't offered one next time but left standing. So the humble and nondescript beer crate came into its own on our beach.

But to return. The long and mostly warm summer evenings were the best of all times. I had collected a number of friends around me, in the main youths of my own age. They were generally members of the Leigh Sailing Club, owning or sharing sailing dinghies, and they usually worked in London. When most of the customers had gone home around seven, Mother didn't mind them coming on the beach and a circle of crates soon formed, cigarettes were lit and, had I smoked – which I did not and never have – I doubt I should ever have found it necessary to buy a packet. With cigarettes so cheap it was customary to hand them round to all and sundry without question.

I don't remember now what we talked about particularly – life in general, boats mostly, I suspect – but the conversation never bored. One among them was Alan Shiers, a gifted musician who could play the violin and mandolin beautifully and also get a tune out of anything that was playable. Around this time ukeleles and banjuleles were all the rage, and the popular sheet music of the day had the finger positions in dots marking the chord changes, making it quite easy to accompany the voice or a melody instrument. In the late summer evenings little groups formed among the tents on the Westcliff beaches and the strumming of these versatile instruments was part of the late night scene, after the 'Minstrels' – who performed nightly from a hut just over the breakwater from our beach – had finished.

It wasn't long before the craze spread among us. We, myself included, bought a 'uke' and under the skilled tuition of Alan soon learned to accompany all the popular tunes of the day. The half-dozen of us that took it seriously formed a group in much the same way as the youngsters of today (except for the gyrations). We added our contribution until quite late into the night, and as we had no night watchman then, it was an advantage.

The music, of course, attracted many teenagers of both sexes to the 'white bar', three white-painted rails on posts that separated the end of the Westcliff promenade from our beach and acted both as barrier and boundary. Several of the more attractive girls found their way onto our side of the 'bar' and joined our group, while the others remained on the prom side.

Our problem was that until Mum was safely on her way home, we on our side had to behave as though we didn't know them. It was one of Mother's characteristics that while she seemed to allow my sisters every opportunity to meet my boy friends, girls were a menace and danger, to be avoided at all costs, and while I am prepared to admit she might have done it for our own good, it built up an unpleasant barrier of deceit. Lack of communication with her led both my brothers and me to feel we could never really confide in and talk to her. I realize now that this discipline and fear, and the fear of the consequences that it instilled in us, was definitely for our own benefit, as in those days the code of morality was very different and the penalties for breaking it very high. But it didn't stop us from enjoying the girls' companionship. The group grew and prospered and gave us all a lot of fun and enjoyment, but one by one various members paired off or left and were not replaced, and with the end of each season it gradually faded out.

With the coming of the autumn, dancing became all the craze and at least every Saturday I and several of my friends attended the Leigh Sailing Club dances at the very popular 'Parochial Hall' (now St. Clement's Hall), Rectory Grove, and many happy times were spent there. I had started to learn an Hawaiian guitar and practised a couple of hours after tea, much to the rest of the family's annoyance, but I tried very hard to learn. Later I was banished to 'the shed' and on cold winter nights my fingers were so cold I couldn't play it, but continued to persevere with it for at least three years and I began to feel quite pleased with my efforts.

One winter's day I was practising when a fellow I had a slight acquaintance with, but didn't know particularly well, attracted by the sound came to the shed door and listened to my efforts. 'I like that,' he said. We got chatting and the upshot was I loaned him a spare guitar I had and a 'tutor' on how to play it. He mentioned he had never played a musical instrument but the sound pleased him. He thanked me and went his way, leaving me to wonder whether I had been foolish to loan the guitar and book.

However, six weeks or so later, he turned up, but no guitar. He apologised for not bringing it. I asked how he was getting on with it. 'Quite good, I think,' he replied. 'I can play "The Hilo March" and "On the Beach of Waikiki" and several others in your book.' These were quite difficult pieces and ones I had struggled with for months. A little doubtful of his claims, I arranged a meeting at home and shortly after he turned up, both with my old instrument and a remarkably unusual guitar, the like of which I had never seen, that he had bought.

We sat down and started. The music flowed from his hands in such a way that even my special guitar records seemed like the work of amateurs. I listened entranced, but almost in unbelief, then with a growing feeling of dissatisfaction and dismay. I realized that however much I tried it was a complete waste of time if he could do in six weeks what I was still struggling with after three years. It was foolish of me to continue and from then on I lost all interest in it, apart from occasionally picking it up, and I finally packed it away for good.

The summer months from June until the end of September were Mother's. I gave my time and labour almost entirely to her and the beach free. I had no wages; my only source of income was the ferrying services I provided for boat owners in the vicinity, for the small fee of threepence each. It was necessary to keep my old dinghy almost always in readiness and it was surprising how many seemed to want to go aboard, right in the middle of dinner or tea. But it was all part of the service. I would also pick up extra by sinking moorings and fixing running mooring ropes, bait digging etc., but the main income from tents, deck-chairs, boat hiring and the winter storage of boats was Mother's, for the family's keep. She in turn worked and looked after me and paid the rent and other expenses for the whole year, not an easy or enviable job and certainly not at that time appreciated by us as it should have been, and she only ever bought bare necessities for herself.

From the end of September the boats were packed away, the tents taken home and sorted out for the repairs they nearly always wanted. The deep open hem at the bottom we filled with sand. The fastenings were always in need of repair, so later they were sent down to the sailmaker and repaired at his leisure during the winter. But once this was done, until the following May, the beach was mine and Mother seldom visited it except to bring me meals when I was very busy. There was no understood partnership; it just developed that way. After Dad died and she took over, it was naturally expected that, as the eldest son, I took his place and my efforts benefited us all, like Mother's, to keep the family. These were concentrated on the summer months and the few boats I stored and looked after for the winter.

Now I had increased the storage of these craft to the beach's full capacity, and every weekend from October and November they were fully occupied by a crowd of boat owners, mostly all Leigh Sailing Club members, a large section of whom, including the 'Commodore', used the beach almost as a second headquarters. They all helped each other to have their yachts up, and secure them for the winter ready for work on them in the spring, and I supplied the gear, rollers, planks and tackle for this work.

This also helped Mother's income, but apart from an occasional 'tip', I still had very little pocket money for myself. I dug bait; sometimes I would dig for five hours. This would fill a gallon bucket and, shared out in lots, fetch about fifteen shillings, but fishing seemed out of fashion and sailing the more popular sport. I don't think that if I had had the initiative or the money to buy and use a boat like the previous 'A. J. Soper', it would have been in demand. In any case, I expect that the proceeds would have gone into the family exchequer. I did a bit of fishing but usually the catch was only enough for the family and aunts and uncles. I looked around for a source of personal income, to be a little independent, but other than getting a job elsewhere – and I had no skills or training – this was unlikely and, in any case, I felt it my duty to visit the beach every day to look after the boats stored there, particularly during the very high tides or when heavy gales were around. Not only during the day, but many a night in the depths of winter, I would go back and wait until I was sure no damage would come to my flock, the owners themselves blissfully asleep and unaware of any danger to their craft. I never told them and I doubt they ever knew, but it make no difference to my lack of income.

Then a customer gave me an old dinghy. It had come ashore on the sea wall and was badly holed and damaged, he thought beyond repair. But it was a challenge to me and after a great deal of work, and revealing more skill than I thought I possessed, I repaired, painted and varnished it until it was almost as good as new. It took most of the winter but I sold it without difficulty for a good price the following spring. This opened my eyes to the possibilities of buying and repairing boats and it became a profitable source of income. When a few years later a very nice 20 ft. motor cabin boat came ashore one night and smashed a large hole in her side the owner offered it to me for a very low price, he was so 'fed up'. I patched the hole with a large sheet of waterproof canvas and floated and towed it to our beach. I spent the whole winter

179

working on it, and by the following Easter I had a boat to be proud of. I kept it for many years. I called it 'Daydream', for I had long wanted a boat of my own and this was everything I desired. I even sold it once and bought it back again, I was so happy with it.

Another small source of income I developed was making model sailing boats for Christmas presents. A customer, seeing me making a small model for a gift, asked if I would make a nice model sailing boat for his son's Christmas present, about 2 ft. long. I agreed and by the following week it was finished. He was delighted with it and the price, £1 – in fact so pleased he took it to his yacht club to show other members, and this resulted in a flood of orders for them, some twenty or more. I was able to speed up as it took no longer for paint to dry on one or many. I cut the sails and Mother machined them and I had them ready in time for Christmas. The demand died out after the holiday but a few weeks ago (in 1981) my brother met a man who recalled his father buying him one and it was still in his possession waiting for his grandson. But the following Christmas this income was lost when German manufacturers produced a pressed fibre hull with standardised and stamped-out sails and gear, a model yacht of similar size at about half the price of my hand-made individual models.

However, I did get an order to make a model liner, complete except for deck fittings, winches etc., from a Mr. Morris, whose son was resident engineer to a shipping firm in West Africa. He had a great deal of spare time and wished to make and fit all the more detailed and intricate metal fittings on his lathe to complete it. I was given detailed plans and taken to London twice (the first time in my life) and shown wonderful models of ships and liners. I was extremely doubtful that my efforts would in any way reach his requirements but agreed to try.

I surprised myself, probably more than Mr. Morris, with the results. In about three months I produced a model that lived up to his expectations and beyond mine. I got so involved in it that when it came to parting with it I was heartbroken. It was carefully packed in a box I made, addressed to Lagos, West Africa, and despatched to London. I charged £4 10s. for making it, a ridiculously cheap price for the work involved, but Mr. Morris was a regular occupant of a beer crate by the shed door, and I had had two trips to

London at his expense, so I didn't like to charge more. When it was finally finished it must have been worth a great deal of money, especially today. I wonder whose sideboard it adorns now or where it rests in the world?

Money in this narrative seems to become out of proportion to its importance. My wants were few; I neither smoked nor drank other than tea or minerals, I had no fares to pay, no expensive clothes or hobbies, no food or lodging to pay for. Birthday and Christmas presents supplied the simpler things and, other than presents in return, which I mostly made myself, I had no serious need for a lot of money.

In fact I could even save with no sacrifice involved. But while we had never known real poverty, with Dad's early death the necessity of being careful was deeply impressed on us all. Saving became a part of my life and I practised it in spite of it not being really necessary at that time. But as time showed, later it was the foundation of my future life.

It gave me the drive for fresh efforts and each year as the spring came round I started decorating and repairing more and more of the boats in my charge on the beach. I did a good job at a cheap price; my overheads were nil, and many of my customers found it far easier and quicker to give me the job instead of struggling at weekends and holidays themselves. As time went on, I found it meant almost every hour of daylight to cope, and Mother, God bless her, walked from home every day with a hot dinner or something to eat, so I wasted no time going back and forth, and for three months or so my life was one hectic rush.

When the weather was fine, every minute was precious; I couldn't do enough. But some days, being open to the elements, the rain spoilt all my paint, other times the wind whipped up the sand and stuck to it and often it tore off the covers I had so carefully laid over my work. The trains belched black smuts, sometimes all over my carefully painted decks, dogs cocked their leg and small boys never took my word that it was wet paint – they had to try it for themselves, and it wasn't only small boys either.

Some springs were marvellous. I remember on my twenty-first birthday, 20th March 1924, some customers insisted it should be a day to remember, hired a hall and band, and it eventually ended in a gathering of both Mother's and my old established 'beach people'. We had a wonderful time but, more particularly, I recall how I begrudged leaving the job I was doing early, because the weather was as fine and warm as a midsummer day and every minute of this counted.

Life on the beach had now settled down to an ordered routine. Both Mother and I had more or less reached the full capacity of its possibilities. There was no room for more tents and I could undertake no more under the prevailing conditions. Even if it had been possible, the ever-growing shadow of the promenade extension to Leigh hung over us. It had been always in the background even before the 1914-18 War: Southend Council, on taking over from the Leigh Urban District Council, had made this a promise. The war, of course, made this impossible, but now once again the project was resurrected and various grandiose schemes were mooted, such as enclosing large areas of sandbanks, installing turbines in the retaining walls to generate large quantities of electricity by the action of the tides, and forming a huge, tideless lake. Sums of several millions were tossed around by its advocates, the Council paid out thousands of pounds of ratepayers' money to consultant engineering firms, the *Southend Standard* devoted whole pages to plans and correspondence, and for a while it seemed it would become reality.

But the crunch was, who footed the bill? With the depression of the 1930s, heralded by the General Strike, it remained a dream but never quite forgotten, and we lived in fear the whole time we occupied the Beach that the former promise would be kept. Under these conditions neither Dad, Mother or I ever felt really secure and all we did was only temporary.

So things continued, apart from minor happenings, for the next few years, and these while it was in my period of occupancy. One day in the autumn I was amazed to find the tide was at high-water mark one and a half hours before it was due. As I watched it continued to rise – soon it was over the beach, it got deeper and deeper and eventually the shed was under water to the depth of two or three feet. The cinder path and promenade disappeared and all the boats stored for the winter floated off their chocks and finished up in an untidy mess on top of each other in the highest corner. Fortunately it was calm, otherwise it would have been even more of a disaster than it already was, but even so, all my tools were under salt water and everything in the shed, including many tents that I had not taken home and much else, was saturated. Many of the larger yachts, now at all angles, would require impossible efforts to put them back into their ordered places and the situation looked hopeless when the tide receded, so much so I just left it, got on my bike and rode along the promenade to Southend to see how others had fared.

I shall always remember my first sight of the sunken garden at the shore end of the pier, now a pleasure ground, but at that time a beautifully kept garden. It was full to the brim, and all that was above the lake of water was the red roof of a building; the tops of half a dozen fir trees, like small Christmas trees, were sticking out of the water. The tide created havoc in Old Leigh and the boat-yards, but on the following Saturday and Sunday a crowd of members from the Leigh Sailing Club turned up and we hauled, levered, pulled and lifted the boats into some semblance of order for the rest of the winter. But it took weeks to dry the contents of the shed and clean the salt and rust from my tools.

Another occasion, while it had no disastrous effect like the high tide, but was sufficiently interesting to remember, was around early February 1927. The previous evening there had been a bitterly cold east wind, and a most brilliantly clear sky as I walked home foretold a severe frost, but next morning I was amazed to find the whole of the foreshore and right out to the 'Ray' banks looking like an arctic waste of snow and ice. The last of the ebb tide had frozen over to the depth of a foot or more, a sight I had never previously seen, and for several days afterwards large chunks of ice floated around and many wild-fowl came almost to the beach for food.

In complete contrast was one Christmas Day in those years. As was my normal practice, every day by force of habit I walked to the beach and this day was no exception. It was bright, warm, and the sun shone from a cloudless blue sky, and sparkled on the incoming tide as it crept up the beach, a day that by the vagaries of the elements had been plucked out of summer. The promenade and cinder path became alive with visitors. I expect the many Westcliff hotels and boarding houses were filled for the holiday and to my surprise a party of young people called over the white bar, 'Can we hire a boat?'

183

'Yes, if you help me launch it,' I replied. Off came the tarpaulin covers and willing hands lifted one of our rowing boats and carried it to the water. A small crowd gathered to watch, the idea seemed to catch on, and the other three were let also and, on their return, hired again by others. I arrived home at 3.30 for my Christmas dinner to be greeted with sharp words from Mother, but when I placed twenty-five shillings in her hand and said, 'That will pay for some of next week's dinners,' she cried, a very, very rare occurrence.

Mother never seemed to get ill and I very seldom. The only occasion I can remember when I missed my regular daily visit to the beach was when I poisoned my foot, and it stopped me going for a week or more.

About two hundred yards wide and extending a quarter of a mile or so directly off the beach was a slight depression in the otherwise flat sandy seashore. It contained black, smelly mud and was by some action of the tides filled with empty clam shells, razor sharp and laying thickly at all angles, some sticking up like vicious teeth to hurt and cut any unwary, bare-footed human. It was a formidable barrier to the hard clean sands that lay beyond, in particular the magnet of the 'Ray', so it was best negotiated with sea boots or paddlers to cross it, or better still go round it.

For some reason, one day I didn't heed these precautions and cut my foot badly on one of the shells. That night my foot and leg began to swell and I was in agony. The pain grew with the size of my foot and leg and I was unable to get out of bed. Mother left me food and drink, as it was in the middle of her season. A large swelling about the size of an egg took the place of the cut. It seemed soft and the pain was still great, so I got a large needle from my brother and pierced it to relieve the pressure. It burst, smothering the sheets with blood and matter, but easing the pain, and after soaking in very hot water it started to heal. I cannot understand now why we didn't call a doctor and I think I was lucky to have recovered so quickly as I did afterwards.

I expect many others could have suffered too, as it must have been a deadly trap caused by the pollution and germs lying in this filthy tract of mud and shells as a direct result of the ever-increasing number of house boats that were filling the foreshore and marshes from the cockle sheds onwards. Untreated sewerage from this source floated down on the tide. The weird and wonderful collection of yachts, ancient barges and derelict craft of all descriptions that had long ceased to be seaworthy was matched only by the variety of their occupants from all walks of life. Living was in the main primitive – no tap water except that carried from the cockle sheds, and no heat or light usually, other than paraffin or candles. All rubbish went overboard. In bad gales and high tides they got little rest, but perhaps the summers compensated. In most cases I think it was necessity rather than a gipsy existence that made them live there. They were a thorn in the Council's flesh and as far as I am aware paid no rates or mooring fees. After much litigation the Council finally evicted them, a pity in some ways as they added interest and colour to Old Leigh, particularly as many cultivated little gardens on the bank or grew flowers in containers on their decks, and even now some of these flowers bloom in patches in an alien environment of wild flowers along the bank.

The stories of many of these house-boat dwellers would make interesting reading and would, I am sure, make a wonderful book. I was too far away to know much of them but I did meet and know three of the inhabitants of this colony.

Charlie Stamp was a familiar sight in his cap and blue jersey and could have been easily mistaken for a fisherman, but his background I think was far different. A cheerful, carefree bachelor of middle age, he lived on his little boat. He did no work and spent most of the winters wild-fowling for pleasure and the summers pottering around. He was a most enjoyable and interesting man to talk to on almost any subject, until the fateful day when a large yacht moored next to him.

The owner's niece, who was secretary to a famous author of boys' books, often visited her uncle and these visits now became even more frequent. Charlie fell for her charms, invited her to tea and became a married man. He gave up his boat and built a wooden house – it looked mostly of driftwood – just inside the sea wall on Canvey Point. It was a sinister black, tarred shanty against the evening sky and perhaps reflected his feelings. It was all wrong from the very start for both of them. The solitude and loneliness of Canvey must have been torture for her and he never accepted the loss of his freedom or the responsibility of matrimony, so there was little happiness in their lives.

It might have been my own father's story told all over again. But I remember him more for a strange claim he made one day when I invited him aboard my boat in Oyster Creek, near his house on Canvey. He was delighted to see me. We discussed old times and got quite intimate and he started to tell me of strange visions and dreams of buried treasure which he was trying to locate near some mounds of imaginary red earth. It is now a fact these red earth hills have been found and are the workings of ancient salt manufacturing (but as yet no treasure). But more extraordinary still was his claim that a Viking warrior had met and conversed in sign language with him near Canvey Point.

Later, I understand, Mr. Wentworth Day, the well-known Essex author and authority on spirit phenomena, investigated his story and agreed that there was more to it than could be accounted for by strong drink, as Charlie was teetotal and far too practical and sensible to suffer hallucinations. Certainly his sincerity and belief seemed very convincing to me. Maybe there is more in heaven and earth than is dreamed of in our philosophy.

Another inhabitant living on a discarded and dilapidated wreck that scarcely warranted the name of house-boat was a middle-aged woman and her son of about twelve. They were reputed to be White Russians (as opposed to the Reds) and part of the flotsam of the Russian Revolution of 1917-18. This was only hearsay, as far as I know, but a number did come to England. How they got here I never knew. I doubt whether they were legally allowed in England. Whether she was mentally afflicted or could not speak a word of English I also don't know. She walked around always in an old black dress with the same black, broad-brimmed hat pulled around her ears, with a scarf under her chin, her reddish purple face just visible. It had all the appearance of severe heart trouble, but she walked for miles round Leigh and I never saw her speak to a soul. Had she done so I am sure many people would have helped her. When the house boats finally went, she or the authorities found an old wooden shack at Daws Heath, which eventually got lost in a thicket of brambles and trees, but she still walked into Leigh every day and was a familiar traveller along the London Road, sometimes with a handful of herbs or flowers to sell, a typical picture-book Russian peasant to the last. I would have loved to know her true story and what happened to her son, who I think left her on her own a little later. An unsatisfactory story with no beginning or end, hardly worth recording other than it was part of the house-boat era and the cruel tricks of fate.

Towards the marshes end of the colony, moored tight to the bank, was a wooden shed-like structure built on a flat pontoon, proclaiming to the world at large on a big board 'DAUNTLESS BOAT STORES, PROPRIETOR W. CLAYTON'. He was not in actual fact a house-boat dweller, he lived in Westcliff, but as he spent most of the hours of daylight there I always considered him as belonging.

I never knew him previously, but from odd bits of information I gathered he had been employed in a bank or some such profession. One day on Westcliff jetty he met three local boys, all keen on boats but without them. He had no knowledge of sailing or the sea but was persuaded by them to buy an old yacht, 'The Dauntless', on the understanding that they took him sailing. This worked satisfactorily, although I believe on one occasion they all came near to drowning, getting lost in a fog while walking ashore and overtaken by the incoming tide. What happened between this period and his appearance among the house boats I have no knowledge, but he appeared to be among those who had opted out, like a number of others, from city life for the freedom of the seashore and had bought this 'mixed marriage' of shed and boat to start a business.

Whether the purchase of some four hundred ex-Government army surplus oil lamps persuaded him to start, or was only his first stock, I can't say. They were not the usual hurricane lamp with the round globe, but a much more attractive, four-sided glass and galvanized type, and today would fetch quite large sums as collector's items. As it was, they sold like hot cakes to house-boat dwellers, yachtsmen and fishermen and he could have sold many more. It opened his eyes to the possibilities and he was soon selling ropes, paint, chain, paraffin and the hundred and one other things connected with houses and boats.

Other than the sailmaker, he had no competition and I transferred most of my business to him. We got on extremely well; he was an educated man and interesting to talk to. Unfortunately his appearance was spoilt by his eyes. One was almost permanently shut and the other didn't seem to locate itself properly, which gave him a somewhat sinister look and was a severe handicap. But once acquainted with him, his charm overruled all else and we became very friendly. When occasionally he was a visitor to the Beach he was accorded the privilege of a beer crate and tea by Mother until, as his business had expanded far beyond his present capacity, he suggested he should buy a barge and moor it at the further end of our beach and transfer his store there.

Of course, this was impossible under the terms of our contract with the Railway Company and against all Mother's ideas of keeping the beach private. She also feared he might approach the Railway Company direct to carry out his plan, which frightened her even more, so he was no longer made welcome. In any case, it was quite impracticable without great expense, as mooring such a craft in such unsheltered waters would have put him in constant trouble. I was able to make him see reason in this and he decided to rent an area of foreshore adjoining or near where Johnson & Jago's boatyard is now, and erected a large boathouse on posts above high-tide level.

He continued to stock all boat gear, but now with the help of his early shipmates and a skilled young boatbuilder, turned his attention to building straight-sided, flat-bottomed dinghies, a remarkable innovation unknown in Leigh and almost a sacrilege. They looked home-made boxes in the locals' eyes but later, mass-produced in large numbers and sold cheaply, a large market was established and they were sent all over England by rail and even overseas. His success encouraged him to start building a small but extremely roomy 16 ft. clench-built cabin cruiser and from these a larger cruiser, the well-known 'Dauntless', emerged. Now four hundred or more float or rest around our shores and are still much sought after, perhaps not quite so remarkable in these days of moulded fibre glass but a very considerable achievement for all that.

He sold out in Leigh and moved to even larger premises by the bridge at Benfleet. I lost track of him but understand that, having later disposed of his interests, he moved to Wales and died in an accident on a slipway in another boatyard he had an interest in. I have no real knowledge of the true facts. He was the 'Henry Ford' of the 'flattie' and made 'Dauntless' a well-known and respected name among the yachting fraternity.

I have often wondered if his success came by chance or by a clever business instinct – probably a bit of both. Even his idea for a boat store on the beach (other than from a barge) was basically sound.

Our Beach in the winter was now filled to capacity with boats and the Chalkwell beach just over the breakwater was also quite full, with the added advantage it was free. The nearest other store was 'King's', a boatbuilder on the promenade below where the Pavilion now stands, and they kept a minimum, mostly for their own needs, so paint, chain, rope and anti-fouling were in growing demand. I toyed with the idea of supplementing my income and starting such a store but it would have meant building another larger shed or increasing the original. It was against the terms of our agreement and the threat of the continuation of the 'prom' to anything permanent, and Mother's immediate dismissal of any such idea, finally made me realize it wasn't to be.

But an opportunity presented itself in the shape of a Mr. Psaila (I think his parents were South American), a self-employed photographer who carried on business from the first floor of a stable behind the butchers on the corner of Leigh Road and Lansdowne Avenue. He collected and printed films on a twenty-four hour service from quite a number of the local chemists' shops. Each evening he collected and the next day in the afternoon returned them. It was a difficult and tiring job, collecting during the day and developing films late into the night, with none of the modern methods of today available, and his premises looked like a photographic laundry of drying films. He approached me, suggesting I also collected films on a twenty per cent basis. Mother, while not particularly enthusiastic, agreed, so I erected a large canvas sign 'FILMS DEVELOPED. 24 HOUR SERVICE' on top of the shed. A little later a chemist friend offered me films on commission and sale-or-return terms, so I was in business.

It worked fairly well but had its snags. The chief difficulty was the impatience of the customers. Films were handed in late in the evening; they would be there early next morning worrying to collect them and come back several times before they finally arrived.

Then there was the fitting of films. With so many makes of camera and so many sizes of films, I found great difficulty at first. Mother would have nothing to do with it, so it meant being more than ever tied to the beach, even when the tide was out. My income from this source averaged £2 or less a week for the summer. I carried on for about three years but I think new methods put Mr. Psaila out of business, so I discontinued it, with almost a feeling of relief.

The Path of True Love Never ...

Among the regulars on the Beach were a delightful and quaint old couple, Mr. and Mrs. Curtis. He was enormously fat, particularly around his tummy, balding with sparse grey hair and a huge walrus moustache and quite short. He was the exact opposite to his spouse: she was tall, thin as a lath, with not an ounce of fat on her. They made a complete comic postcard couple when in bathing costume on the seashore, and to make it even more authentic, his bathing costume was a genuine antique, with the horizontal stripes so loved by those who produced these comic cards, and hers was of much the same period. Many were the smiles and remarks of the other customers when they appeared for their 'dip in the briny', which they did regularly. They were a devoted and harmless old pair. She ruled him with a rod of iron but it made little or no difference to his happy temperament, and neither gave Mother the slightest trouble, which was the reason they were there as regular customers for a month each year for several summers.

But I doubt I should have even remembered them except, like so many of my memories, it was in association with other incidents. Least of all would I have guessed they could have affected my first venture into romance (such as it was). And it came about in a strange and unexpected way.

Sometimes my route to the beach in the mornings took me down Grand Drive and along Grand Parade. On this particular morning, as I passed towards the junction of Leigh Cliff Road and the Parade, where there was at that time a large plot of land extending back some hundred and fifty feet from the Parade. At its northern end was the flank wall of a very large house with a number of windows which then overlooked the sea. I glanced up and was horrified to see a very small child climbing out of a tiny window on the top floor.

Realizing he was in imminent danger of falling, I ran up Leigh Cliff Road and banged heavily on the front door. It was opened by a charming young girl. I quickly explained what I had seen; she screamed and started in a panic to rush for the stairs, but before she could reach them I grabbed her. Holding her, I explained that I would go round the side way and, should he fall, try to catch him, and she in her turn must approach him quietly and without panic and entice him to come to her.

All went well, and shortly afterwards he climbed back in and was brought downstairs by a very greatly relieved big sister, who was full of thanks and praise. That, I thought regretfully, was the end, as I could find no excuse to prolong it further (although I tried quite hard), but I did mention I was on my way to 'our beach' at Chalkwell, with some undefined hope I might see her again.

To my surprise and joy, late that same evening who should turn up but my acquaintance of the morning, complete with her parents, both of whom were full of gratitude, having heard the story, possibly enhanced but certainly not lacking in detail of my efforts of the morning. I suppose their praise helped to persuade Mother to let a tent to them and to my joy, having already decided in my own mind that a closer acquaintance with the daughter was most desirable, possibly shared by her, they became customers.

From then on things went along quite nicely. We got very friendly, talked a lot but never seemed to be able to be alone together. If it wasn't her parents; it was Mother. She always seemed to find something that urgently wanted doing whenever the situation or the other parents allowed us to get together, and all in all it seemed our chances of a close friendship were not to be.

Until one miserable, cold, windy day. The beach was empty of customers except for Mr. Curtis; the others had all packed up early and gone, even the young lady's parents. Mother was tucked up out of the wind in 'the shed' and at last we had the beach to ourselves.

She was sitting alone in their tent and I slipped in beside her. At first we sat and talked. I edged closer, she didn't move away, neither did she give me any encouragement. Bearing in mind we were both young, inexperienced and both extremely shy, this was not to be wondered at. She was a lovely, round, cuddlesome little creature and I desperately wanted to do just that, but feared to upset or frighten her. So there we just sat with the precious moments slipping rapidly by. It is laughable now, but very real and serious when one is very young as we were then. The wind was blowing hard; grey, angry clouds scudded across the sky. The rough sea was pounding on the shore filled with – and ready to pile up – great heaps of seaweed to make hard work for the morrow, but as far as I was concerned the sun was shining and everything was lovely. It only wanted my arm around her to make it perfect, but I didn't dare.

Our minds on other things, I was suddenly brought back to reality. I looked out and there, like Neptune arising out of the deep and advancing up the beach, was Mr. Curtis, totally and blissfully unaware that his ancient horizontal-striped bathing costume had finally succumbed to old age. The cotton that held the crotch and inside legs could no longer stand the strain of time and his increasing girth and had given up. It had now become an open shirt and as he left the water the last wave playfully lifted it above his waist, where it lodged on his extremely large tummy and there remained.

He picked his way carefully up the beach straight in front of us, completely naked from the waist down, and in the words of a well-known T.V. comedian, 'not a pretty sight'! I was horrified and just stared in stupefied wonder, unable even to think. As he passed about a yard from us and continued to his tent my companion, with a stifled 'ooh no', flung her arms around me and buried her head in my shoulder, thereby achieving the result in a moment that I had contemplated for so long. After some while – quite a while – she murmured, 'Is he gone,' but made no attempt to see for herself, which suited me admirably.

But it was the only time; Mother and her parents saw to that. She was a nice girl but in Mother's eyes all young girls were a 'snare and delusion', to be guarded against, and I suppose in the opinion of *her* parents my prospects of being a suitable suitor for their daughter's hand were nil. As far as either of us was concerned, we never thought that far ahead, we were just interested in each other. But with opposition from both sides and the end of the summer the romance faded out and ended, but with the conviction that from then on I would do my courting in the winter when neither Mother nor Mr. Curtis was around.

I never did quite understand the reason for this antagonistic attitude Mother took towards girls – not all of them, but with an uncanny foresight towards the ones likely to become involved with me, although perhaps not really so surprising when I was within her vision for most of the day, seven days a week, for most of the summer. And to be perfectly honest, the beach was a business, and to her more than that, it was her life and therefore not a playground. She didn't mind a general contact with them, only if she thought I was getting involved too much – a very easy and frequent situation during the holiday season, combined with the fact that I was young, healthy, strong and suntanned, but mostly because of the environment being so different. The holiday atmosphere and the added attractions of romance, warm summer evenings and moonlight swimming in the quiet waters, all added up to a trap very easy to fall into, and perhaps in retrospect she was wiser to this fact than me.

Strangely enough, she never made things difficult for my sisters, in fact almost encouraged them, and the same attractions gave them equal opportunities of meeting my male friends, but they were out at work, not on the beach constantly under Mother's watchful eye. Both of my brothers were also at work and had their boats and free time and were not tied to the beach in the same way as I was.

Mother's attitude, right or wrong – (at this age I am able to concede she was right) – built up a wall of deceit between us, which I very much regretted. I would have liked to have taken her into my confidence; I felt she should be interested and encourage my various friendships, instead of being so difficult and placing so many obstacles in their way and invariably frowning on them as I grew to expect. Maybe I was too naive to realize all the complicated reasons for her, to my mind, unreasonable objections to romance. I found ways round them, in fact they encouraged it to a point, as it added spice to thwart her. But I would have much rather had her confidence, and this, it seems, was in the mind of one particular romantically inclined young lady.

It started when a local family had a tent for the whole season. They were delightful people and, occasionally at first, but with growing frequency, they were visited by this tall and extremely athletic girl. She swam like a fish, played tennis, hockey, netball and all other female sports with great skill. I grew to admire her and I often used to chat with her but no thought of romance entered into it. Her exclusive boarding school education and quite obvious expensive way of living placed a barrier between us, but other than that she just wasn't my type at that moment. That was the situation when 'her family' decided to go away for a month and asked Mother if she would mind 'Kathy', the young lady in question, using the tent during their absence, and Mother agreed.

Kathy came weekends and evenings by train from her home near Upminster regularly, had her swim, then usually a chat with Mother or me and then set off back home. This became normal routine until one evening, when I noticed her and Mother engaged in deep and serious conversation. Not wishing to interrupt I left them to it, coming back later. They were still seriously involved but, seeing me, broke off and Kathy left to catch her train. Mother looked a bit flustered. I knew something was coming but it was the last thing in the world I would have even guessed at.

'Sit down,' she said, indicating the beer crate Kathy had just vacated. Then it came straight out: her manner gave no indication of her feelings. 'How would you like to marry Kathy?'

I had never even contemplated the possibility, far less thought about it. 'I don't know. It's a load of nonsense, anyhow, to talk about it. Why should I?'

'Well, she wants to marry *you*,' said Mother, and she unfolded the reason for the deep and serious conversation I had previously witnessed.

Kathy had come straight to the fountain head. Whether she had spotted the state of affairs between Mother and me, or it had got to her ears by other means, she determined to go her own way about the matter. She approached Mother openly and completely knocked the wind out of her sails (and incidentally nearly capsized me in the process).

Kathy had not beat about the bush. She said quite straightforwardly, as one used to getting her own way, that she had grown very fond of me and would like to marry me, hinting perhaps my own lack of initiative was due to the difference between us in social standing, which she assured Mother was of no matter. She asked Mother's opinion, whether she would mind and whether she thought I would be agreeable to such an arrangement, or had spoken or hinted at any romantic interest in her. She went on to explain she had already discussed it with her father, a widower and a very wealthy man, and it seems, as he invariably gave in to all her whims, she had won him over on the recommendation of the family she visited on the beach.

Her father, a building contractor, was quite willing to employ me with the view to a partnership later, as he had no son and, she added by way of an afterthought, she would inherit most of it. In any case, not only that, her father would give her a house, one on the estate he was building, so no problems would arise in that respect and the whole thing seemed a most business-like and satisfactory arrangement.

It only remained now for Mother and I to agree and everything would be taken care of. She would leave it with us to discuss and consider and, if satisfactory, meet her father. No wonder Mother had looked serious and, for the once, we talked openly and in harmony about this amazing proposal.

When we had both got over the first shock, we discussed the situation and both agreed on one thing – the honesty and straight-forwardness of Kathy. Then we realized, that to someone who had always had their own way, it was not perhaps so surprising after all. Mother was pulled two ways; it would have been almost impossible to find a replacement on the beach for me and her business would surely suffer. On the other hand, she could offer nothing like the prospects for my future as outlined by Kathy.

But eventually, when it became my turn to have some say in the matter, I had little or no doubts. I had no intention of settling down to a normal job depending entirely on someone else. At least I was my own master most of the year, and money or future prospects played no serious part in my life at that time. But most of all, I wasn't romantically attracted to her and I was sufficiently young to think that important.

Possibly too, my pride was somewhat shaken that I hadn't been consulted first in the scheme of things. But I was equally flattered that she liked me sufficiently to declare it openly to Mother, and it pained and embarrassed me that it was my intention to refuse what in any terms was a sincere and very advantageous offer. Had I been really in love with her it might have been different; there is no accounting for what one does in that state of mind, but as it was I had no hesitation in telling Mother my views – a decided 'No'.

I could see Mother was greatly relieved. I have little doubt that was what she wanted but could find no good reason for saying so. Kathy was a fine girl and had no faults other than that she was the pampered daughter of a father who spoilt her. There was nothing Mother could reasonably find to pick on and secretly she was, I think, delighted Kathy had come to her direct and offered what appeared to be such an attractive future for me, but was equally relieved her mind had been made up for her by my reaction.

I was both too cowardly and embarrassed to face Kathy, so I made a point of finding a job away from the shed at her usual evening arrival times. Three evenings later, when she did appear, it was Mother who had to break the news of my unwillingness to enter the state of matrimony with any girl. She told her that had I contemplated such an idea, I would have been delighted to have accepted her wonderful offer and that I hoped we could still remain good friends and she would continue to come on the beach as usual.

I think that she also had had time to review her ideas and when I did arrive, after a reasonable interval, she was much the same Kathy we had previously known. The following year she visited us and introduced a tall, good-looking young man as her husband, so she didn't die a brokenhearted old spinster after all. Looking back now, it all seems so silly and unbelievable but I can't help occasionally contemplating what, where, or how my future would have ended, had I said 'Yes'.

The Beach had now little scope for expansion and, with limited facilities available to me during the spring I was, of course, dependent on the weather. In bad years it became difficult, or even impossible for me to cope with the work of fitting out and painting my customers' boats in the open, yet I could see no alternative, and my income suffered in consequence. I was beginning to learn that money plays quite an important part in one's life the older we grow. Clothes, dancing, parties, presents; all took their toll but my income depended for the most part on four months of the year and I saw no way of altering the situation without encroaching on Mother's preserves and that would have only reduced her income. True, she had every available tent now let for the season, but that again was only four months, and the younger members of the family were still dependent on her. It slowly but surely began to sow the seeds of unrest in me. They crept in so slowly, at first I was almost unaware of their presence.

Except in a very subtle way, nothing appeared changed. The tides didn't alter, most summers the sun shone and the beach continued its well-ordered life with Mother at the helm. To all outward appearances I was contented enough and still enjoyed the carefree existence that was the envy of my friends, but an element of discontent and resentment crept in, but possibly more – a greater realization that there was little or no prospect of an independent future, or of living my own life free from the ever watchful eye of Mother. She had not the slightest intention of relinquishing any of her power: the Beach, during the summer months, was her life. She had now got it – barring anything unforeseen – just as she planned, with every tent let for the season to better class families who gave little or no problems, paid mostly in advance, and usually left early. The children were fond of her, the parents brought her little presents or tasty morsels and sweets, and she reigned like a well-loved queen over her subjects. It sounds almost like a fairy story the way I tell it (but ask anyone who is still alive and a customer of those days and they will tell you it was so), and as far as I could see it was likely to continue so for many years to come (and no costumes and towels to wash either). I, of course, knew it couldn't continue for ever, but at least for the foreseeable future there would be no change.

The mere fact that the tents were now all occupied by a very proper, middle class family society excluded even the excitement of meeting old, regular, short-term customers of the odd assortment that used to occupy the tents. They, and particularly their daughters, disappeared. No longer were there the parties out to the Ray sands, or the carefree atmosphere of people on a seaside holiday and determined to make every minute count; it was now more a small, select, social club and from, both Mother's and the customers' point of view, highly desirable that way, and that's the way it continued ever after.

During the summer holidays every inch of the Westcliff and Chalkwell beaches overflowed with visitors. At least five or six sailing boats, carrying about twenty passengers each, plied for hire between our beach and the Crowstone. The 'Coronation', the 'Albatross', the 'Warrior', the 'Peggy', and 'Faith' were some I remember, and they were always full on fine days. 'Uncle Sam's Minstrels' in a large hut just over the breakwater on Chalkwell Beach was packed with large crowds until late at night, and midnight bathing became extremely popular. But all this in turn made my job of policing and keeping off intruders even more difficult.

Frequently, with the milling crowds on the Chalkwell beaches, a tiny empty stretch of clean sand at the end of our beach became a magnet for those who in increasing numbers were questioning the rights of an unequal society to anything. I was constantly chasing off intruders or involved in trouble with them, so much so I grew to hate and detest the job and the everlasting arguments that accompanied it.

Previously I had never questioned that I should spend twelve or fourteen hours a day, seven days a week, on top of my previous stint of four months of much the same hours doing up boats. But the feeling that I also should have a holiday like those around me began to unsettle me and add to my dissatisfaction, though I felt I dare not leave the Beach.

Somehow I voiced this desire when chatting to one of Mother's customers, an interesting man, who also owned a small barge yacht, recently built for him by a local firm to his own design. It had hardly been on its mooring just off our beach a week when I noticed it riding sluggishly and found it half full of water. Baling it out, for the next fortnight I watched carefully for leaks but it remained quite dry, and the incident was almost forgotten.

Then one day it again filled with water and sank. It was taken back to the boatbuilders but they could find nothing wrong and no leaks, so it was brought back and for some while remained quite watertight. Then one day I noticed it deeper in the water than it should have been and, although the sea was quite rough, I launched my dinghy and got aboard. Opening the cabin I found it half full of water, but not only that, I found the reason for it. In its building the centre-board casing was completely out of keeping with normal design and had been fitted forward of the mast for some unknown reason. Every time the bow dipped in the heavy waves, so a spurt of water shot up through the hole on the top of the casing that allowed the chain for raising and lowering it to pass through. This, of course, it did in ever-increasing amounts as the boat sank lower in the water. But until it was very rough, it had shown no indication of this fault and puzzled us all. This totally unsatisfactory state was overcome by taking out the centre-board and fitting lee-boards in its place and it gave no further trouble.

This led to a considerable understanding between the owner and me, and eventually in conversation I came up with my wish to get away from the beach for a few days. He suggested he could help; it appeared he either owned or was director of a small shipping line trading between London and Antwerp. To my surprise he offered me a trip on one of his ships and even offered to extend the invitation to any friend I wished to take.

It was too good to miss, and Mother said she could manage with Vincent's help for the five days we would be away, so I asked Ernie Tozer, one of my special friends, to come with me. Being in the insurance line, much of Ernie's time was of his own choosing; a time and date was agreed and in due course we set off for London Docks. We found the boat, a small, dirty, steam cargo vessel and met its skipper, a Yorkshire man, Captain Earnshaw, who explained that we had been signed on as first and second stewards, but were not expected to do anything. He also said he was giving up his own cabin for us so that we should be comfortable – a very kind action on his part.

As the vessel was still loading, he suggested that we spend the rest of the time in London, and Ernie, being familiar with and born in London, took me around many of the places of interest and this was almost a holiday in itself. We got aboard about nine o'clock in the evening and awoke next morning to the thud of engines as she got underway. There was a mass of shipping all on the move and, to make matters worse, a heavy fog encompassed us. Foghorns of all nations seemed to be going full blast, chiefly because most of the ships underway were signalling their intentions by this means. The fog was so thick that the whole way down the lower Thames we never saw land, least of all our beach.

With the foghorn going steadily at intervals, we made our way into the North Sea. That night, with the steady hammering throb of engines that seemed directly beneath our cabin, I never slept a wink and was glad to get up at first light. We joined the Captain at his table with a huge breakfast but the fog never lifted until, with the sound of church bells in the distance, we arrived at Antwerp. Whether it was by accident or design, I don't know, but they were holding a 'World Fair' there. The weather was intensely hot, but we had a wonderful time during the one and a half days we stayed. It was all too short.

On the way back down the 'Schelte' there was a long strip of sand much like Canvey Point stretching into the river. We had to pass very close to it and I was intrigued to see some of the crew-men leaning on the rails passing a pair of binoculars around. On enquiry the Captain said that it was a nudist colony, and as we got closer we could see both men and women running around with no clothes on. I was more surprised to see quite a number of what seemed young men in clerical garb amongst them. The Captain explained that they were Catholics in training for priesthood and for the first part of their lives they had to learn to overcome temptation. Whether this was so, or whether they were a special sect, I don't know; I hadn't heard of it before or perhaps he got his facts wrong, but he believed it.

Once again when we reached the mouth of the river we found thick fog, once again we saw nothing of the crossing, and that night the thumping of the engines allowed no sleep, but my companion slept like a log. The fog followed us all the way up the Thames, so we saw no more than on our trip down river, until we reached London and docked, each with a bottle of scent, bought chiefly because it was duty free but also a present to Mother. I am not sure just how much I enjoyed it but it satisfied me and was my first holiday.

I had only been home a few days after my holiday, and that is the reason it calls to mind an incident that puzzles me to this day – it 'rained frogs'. A statement like this immediately conjures up in the mind a vision of large green frogs descending from the heavens upon unbelieving people on earth, but in this case in reality it was not so, and it happened this way.

The fine weather we had had and the direct cause of the sea mist that dogged our trip continued. When, after a lovely warm morning, a large black cloud appeared, I thought it heralded the end of our fine weather. It crept slowly across the sky and emptied itself suddenly in what seemed a cloudburst. Everyone rushed to find shelter and those caught along the cinder path were saturated. It was over in ten minutes but more water fell than in a day's rain. Immediately afterwards, the sun came out, hotter than ever, and everything was steaming with the warmth. It was then I saw several people stopping and looking down, and one or two children excitedly collecting something in their sand buckets. Being curious, I walked up from the shed to the cinder path and lower entrance to Chalkwell Bridge and a curious sight presented itself.

The railway grass embankment (there was no Chalkwell Station then), the cinder path and lower slope of the bridge were alive with tiny black frogs just out of the tadpole stage. There were literally thousands, or so it seemed, everywhere, but in a very short while only those that had been caught by the many children remained. Most of the others found shelter in the long wet grass safe behind the railings of the railway. A man sheltering close to the wall of the bridge was telling people he saw them falling in the downpour but few believed him, myself included. However, I cannot think of any other sensible explanation, and it seems in recent years many cases of such happenings have been authenticated, both with fish and frogs, but I've never previously heard of it in Leigh, and it is perhaps worth recording.

My holiday contented me for that season and, with the coming of autumn and winter, the old order resumed and my biggest worry, that of keeping the beach private, was removed. The boats were hauled up and packed away for the winter and I was more or less free until the following spring, although every day I would go both morning and afternoon to check that everything was safe. I had long given up my evening trips to the Southend School of Art but the knowledge, and more particularly the skill and patience, I had learned in the making of jewellery and fine art work gave me an urge to do what I seemed best at – model making. So when I was given a book containing a scale model of 'The Royal Charles', a seventeenth century 90-gun ship of the line, I started making it in the shed. It gave me not only a good reason for my daily journey, but filled the winter months and gave me considerable pleasure. It took the whole of that winter and early spring to complete the hull alone, and the whole of the following winter to complete the rigging, etc. It also led to a number of enjoyable trips with another good friend, Eric Page, to London museums to study in precise detail much of the rigging, etc. I still have the finished model.

Eric Page was the most studious and intelligent of all my friends and I envied and admired his capacity for general knowledge and learning, and mention of him brings to mind another curious happening. This time I never witnessed it, and only have the word of Mr. Arnold, the man who told me. He was a customer, a fine, bearded tall and aristocratic-looking man. Retired, he spent quite a lot of his time both on his boat and with me in the winter, chiefly to escape his wife, equally aristocratic but in my eyes far less likeable, and who never forgave her husband for the 'Farrows' Bank crash that reduced them to living in a bungalow in Nelson Road.

On one of his visits he told me that he had gone to the coal shed a few days before and was bringing in two large lumps of coal on a shovel. One of them fell and shattered on the ground, revealing a large mummified frog or rather, perhaps, a frog colourless and looking much as if it was made of dirty white rubber, apparently lifeless and withered but soft to the touch. Putting it aside in the greenhouse, he said nothing to his wife, as even in trivial matters of this sort he had learned that 'a still tongue makes a wise head'. But that very morning he had gone to the greenhouse and found that the creature was no longer where he had placed it, but a frog of normal colour and size was hopping around quite happily on the floor. The door of the greenhouse had never been opened and nobody, least of all his wife, ever went in it other than himself, and he was totally unable to explain the mystery. I suggested that perhaps he had dropped the coal on a frog, but it did in no way account for its appearance when found and it bore no signs of injury. We puzzled over it and I even had my doubts as to its truth, or possible exaggeration, yet knowing Mr. Arnold, couldn't doubt he was telling the truth.

I was so taken by this story that when Eric arrived in the evening I was full of it. He, like me, expressed his doubts as to its authenticity but said he would discuss it with his friend, the curator of the natural history museum in London, next day. I couldn't wait for the next evening to come round and was delighted to see Eric arrive at his usual time. And he had news for me. His friend the curator had said that it was more than probable it was true. It was known as 'suspended animation' and the creature could have been in that lump of coal for 35,000 years or more. There were several known cases of much the same thing. His one regret was that he had not been able to see the frog, but Mr. Arnold had let it go after finding it alive.

I still, in spite of all this, couldn't bring myself to accept it, until some months later I read of a case of two lizards found in a solid block of slate in a quarry somewhere in America. One of them survived and expert scientists claimed they also could have been many, many thousands of years old in the same state of 'suspended animation', so to some degree this was additional proof that it could have been so. But even now it takes an awful lot of believing and, as I sit here recalling it, I can't help but wonder what sort of world we might find in 35,000 years if the same thing could happen to us. Even now in America they are investigating its possibilities and it certainly gives room for thought.

A Distant 'Splash of Colour'

Sometimes the nostalgia of my boyhood leads my footsteps back through Old Leigh. I wander along the High Street but there is little left of the Leigh I knew. Gone is 'Lumpy' Cotgrove's little fish shop, gone too is Tomlin's coalyard and Juniper's shop, where it is reputed that Constable stayed when painting one of his perhaps less famous pictures, 'Hadleigh Castle'. All the little tumbledown wooden and lath and plaster cottages that housed the fishermen and others that dwelt in or around are gone. It started with the coming of the railway and was effectively continued by the twentieth century planners and sheer neglect.

When I reach the 'cockle sheds' it has a more familiar look, but that is only because the piles of empty cockle shells haven't changed; the sheds have. No longer are they the tumbledown, awry, tarred shacks of those old days, or their boats the small, odd, assorted craft whose crews scraped up the cockles with rakes to supply the holiday crowds of Southend.

I continue on the narrow strip of road still haunted by the ghosts of that motley collection of things that once floated, the house-boats, and eventually reach the boatyard and Leigh Railway Station.

But I see it as it was – no yard, no station, just the further end of a path that led only to the sea wall and the tracts of marshland it enclosed, the vast flat expanse, broken only by the two elms and black tarred barn that sheltered between them in the far distance and gave the name of 'Two Tree Island' to posterity. Snaking like a thin ribbon through this marshland, silent except for the cries of the seabirds, the seawall meanders through it on its seven-mile journey past 'General Booth's wharf' to Benfleet.

As my eyes follow that ribbon, once again I am reminded of a curious and vivid dream I had several days before my twenty-first birthday. Not the ordinary, incomprehensible, incoherent and jumbled up mixture of nonsense, with neither rhyme nor reason that comes to us with sleep. This was so different, that it will remain permanently in my mind to the end of my days. Fact and fantasy were entwined so closely in it that it was difficult to say where the one started or the other finished. But let me tell it.

In my dream I had wandered through the Old Leigh I have described and had walked the short distance along the sea wall that brought me to the sharp bend that led westwards through the green marshlands divided neatly by the dykes that drained and separated them. It was eventide and the sun low on the horizon and as I gazed into the far distance it lit up three patches of brilliant colour in succession, extending the width of the marsh. They were so far away but I determined I would get there and see for myself what caused this most beautiful picture of startling yellow, mauve and red, that called so insistently.

With one thought only in mind – I must get there – I hurried along the narrow uneven walkway on the sea wall. The way seemed long and tiring but I was winning, and as I drew nearer I realized they were fields of the most gloriously coloured flowers, much like illustrations now used for the advertisements of the bulb fields of Holland but, of course, at that time never seen or heard of in England. Getting ever closer, I found them to be the tall 'Evening Primroses' that were quite popular then but are seldom or never seen now.

I was determined, having come so far, to take a huge bunch home, so climbing the stile across the footpath that protected the flowers I clambered down the grassy slope of wall and in amongst them, only to find that those immediately within my grasp were withered and dying. A little further on they looked better, so moving on I started to pick them but then doubts entered my mind – surely those further on were even better and the colour brighter, so I moved on, throwing those I had picked away.

I was right; those yellow flowers right close to the next field of mauve were quite perfect, but did I want yellow flowers? They weren't nearly as nice as those adjoining, so I climbed over the next stile into the next field and was among the same 'Evening Primrose' but of a different hue. The same disillusionment and dissatisfaction that had happened previously occurred, although as with the others they were perfect as I neared the gorgeous red ones. But I was now equally sure that it was the red that should be my ultimate choice, so once again I crossed a stile into the next field, with exactly the same thing repeating itself.

Now I knew that the best ones would be the furthest away, so I pushed forwards and as I made my way towards the further and more perfect flowers I became increasingly aware of a terrifying fear. Some sinister presence was overtaking me; I was too frightened to look round; it was getting closer. Abandoning all thoughts of picking the flowers I had so carefully selected and come so far to get, I hurried once again over a stile into the next field, a field of tall waving corn. 'The presence' was getting ever closer and in a panic I slid down the bank. Surely if only I could reach it in time I could hide in safety within it?

But whatever it was that was striking terror in my heart – and I dared not look – was almost on me. I remember only putting both my hands forwards to part the growing corn and dive into its shelter when 'it' caught me. I awoke in shock and terror, covered in perspiration, not then even sure whether it had actually happened, it had been so real. It puzzled me considerably, as if in some way it was intended to be either a warning or message that should not be ignored. Whatever its reason, unlike most dreams it remained vividly with me and refused to be forgotten, and still does.

Some sort of answer came later in a roundabout way when the summer season started. I was having a cup of tea with Mother in the shed when this new customer arrived. She was old, very old. I doubt she was under eighty, perhaps eighty-five, small and so thin her bones had no flesh, just skin covering them. She had a hooked nose and a long chin that was part of a face like a ripe brown wrinkled walnut and she was dressed in clothes that were probably fashionable twenty years earlier and plainly bought at that time. One automatically looked for the broomstick that had brought her to our door. My thoughts obviously transferred themselves to the youngest of my brothers and sisters playing outside, and behind her back they silently mouthed 'witch' and edged away, half frightened.

But to Mother she was a customer, that was all, and when she asked for a tent for the day and the price was accepted I was detailed off to erect one of our spare 'collapsible' tents for her, and she was installed complete with beer crate in a quiet corner of the beach. She was no trouble, minded her own business, and in Mother's eyes was an ideal customer. It was the beginning of many such visits and, from the very first, in private among us, she was affectionately known as 'The Witch'. As her visits became more frequent we got to know her better. She came not by broomstick but by courtesy of the L. T. S. Railway from around the Ockendon area of Essex. I pictured her in one of the timber and corrugated iron shanties with a small overgrown garden, but later in conversation we found out she lived in a large, neglected Victorian house surrounded by grounds and was the last of a wealthy family.

She would arrive fairly early in the day and, if the tide was in, in spite of her age, undress and then dress for her bathe – because her costume covered her almost as completely as the one she took off. She couldn't swim but waded in up to her waist and bobbed up and down and enjoyed it as much as if she was swimming the Channel. If it was warm she would sunbathe, although her skin couldn't have got much browner than it was. She must have spent hours sunbathing in the privacy of her own home, but she assured us that the salt sea water did her the most good.

She was a vegetarian, a suffragette, a free thinker – whatever that was – and much else besides, but what was more, we found she could tell fortunes and cast horoscopes. No one could deny she looked every inch the part and could have made a fortune at funfairs with a crystal ball. As a special treat she would tell our future on the spot, but the horoscopes took a little longer. She would make a note of month and date of birth etc. in a little notebook and on her next visit bring a neatly written horoscope of the person concerned, but I never quite got over the feeling that she had a book of horoscopes at home and just copied them from it. Maybe I misjudged her.

She also had a wide knowledge of herbs, herb medicines and nature cures, flowers and plants, and it was this subject that brought to mind 'Evening Primroses'. She informed me that they did have very considerable medicinal value. I asked her about them – did they grow in different colours? No, only the one pale yellow. She didn't know why they were called primroses. Apart from their colour they were nothing like primroses, growing as they did on tall stalks in thick profusion. The 'evening' part was more easily explained: the petals remained closed all day, opening only in the quiet light of evening.

My interest awakened her curiosity. She, by some uncanny instinct, soon realized my interest went deeper than a passing wish for knowledge. Without realizing it, I found myself blurting out the story of my strange dream, something I had not even mentioned to Mother for fear she would think it nonsense. Having heard me out in all seriousness, the old lady said she would 'think on it' until her next visit.

Her next visit couldn't come soon enough. Finding me alone she handed me an envelope enclosing written details on 'her thoughts'. She expressed surprise that such a self-explanatory dream should have puzzled me, when it was all so obvious, and she explained it thus:

The walk along the 'Old Town' was my early life, the arrival at the sea wall was my twenty-first birth date, the ribbon of footpath my future, the brilliant patches my ambitions, the long walk and the stiles obstacles to be overcome. My disappointment with the quality of my gains and the everlasting search for something better which, eventually within my grasp, was lost at the last moment, was fear of the unknown, and at last I awakened to the reality of life.

It was an ingenious and imaginative explanation. Everything seemed to fall into place and I wondered why I had myself not thought of it. It was nothing much more nor less than a glorified version of the old adage 'The grass looking greener in the next field', or so it seemed. I was never fully convinced that the description fitted me. I have, as far as I know, never been particularly ambitious or dissatisfied with my lot, or demanded the best in life. But as I cannot think of a better one, and in any case it doesn't much matter now, I'll leave it with you to try and find another.

As the season progressed, so her visits increased to twice a week. She became part of the community. Mother liked her, and she spent quite a lot of time on the privileged 'seat crate' by the shed door. She had had an exciting and not altogether moral life in her younger days, but such was Mother's rigid puritanism that I doubt she was told it all, and certainly what she did hear was never talked of with me. It was a forbidden subject and I on my part was not particularly interested at the time, although now I would have relished every moment of her story. There always seemed a barrier between Mother's customers and mine. I got so much closer to those I counted mine, perhaps because it was men and boats rather than affairs of the heart.

The children no longer peeped round the corners of tents in a self-imposed fear of her, neither did their parents exchange the sly grins that previously followed her, as she made her way in her extraordinary outfit to bathe. She was in great demand as a sooth-sayer and a privileged few of the womenfolk became sure she knew more of their private lives than she ought, but still begged to know what the future held for them.

She was still 'the witch' in secret, if such was possible. I never did know what went on behind those sharp and twinkling eyes. One of the customers who knew about these things assured us she was a 'white witch' and could do nothing but good for those around her, a great blessing, a comfort and relief to us all. She in her turn had found a haven from the deadly loneliness of her secluded and empty home, the superstitious fear of the few coun-try folk around it which, but for that one day she hired a tent on Joscelyne's Beach, could have turned her into a soured and unhap-py hermit. Instead she had found a happiness and a haven where she fitted in and it was with great sadness for all of us that the summer finally ended and the tents were packed away. She prom-ised to return the next year but we never saw her again. But one warm evening of the following year, as I sat alone outside the shed door, I'm almost sure I saw someone or something on what looked like a broomstick pass silently overhead, but persuaded myself maybe it was just a heron going back to the marshlands of my dream.

And incidentally, for those who might be interested, I have recently read that oil of evening primrose is now of vital impor-tance in the cure of certain ailments confined to women. How far her knowledge of this extended I don't know, and in any case it was unmentionable to me, but it now seems likely that fields of evening primroses may become reality and no longer be confined to dreams.

This lovable old character was only one of the many hundreds of customers that came, stayed a little and went. Ninety-nine per cent were just ordinary folk, families on holiday, free for a little while from the humdrum lives they lived for most of the year, but more particularly they were culled and sorted by Mother to be the least trouble for either her or their neighbours adjoining. Occasionally one of two customers, like our 'witch', while still conforming to her standards, were a little different and added interest to our lives 'on the beach'.

Amongst these, one in particular holds memories for me. I have tried to place a date unsuccessfully, but it was certainly before the tents were all let for the season and probably around 1921-22. It was a damp, windy and miserable afternoon, and both Mother and I were tucked up in the shed, the door half shut to keep out the wind, and clutching mugs of tea to keep us warm. The last thing we expected was a customer, when suddenly a resounding knock on the door made us jump to attention. A little, elderly lady, all in black, umbrella in one hand which she had used with such effect, and a large black bag in the other, stood outside. By her side stood a thin, pale, sandy-haired boy with a strangely pointed face and an even longer thin nose supporting large, thick, pebble glasses that hid his eyes and half his freckled countenance. He hung tightly onto the arm that held the bag and kept slightly behind her, as though he was frightened of us, or perhaps the outside world in general.

She wasted no time. In cultured tones and in a manner that showed she was accustomed to having her own way, she demanded – rather than asked – did we have a tent to let to avoid this atrocious weather? and said it almost as if she blamed us for it.

As we had several empty tents Mother, while perhaps resenting her manner, could hardly refuse but informed her she would have to pay for the whole day, just to show she had no intention of being intimidated. The customer agreed without hesitation and paid the half-crown rent and I was detailed off to take her to a tent.

Pointing out the empty ones, I suggested she might like to choose for herself and this she did by selecting the very last one, remarking she preferred privacy for both herself and her son. I was amazed that this rather sad small boy of around twelve years old, with her and now standing listlessly shuffling his feet in the sand, could possibly be her son. The age difference was so great that I thought that at least she must have been his granny, and looking back I can only think that he was born very late in her life. They disappeared inside the tent, did up the fastenings and that was all we saw of them until the evening, when they once again presented themselves and she asked, could she have the same tent tomorrow? which was no problem.

This was the forerunner of many such days. Each day they arrived, she with both umbrella and black bag, in which I assumed she brought their lunch – it was always full. She always went straight into the tent, tied the fastenings, and for the most part remained inside. Beyond a curt 'good morning' to Mother or her neighbours, she remained completely aloof. Sometimes the little boy would sit outside, sometimes disappear inside, always a pathetic, lonely little figure, either too shy or too afraid to make friends with those around him.

The weather was now fine, the beach filling with customers and their children and, as was my custom, in slack periods I filled my old ferrying dinghy with these children. I asked permission of our strange client to take her son with us and, unexpectedly, she said yes.

Frightened at first by the boisterous and noisy children around him, soon he was one of them and when I unloaded my cargo, instead of going back to his mother's tent, he was busily engaged in digging a large hole in the sand with his neighbour's children. From then on the ice was broken and to some degree he became involved in life on the beach. The change was noticeable but his mother remained the same, still out of sight in her tent. As she continued on this daily basis, and Mother was fast letting her tents for longer periods, it became necessary to inform her that she must either take over for a longer period, or until the end of the season. That was what happened, but she was so rarely seen as not to have been there at all, which suited Mother and incited very considerable curiosity among the other occupants of the beach.

Meanwhile, Fulmer, her son (I have deliberately changed his real name so as not to cause any possible embarrassment to his relatives still living), had found his way up to Mother and 'the shed' and she, overcome with pity for this strange, rather lost boy, made him welcome. In turn, Harold and Edna, the two youngest of our family, being of like age, took him to their hearts and he almost lived with us. The change in him was almost unbelievable by the end of that summer, and 'the beach' and the family filled his whole life. When the time came to say goodbye, we were quite heartbroken to see him go, particularly the youngest twins.

Then a strange rumour from one of the other tent dwellers began to circulate, its source the boarding house the strange lady had stayed at. It was said, or perhaps more hinted at, that the lonely occupant in the end tent was the Duchess of C ——, and Fulmer, the pathetic little son, the Earl of C ——. This was in no way reconciled with the fact that his ancestral home, it was also said, had been hotels and seaside boarding houses for most of his life. Mother, for some reason, dismissed this gossip as a load of nonsense. Fulmer would have told her, she claimed, and, the rumour almost forgotten, we knew little more than the day they came. But shortly after they left, I made a surprising discovery.

Their tent had remained empty and a hurried peep inside revealed nothing. It wasn't until I finally took it down that I found, beneath the piece of matting and sand on the floor, a large hoard of empty wine bottles covering the whole area, carefully buried and hidden from sight. The secret she had so carefully kept hidden from us all was revealed, but never once did she give any of us any reason for thinking she was the worse for strong drink, or an alcoholic; neither had Fulmer breathed a word of his Mother's failing. And this, I thought, was the end of this little episode of human frailty.

But it was not to be. The following early summer, who should turn up one day – none other than Fulmer. A bigger, more robust, livelier copy of the original, he informed us his mother had passed away. He was in the care of guardians and now at boarding school (he mentioned a large college in the west country). It had been arranged at his own request that he should spend his summer holidays on our beach if he could have a tent with us. He arranged with his previous landlady to look after and dispense his pocket money and generally take care of his welfare, a task not particularly difficult in his case, as he still retained the hesitant, somewhat frightened attitude of yesteryear.

We were glad to have him and Mother was even more sorry for him now that he was an orphan. He was no trouble; just fell back into place amongst us. He never spoke of his past, or his Mother, and least of all, his father. I realized he must have had or did have one somewhere, and both Mother and I wondered just what there was in that past that he kept so silent about. The few questions we did ask were ignored or answered by, 'I don't know,' or, 'I don't remember,' but as far as we children were concerned, it didn't matter. The present and immediate future was all we were interested in, and the past and his family concerns were of no importance.

And so that summer went by. He learned to swim, to row, to fish and all the other fun that was part of our lives. He was always well behaved, but he was somehow, and I still can't find an answer or pinpoint what it was, *different* from us. I sensed it, but in no way could I explain it. Maybe a different culture or breeding, perhaps his strange upbringing, I just don't know. 'Perhaps,' I said to myself, 'it's the difference in ages.' I was quite grown up; he was still a young boy. I don't think the younger members felt it. 'Mother,' I wondered, 'did she feel it?' But as I couldn't describe it, it was silly to ask – perhaps just a figment of my imagination? Certainly I had no reason in particular for thinking it and it has remained so, without an answer, to this present day.

The summer came and went and, with it, with quite considerable sorrow did Fulmer, and we still knew no more of his private family life and ancestry than when we first met him. Except his full name, and that was extracted from him more by accident than design, when one day my sister was boasting she had two Christian names, Edna Edith Joscelyne, and not just one, and he replied that he had five Christian names, something unheard of and quite outside our sphere of knowledge. We challenged him to repeat them and, to our almost unbelief, he reeled off the following: 'Fulmer, Nigel, Charles, Herbert, Guy C ——— .' For some unknown reason they have remained in my memory ever since.

The following two years he again re-appeared; the same arrangement was made. He took up where he left off the previous year, joined in the general life on the beach, was as little bother as before, and the constant companion during the holidays of Harold and Edna and, as usual, disappeared from our lives at the end of the season. He never wrote or sent a card at Christmas or any time during the winter months that followed. Like the swallows, he came for the summer only.

Then he didn't come; the summer passed with no word or sign of him. So did the following two summers. Harold and Edna were now quite grown up and out at work, in fact all of us thought we should never see him again, and almost forgot him.

214

But Fate decreed otherwise. The season hadn't started and Mother was still at home, when there was a knock on the front door. There, dressed in leather, in the height of fashion with a powerful sports car parked outside, stood Fulmer. Mother, delighted to see him again, invited him to stay to dinner. He had now left boarding school, was a man of leisure with an allowance from his guardians and hoped once again to join us on the beach later in the season. In the meantime he had come to ask Mother's permission and Edna's agreement to take her on holiday in his new car for a fortnight in Cornwall, to stay with his guardians. With the lost, intervening years forgotten, it was all so exciting and sudden and all of us were delighted at his return. Mother, when Edna showed how keen she was to go, gave her permission

'Le Bon Marché' in Leigh Broadway, where Edna worked, gave her her holidays in advance, and with Fulmer staying overnight, all was ready for a start next day. He said little of the intervening years and, the following morning, with curtain-peeping neighbours on full alert, the pair started off, with a roar of its powerful engine, in the bright red sports car of which we had never, in our street, seen the like before.

Then the doubts and fears that had been totally obscured by the excitement of Fulmer's sudden appearance began to form in our minds. He was as blind as a bat without his thick pebble glasses and little better with them. The roar of his engine when he had started added to our worries. When we had last seen him he was a boy, one of the family, and Edna more a 'sister'. Now he was a young man. How would he react to Edna, now a pretty girl? The worries mounted, and even when we received a postcard from Cornwall that all was well, it did little or nothing to relieve Mother from anxiety and the firm conviction she should have never allowed her to go.

Fortunately all our fears were set at rest when they arrived back at the appointed time. They both looked well. Yes, they had had a nice time, but I sensed an indefinable air that all was not well, particularly when after lunch Fulmer decided he must be getting back and hurried off instead of stopping overnight.

Edna didn't seem to want to talk much about her holiday, but bit by bit we learned how they had not gone to his guardians' home but had put up at various hotels at their different stopping

215

places as they toured Cornwall. He told her he desperately wished to marry her and had loved her from when he had first seen her. Edna, with no other feelings for him than the normal affection of an old and trusted friend, was shocked and dismayed, but Fulmer, hoping he could change her mind, persisted in continuing the holiday with that hope. Edna, however, could not and had no intention of allowing it to develop, so most of the enjoyment of the holiday was spoilt in an atmosphere of disappointment and unhappiness that affairs of the heart so often bring with them. Added to this, she was terrified at his driving. But she was loud in her praise of his conduct. Other than kissing her, he had behaved himself as a perfect gentleman in every other way, treating her with courtesy and always arranging separate sleeping apartments wherever they stayed overnight.

She was glad to be home, and had no intention of changing her attitude towards him. That, it seemed, was the end of both romance and Fulmer, as we never saw him again, which in a strange way pleased me. I never did quite overcome that indefinable doubt that, without reason, I had about him.

Did rumour lie when it hinted at his ancestry? Was his mother Countess of C —— ? Was he Earl of C —— ? Recently I determined to find out and asked my sister-in-law Rhoda, who was a frequent visitor to Southend Public Library, to investigate for me. There, sure enough, in Burke's Peerage and Baronetage, under the direct line of the sixth Baron was his father's name. At least I assume so, as all but one of the five Christian names were the same, and other interesting facts emerged, quite unnecessary to repeat, but which provided answers for much of the secrecy we had encountered. He was as rumour claimed. It is an intriguing thought that had the course of true love run smoothly, we might have had an earl in our family. But stranger still – amongst the descendants listed was the name Evelyn Caroline *Jocelyne* C ——.

Curiously enough, although none of us realized it, some of that time Fulmer was mixing with his own fraternity and class. The aristocracy was then a distinct and separate layer of English society – but perhaps the same rules did not apply to our beach.

Lady Dorothy Moore, a very beautiful brunette, was both a good Christian and equally good Catholic, and if proof was needed, although she was so young and lovely, six small daughters, the

216

eldest about ten, showed she upheld her faith and had tried hard to produce a son and heir to continue the line and family, but until that time without success.

As a patron of St. Edith's Convent in Glen Road (five minutes or so from the Beach), she stayed for her children's holiday with the Sisters of Charity that were its inmates. For a number of summers she had a tent on the beach with us. Sometimes the Mother Superior and others of the chosen, their robes of many layers and Dutch-style starched bonnets blowing in the breeze like ships in full sail, would accompany her, but mostly she cared for the family herself, and a better behaved little family would have been hard to find. Then they stopped coming, as was so often the case on the Beach. Perhaps I must also get Rhoda to do a little more research to see if the male line was eventually established, if this little story is to finish properly.

In the adjoining tent was also another we treated with respect a little above the average (knowing our proper station also) – Miss Marie Clare, who played the leading role in the long-running theatre hit 'Rose Marie'. Built on more substantial lines, and maybe a bit older, she was equally as lovely to look at and very friendly and nice to all of us, and Mother in particular. Her two children and the Moore's children, and quite often Fulmer, were regular passengers in my row-abouts together.

On another occasion we were surprised by two elegantly dressed chauffeurs asking if we had a tent for hire that afternoon. When told 'yes', they disappeared, only to return a few minutes later carrying a large luncheon basket and followed by several people in flamboyant clothes, leading them a lady dressed in dark clothing. I showed them to a tent, the chauffeurs returned to their cars, and the party proceeded to enjoy a wonderful lunch, if the champagne bottles I found afterwards were any guide. We hadn't the slightest clue who they were, but some of our customers recognised the lady. It was Marie Lloyd, the Music Hall star. On leaving, she thanked Mother and said they had been told in London they would find privacy and comfort on our beach, so our little corner wasn't quite so local. It was the last time we saw her.

Other than the general strike the following year [1926], things took their usual course. As far as the strike was concerned, it had no effect on the Beach at all, and if it hadn't been for newspapers and none of the usual activity on the railway adjoining, I would hardly have been aware of it, such was our isolation from worldly affairs. Neither prosperity nor the coming Depression seemed to shatter our immunity. People still had their boats and their holidays irrespective, and after a busy spring, once again summer with its old problems came round. The everlasting chasing off of trespassers and the ever-present difficulty of keeping both adults and children out of customers' and our own boats as they roamed the mud, and deposited most of it in the dinghy of their choice – aroused once again the dissatisfaction and killed much of the enjoyment I used to feel in those earlier years.

Looking back, perhaps I worried unnecessarily or was too conscientious. Maybe I should have shut my eyes to it or left matters to take their own course. I didn't know, and still don't know, whether the fault lay within me or the circumstances I found myself in; I was, I think, as equally 'mixed up' as the youth of today. Perhaps it was all part of the 'growing up' process, but it seemed the old joy of life was slipping away and an unknown lack of future was confronting me. An overwhelming desire to be free of the Beach and its difficulties haunted me. I lost sight of all the good things – my freedom from travelling, the sun, the sea, the lovely summer evenings, all these were lost in a darkness of self pity. I exaggerated its problems and hated each day that dawned that summer, but saw no way out and felt I just couldn't let Mother down either. Perhaps I should have insisted on more freedom away from it, but I had convinced myself that I couldn't be spared or leave it in case something went wrong. But mostly only in the imagination did this happen.

I couldn't wait until the quiet and freedom of the autumn arrived and the summer was over. Then to some degree, working once again on my model and the return to my side of the Beach and customers gave me the peace of mind of those earlier days and the darkness slipped away for the time being. As the winter passed and the following spring approached, I was back to the normal routine of everyday life of quiet enjoyment that existed once the holiday season finished.

My busiest and happiest time was spring, but as the summer approached, so the dread of facing it grew. I told myself, it was only the July and August that was really so bad, and surely it was worth facing just two months for the other ten. This did help to some degree, but the carefree happiness of the early summers remained in my mind and could not be replaced.

With the wisdom of hindsight, I now realize that with the drastic changes Mother had made, the beach was no longer a playground and business as previously. It was now a business only, run on the business lines of a social club for an elite few; it had lost all its old haphazard customers and the light-hearted joy and happiness for both them and me of the old days. It was now to all intents and purposes a separate and complete business, running smoothly and quietly, in which I really played little or no part, other than contributing to its efficiency.

My side of the business was now sharply defined and was a separate entity, paying lip service to the old cooperation and involvement, but not producing enough to meet the ever-increasing cost of living for twelve months of the year. I had no intention of breaking into the savings I had accrued previously, but could see no possible means to improve the situation or foresee a future with prospects of anything different. My sisters were now married, Vincent employed by a local firm of artificial limb makers, Harold, a carpenter in the building trade, and his twin sister Edna working at Le Bon Marché, drapers in Leigh Broadway. Both Vincent and Harold had their own boats and were completely free to use them evenings and weekends, and the strange feeling that I was a husband, rather than a son, in Mother's eyes, seemed to add to all these self-made fears.

Added to this was an increase in the irritating trick of not returning our rowing boats, a practice that had developed in more recent years. We still had four and, with a large painted notice on the shed, 'ROWING BOATS FOR HIRE', we still had quite a steady and lucrative trade with them, including a number of regular local customers. But unknown visitors were more general. When a boat was hired it was usually one shilling for one person, and sixpence each for each additional one, and it became more and more common for one person to hire a boat, take it some distance along the Westcliff beach, and fill it with members or friends.

Later, the one person would return it, having hired it for perhaps two or three hours at one shilling per hour, and it would then be filled mostly with sand and water up to the floorboards through using it as a communal plaything on the beach. But worse than this, some never returned the boat at all, but just left it when they had used it for most of the tide and then gone home. This made it necessary for me to search the whole length of the foreshore to find and recover it – my own fault, as I suppose I should have made them leave a deposit. I am not suggesting it happened all the time, but frequently enough to add to my dissatisfaction in general.

But deep down, and the root of my discontent, was Mother's antagonistic attitude to my making any lasting relationship with a girl. I was tiring of the odd clandestine, short-lived romances, with the deceit that accompanied them (although I am sure Mother was fully aware of them). My friends of both sexes were now mostly engaged or married but my entire dependence on Mother and the demanding hours of the business gave no possible chance of following my inclinations, even had I been able to afford to, which I couldn't. Mother's possessive attitude had grown with the bondage that held the three of us – the beach, Mother and me, together. Anything that threatened that trio was of necessity a danger and she had no intention of allowing anything to disturb or alter what she had worked so hard for and achieved. It was now her life.

Maybe I am now only searching for excuses for the decision that, should the opportunity arise, and I could leave the beach, I would take it. I told myself the family was now 'off hand', that Mother didn't really need me particularly – someone could fill my place, possibly Vincent, who disliked his job and would willingly take over. Nourishing this ambition in secret, with the season finished, and in a more settled state of mind, I waited in the hope and strange conviction that something would 'turn up'.

Wilfred Watts, perhaps a year or so older than me, although not one of my regular customers, frequently stopped for a chat on the quieter days but had his own circle of yachting friends. He owned a fairly large naval cutter that had been professionally converted to quite a nice sailing yacht with an auxiliary motor, the 'Tee Two'. A year previously, I understand, his grandfather had died leaving him a very large sum of money. He packed up his job, bought a house on Chalkwell Estate, married, and had a very nice auxiliary sailing yacht built at Cole and Wiggins in Leigh. Painted all black, it was named 'Night Hawk' and was a fine vessel.

Circumstances led him to hire, rather than sell, the 'Tee Two' and opened his eyes to the then unfilled market open to such demand, and soon he was considering its potential lucrative possibilities. With a year of freedom he became bored and his money idle; he decided to start his own business in the hiring of a number of cabin cruisers in and about the Thames Estuary and East Coast. He now had three cabin yachts, based at Paglesham, where the tide remained in at all times, and intended buying more. He asked me if I knew of someone who would take over the running and upkeep of them, both during the winter and summer months. Almost to my own disbelief, I found myself offering my own services to him, and from the next first of January, 1929, I took over and left the Beach for pastures new.

My leaving opened up a completely new chapter in my own life, too long to record here, but the story of Joscelyne's Beach does not end there either. When Mother got over the shock that I was leaving, she was very angry and upset, feeling I had deserted her, and as I couldn't fully explain my own reasons I felt both sorry and guilty. But Vincent was delighted and full of enthusiasm to take over and somewhat reconciled Mother to facing the coming summer.

It did, in fact, have little or no effect on the way she ran the Beach, and the changes Vincent instituted she accepted almost without question. He insisted on a weekly wage, cut out most of the work and repairs to customers' boats, and persuaded Mother to sell all the rowing boots (not an unmixed blessing). With stakes, rope, and fencing he shut the beach off from the cinder path and erected, mostly with driftwood, a castle-like structure with a door at the entrance with a 'customers only' sign, and turned the beach into an almost 'no go' area.

Local councillors wrote to the *Southend Standard*, and residents who had no access to it complained to anyone who would listen. Nothing was ever done about it and Mother and her flock remained secure behind her barricade, while Vincent, cutting out all ferrying services, sailed around most of the time in his little sailing boat. Mother had found a treasure, in the shape of a Mr. Cobb, who not only looked after the beach all day, but stopped all night as watchman. He was loved by everybody on it and kept off the few strays that found their way onto the beach.

This arrangement seemed to suit Mother even better. She reigned supreme for the summer months among 'her people' and this happy state of affairs continued until the beginning of the Second World War, when the whole coast of Essex was closed and for, I think, thirty miles inland, was declared an evacuation area. Although 'the shed' remained quite safely, the beach was never used.

After the Second World War, Mother once again took up the reins and almost returned to the previous pre-war conditions. Although now well over seventy, she made the journey each day from Leigh Cliff Road, from her new home that Harold and I had built for her in 1931. But the forces I had myself anticipated grew and an awakening social conscience was preached, and now practised by the newly returned Labour government, who began to put their theories into practice – and one of these was public ownership and compulsory purchase. Mother never thought it could happen, but it did. 'The Powers that Be' took away her beloved beach, not even consulting her, let alone offering any compensation for either her equipment or loss of livelihood, and only when she read it in the *Southend Standard* did she realize it was no longer hers. She died the following year: everything it seemed she had lived for had gone. But even now, after all these years, it's still 'Joscelyne's Beach' among those who remember and pass by.

TELEPHONE NO. 4948

ARCHIBALD GLEN,
TOWN CLERK AND
CLERK OF THE PEACE.

REGISTERED POST.

GAH/GC/124/23/1.
Encl.

TOWN CLERK'S OFFICE,

SOUTHEND-ON-SEA.

27th November, 1948.

Dear Madam,

Beach at Chalkwell.

I refer to my letter of the 6th ultimo. The appropriate Committee have now had before them your letter of the 28th September, and the Council have accepted their recommendation that your application for permission to remain in occupation of this beach after the end of this year be not acceded to.

With regard to the disposal of huts and tents mentioned in your letter, the Committee decided that if you care to let them have full particulars of the items of which you wish to dispose, together with the price you require therefor, they will be prepared to consider the purchase of the same.

I enclose formal Notice to Quit the beach and to deliver the same to the Corporation on the 31st day of December, 1948.

Yours faithfully,

Town Clerk.

Mrs. E. E. Joscelyne,
24 Leigh Cliff Road,
Leigh-on-Sea.

CORPORATION
Death Warrant
Curse them
FROM
Vincent

E. R. JOSCELYNE

Following the Second World War, Britain's railways were nationalised.

In November 1948, Southend Borough Council declined to renew the annual lease on Joscelyne's Beach, which had been in the family's hands for 39 years, and in Mrs. Joscelyne's name since 1917.

This is the Town Clerk's letter, addressed to Mrs. Ellen Elizabeth Joscelyne. Arthur's younger brother, Vincent, scrawled over the accompanying Notice to Quit the words 'Corporation Death Warrant, Curse them, from Vincent'

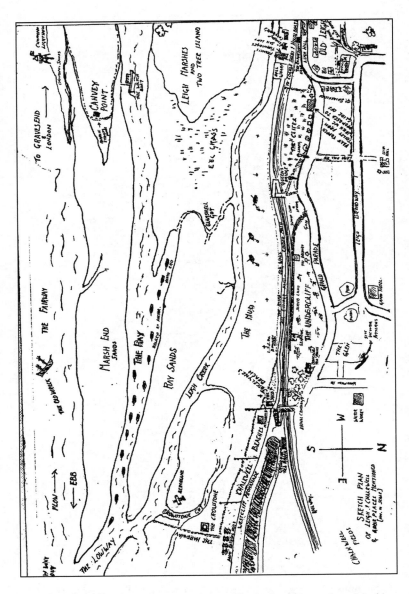

Arthur Joscelyne drew this map. Unfortunately, the lettering on the original is sometimes too small to read. Joscelyne's Beach is marked in the left centre